PRAISE FOR
AMONG THE MAASAI

"This is a credible, brave work that reflects the stark realities faced by girls from the majority of Maasai society and the hurdles they face to achieving educational liberation."

—NENGAI LAZARO BENTON, English teacher and graduate of the Maasai Secondary School for Girls

"Juliet Cutler's insights into the lives and challenges of the Maasai people make for a compelling read and honest look behind the veneer of village life often seen by tourists."

—LISA BROCHU AND TIM MERRIMAN, PHD, coauthors of *The Leopard Tree*

"A thoroughly engaging and meaningful look into the struggles confronted by many indigenous societies today and the challenges faced by the educators who are at the forefront during these rapidly changing times."

—KENNETH CUSHNER, EdD, author of *Teacher as Traveler*

"This fascinating memoir chronicles the courage and tenacity of a young couple teaching in the heart of Africa. Juliet Cutler presents a frank account of the moral dilemmas she encounters as she plunges into a tribal society where young girls face many challenges, yet generosity thrives. Prepare to be inspired by the true stories of girls who struggle against repressive traditions to become educated young women making a difference in the world."

—GAYLE WOODSON, author of *After Kilimanjaro*

"With courage, Juliet Cutler confronts the complexities of privilege, race, culture, and self-doubt, as well as the paradox of helping others. She emerges transformed by lifelong friendships and with the conviction that empowering local leaders makes a profound difference. *Among the Maasai* is a compelling must-read for anyone working in developing countries."

−DEB GRIFFIN, LCSW, former chair of La Gonave Haiti Partners

"Few writers are gifted with Cutler's graceful ability to step back when necessary, balancing between her roles as narrator, observer, and participant. *Among the Maasai* is a must-read for anyone dedicated to the uplifting of women by women, the gender-education gap, and the beauty of perseverance."

−CAMILLE GRIEP, author of *New Charity Blues* and *Letters to Zell*

"This brave and heartfelt account of Juliet Cutler's journey in Tanzania is an inspiring and important work. Through the intersection of her story with the extraordinary experiences of her young Maasai students, Juliet reveals the transformative power of education."

−HERTA FEELY, author of *Saving Phoebe Murrow*

"Juliet Cutler observes complex juxtapositions—intersections of wealth and poverty, modern and traditional, insider and outsider. She asks herself difficult questions—about her place in the business of helping, her motives, and the limits of her role as a teacher from a different culture. But there is powerful sophistication in her questions and in this beautiful account of transformation."

−DAUDI MSSEEMMAA, senior adviser to Mwangaza Education for Partnership

"This book is beautifully written and should be on the prescribed reading list for all schools. . . . It made me laugh and cry as I feverishly turned the pages. . . . I loved it."

−LUCINDA E CLARKE for Readers' Favorite

AMONG THE MAASAI

AMONG THE MAASAI

A MEMOIR

JULIET CUTLER

SHE WRITES PRESS

Published 2019
Printed in the United States of America
ISBN: 978-1-63152-672-5
ISBN: 978-1-63152-673-2
Library of Congress Control Number: 2019938034

For information, address:
She Writes Press
1569 Solano Ave #546
Berkeley, CA 94707

Interior design by Tabitha Lahr

She Writes Press is a division of SparkPoint Studio, LLC.

For the students and graduates of
the Maasai Secondary School for Girls

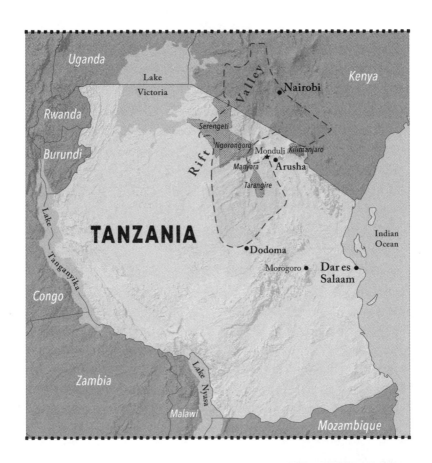

Uganda

Lake Victoria

Kenya

Nairobi

Rwanda

Burundi

Serengeti

Ngorongoro

Monduli

Kilimanjaro

Manyara

Arusha

Tarangire

Rift

Valley

Lake Tanganyika

TANZANIA

Dodoma

Morogoro

Dar es Salaam

Indian Ocean

Congo

Zambia

Lake Nyasa

Malawi

Mozambique

 Select Parks and
Conservation Areas[1]

Traditional Maasai
Territory[2]

AFRICA

Tanzania

"The choice is not between change or no change,
the choice for Africa is between changing or being changed."
　　—Julius Nyerere, President of Tanzania, 1964–1985[3]

"One child, one teacher, one book, and one pen can change
the world."
　　　　　　　　　　　　　　—Malala Yousafzai[4]

❖ CONTENTS ❖

FOREWORD

Education has the power to transform. There are many ways that I know this is true. In 1999, as a naive twenty-something American teacher, I went to Tanzania to teach at a school for Maasai girls with this conviction, and today my experience has borne out what research in the field of international development confirms: the single most transformative intervention for poverty alleviation is education, particularly for girls in the developing world.

As anyone who has ever taught will tell you, learning is frequently a reciprocal process. Teachers can be transformed alongside their students, and perhaps there is no better testing ground for this than in an unfamiliar context, when teachers step outside of what is comfortable. Though my Maasai students probably didn't realize it, they certainly taught me as much as I taught them. From them, I learned about determination and hope, about community and family, and about generosity and hospitality. I learned that poverty and wealth are about more than money, and that walking with people is far more powerful (and difficult) than offering charity.

When I first conceived of the idea for this book, what concerned me most was accurately conveying the reciprocal learning that took place between me and my Maasai students and Tanzanian colleagues. It felt like a tremendous responsibility to tell this story, and I frequently sought their counsel and advice throughout the writing process.

Some chapters describe events that I heard about from them and are, therefore, based on interviews. In translating these interviews into narrative form, I took some liberties in describing scenes and emotions that I was not present to witness. Several Tanzanians, including most of those described in the book, have reviewed the manuscript and provided insights into my descriptions. I have made every attempt to make the descriptions as accurate as possible based on their feedback. However, any inaccuracies are certainly mine.

I must acknowledge that I am neither Maasai nor Tanzanian; thus my descriptions and characterizations throughout the book are written from my perspective as an American woman who lived in Tanzania for the better part of two years and who has remained connected to the country as an advocate and fundraiser for twenty years. I have made every effort to write an evenhanded and objective account of what I have experienced and come to understand about Tanzania and the Maasai. Nevertheless, it would be impossible for me to entirely cast off my cultural biases and opinions about issues such as female genital cutting, polygamy, early marriage, gender discrimination, and certain Tanzanian policies related to education. In the presentation of these issues, I have endeavored to be as transparent as possible.

In many cases, I have changed the names of characters and the locations of events to protect the privacy of my former students and colleagues. In addition, some characters represent composites of more than one person; this was also done to protect identity.

The proceeds from the sale of this book will be donated to support education and women's empowerment in Tanzania. It is with great humility and respect that I tell my story and theirs.

—Juliet Cutler
September 2019

A SCHOOL FOR MAASAI GIRLS

It took Neng'ida, Miriam, and many of their classmates more than a decade to tell me their full stories. By then they were in their midtwenties, and I was in my midthirties. Though we were still young, we'd been tested, and through this, we'd come to trust one another. We understood that though we came from vastly different places, our lives had intersected for a brief, seminal period in time. We'd shared something—we'd all been transformed by a school in the heart of Maasailand.

Within a few months, at the end of 1998 and the beginning of 1999, we all left our respective homes to follow the pull of something we felt was greater than our individual existences—perhaps it was a desire to help others, or a belief that our lives should be lived on the edge of what was possible, or maybe we simply sought knowledge or a better life. In some cases, including mine, the allure of adventure held sway.

My students' motives certainly fell into much more immediate and pressing categories than my fanciful and high-minded reasons. At the age of fourteen, Neng'ida ran away from her father and a marriage he'd arranged for her. Half a world away, at the age of twenty-four, I thought I could help. In some ways, I was right, but in many ways, I would learn, I was wrong. Helping others and empowering others are not always the same thing. Neither are simple matters, particularly for outsiders, but I didn't know this yet. If I had, I might never have gone.

That said, Neng'ida, her fellow students, and I all guilelessly stumbled our way toward each other and the Maasai Secondary School for Girls, and today I believe we would say that we are the better for it. Here's why.

CHAPTER 1:

KUONDOKA NYUMBANI (LEAVING HOME)

While I packed my bags and made my plans, Neng'ida was busy making her own plans. It hadn't yet occurred to me how different the daily realities of life for Maasai girls could be from my own. But soon enough, I would learn. Neng'ida and many girls like her would teach me.

The first and most important lesson, which even today I'm still learning, is to listen. In order to understand how Neng'ida got to school and what that meant to her, I had to understand where she came from.

■ ■ ■ ■ ■ ■ ■ ■

East Africa's Great Rift Valley is an unforgiving place. During the dry season, it is a dusty, radiating cauldron of cracked earth. In the wet season, it is a verdant miracle rising from the very brink of despair. In the middle of this remote place is the heart of Maasailand.

In April of 1984, while the long rains that would bring life to Maasailand poured down, a smaller-than-usual baby entered the world. Born in a mud-and-dung hut known as a *boma*, this baby's survival was not assumed, so her mother gave her an *embolet*, or temporary name—Neng'ida, which means "joy" in Maa. After three cycles of the moon, enough time to be relatively sure that Neng'ida would survive infancy, her mother decided the name fit, and so Neng'ida remained her mother's joy.

Eventually, Neng'ida's mother would have ten children. As the third born, Neng'ida had two older sisters, but in a matter of years she would have another four sisters and three younger brothers. However, Neng'ida's family extended well beyond the children born to her mother. Neng'ida's mother was one of five wives, so Neng'ida grew up surrounded by all her father's children, who numbered twenty-three. His wives and their children, as well as grandparents, uncles, and aunts with all their children, were Neng'ida's family. And, as a Maasai, Neng'ida's family would always define her identity.

By the age of six, Neng'ida was already helping her mother and her older sisters to haul a few buckets of water over two miles from the nearest water source to their home. She would watch her mother use this water with zealous thrift to make *chai* or *uji*, and to cook *ugali* with beans and sometimes meat—all over the hot coals of an open fire. Once a week, there might be enough water to bathe or to wash the traditional red-and-blue swaths of checkered fabric called *mashuka* that Neng'ida wrapped about her spare body as her only clothing.

When Neng'ida wasn't hauling water or cooking with her mother, she might be found hunting for firewood or milking her father's cows or goats. Some days, she would herd the animals to the same watering hole where she collected water for the family. She would walk among the animals with a supple stick in her small hand, swatting the slower-moving animals and peering through the dust at a rolling landscape of open grasslands, whistling acacias, cactus-like candelabra trees, and rocky escarpments.

This progression of daily life for a Maasai girl, whose traditional path would typically include becoming a young wife and a mother, changed for Neng'ida only by chance—a decree came down from the village elders. Every family must send at least one child to primary school. Her father disagreed, mostly because he didn't have a son yet and his daughters seemed too valuable to send to school. They herded the family's cattle and goats, and it wouldn't be long before they were old enough for marriage. He would arrange each of his daughter's marriages—a daughter in exchange for five, maybe six, cows. Neng'ida's father measured his prosperity in wives, children, and cows, and by this measure he was a wealthy man.

However, since the village elders insisted, Neng'ida's father complied. He knew Neng'ida was the right age to start school, and since her two elder sisters could tend his animals, he decided Neng'ida would be the child he would sacrifice to school. He left little doubt in Neng'ida's mind, even at a young age, that he disapproved and wanted nothing to do with her education.

At the time, Neng'ida's mother recognized schooling as an opportunity for her daughter, but she didn't yet know that over the course of the next twenty years she would increasingly insist on education for all her children, and this would drive an irreparable wedge between her and Neng'ida's father. Eventually, Neng'ida's mother would leave her boma and the family settlement with her youngest children. As a Maasai woman who had virtually no means of supporting herself, the degree of her belief in education must have been profound.

Although Neng'ida doesn't remember it exactly, I can picture her on that first day of primary school. Her uniform—a little button-down white shirt, a knee-length blue skirt, and clean white socks with a pair of used-but-shiny black shoes—must have felt foreign and stiff compared to her usual attire. I imagine her standing a little straighter and looking a little brighter as she walked the nearly four miles to her new school—a single, diminutive figure leaving her boma for uncharted territory.

Neng'ida mostly remembers how much she loved school. She recalls the simple concrete-block school building where there were more students than desks and more boys than girls. She sat with other students—two or three small bodies squashed into a single desk, or on a bench behind a crude table. Books were rare, and paper and pens were sparse, so her teachers wrote letters and numbers across a bumpy black chalkboard-painted concrete wall at the front of the classroom.

When she first arrived at school, Neng'ida spoke only Maa, but many of her lessons were in Swahili. Sometimes her teachers explained in Maa, but she often didn't understand. Even so, she remembers diligently copying everything her teachers wrote on the blackboard into a notebook, filling each and every line, front and back of the page. Even if Neng'ida didn't understand what she wrote, she continued, carefully safeguarding her filled notebooks and scrounging for new notebooks when necessary. When she wasn't writing in the notebooks, she was methodically memorizing everything she'd written earlier. This is how she learned to read and write Swahili.

During recess, Neng'ida remembers gathering with a few other Maasai girls in the shade of scrubby thorn trees, arms easily slung across friends' shoulders as they watched a group of boys kick a tightly bound ball of plastic bags across the dusty schoolyard in an improvised game of soccer.

Her life at home didn't change much during these years. She continued to help her mother and her siblings with work around the boma before and after school and on weekends. In years when rain was plentiful, Neng'ida learned to cultivate beans and maize. In years when it wasn't, her tall, reed-like frame grew even thinner.

As Neng'ida neared the end of primary school, she and her fellow students prepared to take the national exam required for graduation. As a girl on the verge of puberty, Neng'ida rarely thought about her future; when she did, she felt a twinge of uncertainty. Students from her primary school seldom scored well enough on the national exam to qualify for one of the very few positions at a public secondary school, and virtually no one could pay the school fees required to attend a private school.

Neng'ida knew even if her family could afford to sell a cow in order to send her to secondary school, her father would never agree. He was expecting to gain cows for his daughters, not lose them. In fact, her elder sisters were already married. Thus, even if Neng'ida loved school, she believed the end of primary school marked the end of her education. In fact, she knew her father was already making plans for her marriage to a man more than twice her age. When she finished primary school, she would be fourteen years old. Among the Maasai, she would be considered ready for circumcision and marriage.

Neng'ida remembers the day that representatives from the Maasai Secondary School for Girls showed up at her school. Though she'd heard about the boarding school, which was only about thirty miles away from her village, she never expected an opportunity to attend the school, but the Maasai Secondary School for Girls was looking for two girls from Neng'ida's village to start Form I (eighth grade) immediately after the primary school national exam. Even though it was a private school, the girls who attended the secondary school would receive full scholarships.

The day the visitors arrived, Neng'ida and her classmates excitedly squeezed into the classroom's doorway to watch as the unfamiliar Land Rover entered the schoolyard. Neng'ida saw the school's logo on the side of the vehicle—an image of a Maasai beaded necklace, or *ilturesh*, with an open book and the words "Maasai Secondary School for Girls."

Neng'ida's teachers greeted two sturdy, well-dressed Maasai women and a Maasai man, who was the secondary school's driver. After an exchange of customary greetings and a brief tour of the modest primary school structure, the group had chai together, all while the students kept a close watch.

Then, one by one, Neng'ida and other interested Maasai girls were called into a quiet classroom where the two women from the Maasai Secondary School for Girls sat waiting. At first glance, Neng'ida thought the women seemed friendly, if not a bit stern, so she kept her eyes on her shoes as she quickly entered the room. She stiffly sat down in front of the women and whispered, "*Shikamooni*," a greeting of deference and respect spoken to elders.

The women began by asking Neng'ida several questions before giving her a brief but difficult written test. Most of the test was in Swahili, but some of it was in English—a language Neng'ida didn't know and couldn't read. Likewise, the interview was partially in Swahili, with a handful of questions in English. Neng'ida felt uncomfortable conversing in Swahili, and English left her mute. She was, however, asked two questions in Maa: "Do you want to go to school? And how do you think your family will respond if you go to school?"

Her answers were brief but emphatically clear: "Yes, I want to go to school, but my father will not approve. I respect him, but I still want to go to school. I think my mother will support this."

After the interview and test, Neng'ida worried that her poor performance, or the fact that her father might not support her education, would disqualify her. What she didn't know was that the school was looking for students just like her—Maasai girls from the remotest parts of Maasailand with virtually no other opportunities for secondary education and families who were reluctant to send their daughters to school.

It wasn't long before Neng'ida and another student at her school received word that they had been accepted to the secondary school—news that in equal parts frightened and exhilarated Neng'ida. Her primary school teachers urged the girls to keep the news a secret. They were concerned that if Neng'ida's father found out, he might prevent her from going to the school, or take even more drastic measures such as sending her off to her husband-to-be overnight. In a few days, Neng'ida would take the national exam at the primary school, and then representatives from her new secondary school would come to collect her.

The day after the national exam, Neng'ida told her parents that she needed to return to the primary school to complete a few final tasks. She left her boma with nothing but the school uniform she was wearing. Later that morning, she climbed into the same Land Rover that had brought representatives from the Maasai Secondary School for Girls to her primary school only a handful of weeks earlier. When Neng'ida arrived at the secondary school a couple of hours later, she believed no one in her family knew where she had gone.

But Neng'ida's family did know, and they were coming for her.

CHAPTER 2:

LEAVING HOME
(KUONDOKA NYUMBANI)

"If your final destination is Dar es Salaam, you are not allowed to disembark at Kilimanjaro Airport," the KLM flight attendant told us, adding that we could stand in the doorway only if we remained inside the aircraft.

Even though darkness had fallen, Mark and I eagerly sought our first glimpse of Tanzania, so we stood with our heads poking out the door of the Boeing 747 that had brought us from Amsterdam to East Africa.

We leaned out as far as possible without stepping onto the stairs that connected the aircraft to the tarmac, and our familiar world to this new foreign one. Though we yearned to run down the steps having just spent more than twenty hours on three different airplanes, the unimpressed flight attendant hovered nearby to ensure we stayed put.

Beyond the small circle of light that surrounded the terminal, we saw a vast blackness filled with thousands and thousands of stars. We smiled at each other. Mark held up his hand for a high five. We felt giddy in the way people who'd been awake for a very long time could be.

"We're here," I said to Mark with a sigh. "Can you smell it?" He nodded. We couldn't see this continent we'd waited so long to get to, but we could certainly smell it. This was East Africa—hot coals and smoke, dry grass and cattle, dusty wind and perspiration.

"We're finally here," I said again and added, "almost," as the stern flight attendant sent us back to our seats to endure another hour to Dar es Salaam.

By then, Mark and I had been dating for a couple of years. Long enough to know that we loved each other and that we would eventually get married, but not long enough to overcome the cautious stance we'd both taken as the result of previous relationships that had felt firm but had fallen short. We still needed time, but we were sure enough that we'd decided to do something largely uncharacteristic for either of us—take a big, relatively uncalculated risk. Individually, neither of us was particularly bold or brave, but together we coalesced.

After nearly a year of planning and preparing, we'd just traveled across the world to teach at two schools in Monduli, a small village in northern Tanzania. Mark would teach mathematics at Moringe Sokoine Secondary School, and I would teach English at the Maasai Secondary School for Girls. However, we'd first come to Dar es Salaam where we would spend less than thirty-six hours on the coast, before traveling inland for a month-long, Swahili-language course in Morogoro. After that, we'd travel north and begin teaching at our respective posts.

When we arrived in Dar es Salaam, we teetered on the very cusp of April 25, 1999. Though it was midnight, and we'd both been awake nearly the entire journey, adrenalin coursed through us. As naive travelers, our impressions of East Africa remained largely shaped by Western literature and journalism. While we knew we were going to the place of Ernest Hemingway's green hills and Jane

Goodall's chimps, we also knew we were going to the epicenter of the AIDS epidemic and to one of the poorest countries on the planet. Nonetheless, we felt eager to experience the authentic and complex place before us.

Once inside the terminal, we quickly focused on the somewhat intimidating matter at hand—namely, passing through immigration, collecting our trunks, and then getting our belongings through customs unscathed. Mark and I had heard from other expatriates that Tanzanian customs officials frequently inspected bags, particularly the bags of *wazungu*, or white people, and sometimes assessed fees if they saw new or even used items that could be entering the country for sale. In some cases, if an inspection dragged on, we'd been told a little "chai," or a bribe, was probably expected, something that rubbed my goody two-shoes sensibilities the wrong way.

However, my bags contained several new bottles of my must-have face cream as well as a couple of new dresses, a pair of new sandals, and an expensive brand-new water purifier, all of which I'd methodically cleared of packaging and tags. This didn't begin to cover all the used items I was sure would seem valuable to any sensible person since I'd obviously gone to the trouble of meticulously choosing and packing, unpacking, and repacking each and every item over the course of the last several weeks.

In the baggage area, Mark and I stacked our enormous pile of trunks and backpacks on two carts. He stood back, looked at the heap, and raised his eyebrows at me.

I sighed, smiled at him, and proclaimed smartly, "We are here for two years. You'd be thankful if you knew how much stuff I wanted to bring along but left behind. I could have filled at least one more trunk."

He rolled his eyes at me and asked, "Are you ready for this?"

I gave him my most confident look and exclaimed, "Ready or not," as if I truly believed we would sneak through customs unnoticed even with our mountain of luggage.

We were, of course, immediately stopped for questioning.

I'd studied enough Swahili to know basic greetings, and I ventured a timid "shikamooni" to the two official-looking Tanzanian men in khaki military-style uniforms who'd stopped us. I knew this was a greeting of respect used for elders and other authority figures such as teachers and parents and, in this case, customs officials.

One of the men quickly responded to me in a garble of brisk Swahili. I froze and stared wide-eyed at him. I had absolutely no idea what he'd just said. He tried again more slowly this time, but I still stared blankly at him. I looked at Mark for help. He apprehensively looked back at me as he wiped away a thin trickle of sweat that ran down the side of his face.

Mark then looked at the official and asked, "Umm, do you speak English?"

The man brusquely switched to English and told us they needed to search our bags while his counterpart lifted one of our trunks onto a nearby table and opened it. I noticed at once that it was one of my trunks, and even though I trembled with nervousness, I smiled slightly to myself.

When I'd packed my trunks in Montana, I'd decided I could potentially avert too much searching if I packed all my underwear at the top of each trunk. I'd read in my cross-cultural training manual that *chupi*, or underwear, ought to be treated with sensitivity in Tanzania. Even though I'd soon be washing all my clothes by hand and hanging them out to dry, I'd learned that only the most uncouth of people actually hung their underwear outside where they could be seen by prying neighborly eyes.

The customs official surveyed my underwear with an upturned nose, removed his hands from the trunk, and then swiftly closed and returned it to its original place at the top of our heap.

He walked back over to where we stood, and I imagined if his black face could have been red, it probably would have been. I looked at my shoes and held my breath to prevent myself from giggling.

The embarrassed man asked Mark a series of questions without addressing me once: "How long will you be here? What do you have in the trunks? Does it all belong to you?"

Mark politely answered each of the man's questions, and then the officials waved us through.

Once we'd crossed the threshold into the main terminal, Mark looked at me with a smirk and whispered, "I suspected your underwear could sway men, but truly I had no idea you were so devious."

I whispered back, "Then I guess you have a lot to learn, my dear."

When we pushed our luggage out of the terminal into the open air, we were immediately greeted, even at that hour, by a throng of Tanzanians. The trepidation that had been gurgling in my stomach since we'd landed now rose to a rapid boil. Some of the men who surrounded us spoke English, but most were speaking Swahili and gesturing toward Land Rovers, taxis, and minibuses. Most of the Land Rovers sparkled like new, the taxis looked to be in varying stages of disrepair, and one minibus listed dangerously toward the rear passenger door.

A man we'd met a few months earlier, Doug, the only *mzungu*, or white person, in the bunch, strode rapidly toward us as he waved off the crowd, a scattering of men now aggressively trying to direct our carts toward the array of parked vehicles.

"Hey, kids, *karibu*. How was the safari?" We'd met Doug and his wife Linda in Santa Fe, when we'd all attended a three-week orientation course. They'd left shortly thereafter for Tanzania. Even though they'd only been in the country for a few months, they were not new to Tanzania. They'd been volunteers in the southern part of the country several years earlier, and they'd also worked in Papua New Guinea. They now had the job of coordinating American volunteers for the Lutheran church in Tanzania.

Both Mark and I had grown up in families that regularly attended a Lutheran church, and though we were both Christians, we approached teaching at parochial schools in Tanzania with some uneasiness. While Mark and I felt committed to teaching in Tanzania as a form of liberation theology in action, we had less enthusiasm for the prevailing model of Western aid in the world—faith-based or otherwise. We knew that a long history of white Westerners had preceded our arrival and that this legacy of sometimes well-intended, sometimes insidious intrusion was unavoidable no matter if we worked for the State Department, the Peace Corps, a humanitarian organization, or the church.

In essence, we now worked for the Lutheran church. That said, I'd come armed with the work of Paulo Freire, a Brazilian educator who'd developed an approach to community development centered on the idea that those who are being helped, in his words "the oppressed," ought to be engaged in solving the problems that afflict them. He advocated for an approach that focused first on listening to marginalized people, and then empowering them to address the issues that they've identified. Freire made the strong argument that anything else is at best condescending and at worst harmful.[1]

Still, I knew in Tanzania, and perhaps even at the schools where we were going to be teaching, there was a pattern of white men and women charging to the rescue, without considering if and how their help might be wanted. Though Mark and I had been invited by the Maasai to teach at these schools, there seemed to be a big gap between my knowledge of theory and the real world. I desperately wanted to do the right thing—to listen and empower, rather than to assume and act—but I wasn't sure I knew how yet. I knew I needed help—mentors to guide me along the way. Even before our arrival, Doug and Linda had started to fill that role, and now standing outside the airport, I couldn't have been happier to see them.

Linda looked back at me from the front seat of their Land Rover. "Good thing we didn't send a *pikipiki* to pick you up, though it would have been fun to see those trunks strapped onto a moped. Did you guys bring enough?"

Like me, she wore the requisite outfit for women here, even wazungu women—a long sundress that covered her knees with a T-shirt underneath to cover her shoulders. Part of our orientation in Santa Fe had included a lesson on Tanzanian social decorum, which dictated that men and women keep their flesh to themselves. No shirtless men and no tank tops for men or women. Skirts were best worn long. Shorts were for schoolboys, and pants were for men only—not women.

Mark and Doug had decided our luggage wouldn't all fit in the back, and Mark was now handing Doug, who had climbed onto the Land Rover's roof, a couple of trunks to strap down. I stood watching, as did most Tanzanians in the vicinity. Doug, a lanky Vietnam veteran, had the uncanny ability to take almost anything in stride with good humor. He now feigned back pain and ribbed Mark as he climbed down from the roof of the vehicle.

During our application and interview process with the Evangelical Lutheran Church in America, Mark and I had received everything from subtle questions about the nature of our relationship to blunt dictates about what was appropriate and inappropriate in a Tanzanian context. We'd been told any public display of affection was a real cultural no-no for Tanzanians. If holding hands in public could cause a stir, then living together before marriage was out of the question, especially at boarding schools, where both teachers and students lived on campus.

We tried to find the humor in this, given that we couldn't imagine how anyone at any time in either of our lives could characterize us as anything but reserved and judicious. Nonetheless, it left us both feeling embarrassed and unsure about how to act around one another in this new context. We didn't want to offend the people we hoped to serve, and we wanted to indicate by our actions that we understood the culture and aimed to fit in as much as possible.

The irony of our situation didn't escape me. I would be teaching the Maasai, who regularly marry off girls to men two or three times their age. At puberty, most *morani*, or Maasai men, have sex with many Maasai women as part of the rite of passage from boyhood to manhood. Most Maasai men have not one wife, but many. And, amid this, the Lutheran church in America was uptight because a young unmarried couple in a committed relationship were coming to Tanzania together.

In truth, all the hullabaloo about the issue had me worried. Mark and I had undertaken this adventure together, and I was already leaning on him for support, sometimes more than I liked to admit. I worried that once we got to Monduli, we'd be unable to spend time together, and that any time we did spend together would be examined, catalogued, and questioned. I already suspected expatriate life might make me feel isolated and sometimes misunderstood. I hoped these feelings wouldn't be magnified by an awkward inability to share my experiences with Mark, even though we'd be living in the same community.

When we first met Doug and Linda, Doug's approach to this issue was to pat Mark on the back and say with a wink, "Remember, no hanky-panky now." Followed closely by Linda's, "Yeah, you two, no touching." They seemed ever ready to lighten the mood.

■ ■ ■ ■ ■ ■ ■ ■

After our first night of sleeping in our humble and separate accommodations, Mark and I received an orientation to Dar es Salaam, Doug-and-Linda style. The "tour" of Dar began with a wrong turn into the city's main market, a place where vehicles are generally not allowed. We rounded a corner and found ourselves facing a pedestrian-only area lined with vendors of every kind. Hundreds of people milled about, shopping and talking.

"Whoops," Doug said as he tightened his grip on the steering wheel.

He turned to look out the rear window, but the crowd had already parted and then closed behind us.

Linda rolled up her window and locked the door, prompting Mark and me to follow her lead.

The vendors grew increasingly agitated as Doug drove as slowly as possible past produce, piles of used clothing, pots and pans, shoes, small electronics, and sundry other items stacked on the ground all around the vehicle. The crowd continued to slowly part as we moved forward inch by inch. Doug smiled stiffly and waved while saying, "*Pole. Pole sana.* Sorry. Very sorry."

People yelled at us as they moved their wares to let us pass. None of us knew enough Swahili to understand what they were saying, but the body language clearly communicated the message. As one or two people waved their fists at us, I began to imagine some of the scenarios my parents, who were not initially enthusiastic about my plans to teach in Tanzania, had suggested coming to pass on my very first day here—namely me getting dragged from the vehicle and beaten. After what seemed like an interminable five minutes or so, we reached the first outlet to a street and immediately took it at a speed that all but squealed the tires. We all breathed a sigh of relief as Linda said, "Alrighty then, that was Dar's main market. Who wants to do that again?"

After the market, we whipped through a sprawling metropolis of extremes, driving past neighborhoods constructed entirely of cardboard, mud, and *bati*—the prevalent corrugated steel roofing. These neighborhoods looked as if they'd been raised up out of landfills. Dust and dirt hung in the air, and humanity oozed from every nook and cranny.

Amid what seemed like a pervasive stream of garbage, I saw people everywhere—walking on the sides of the roads, sitting in front of tiny shops and houses, and boarding overcrowded minibuses, called *dala dala*, that moved the masses from place to place in what appeared to be helter-skelter fashion. Scenes of Dar unfolded just beyond the protective glass of Doug and Linda's Land Rover, and for that I was grateful.

At lunchtime, we stopped at an exclusive beachfront restaurant where white linens, well-manicured gardens, and predominantly Western diners stood in stark contrast to all I'd seen on the other side of the restaurant's razor-wire security fence. I watched the Indian Ocean roll onto the beach as I ate a typical American pizza, wrote a postcard to my parents, and worried about getting bitten by mosquitoes.

While on the coast, I was taking Lariam, an anti-malaria medication that I'd been told could induce dreams akin to an LSD trip. I hadn't experienced any weird dreams yet, but I was beginning to wonder if the drug could induce anxiety, or maybe it was just my orientation to Dar that produced the anxiety. Dar had many of the surreal characteristics that I imagined LSD might precipitate. To my eyes, the real-life, wide-awake Dar radiated extremes of color and sound, beauty and blight, hope and despair. Just then, I felt as if I might like to wake up.

CHAPTER 3:

UNDER THE SOUTHERN CROSS

For the next month, Doug, Linda, Mark, and I resided at a Swahili language school in Morogoro. The hundred-mile drive from Dar es Salaam west to Morogoro filled me with wide-eyed wonder, as we transitioned from the Indian Ocean up nearly 1,600 feet to the base of the Uluguru Mountains. The paved, relatively well-trodden road from Dar es Salaam to Morogoro meant the trip went smoothly and quickly, but I took in every minute. At regular intervals, the tropical landscape parted to reveal one-room houses built with hardened mud and dung and roofed with thatch or bati.

When we stopped for gas, I watched a group of children use sticks to push small toy cars across the pavement. A medley of cleverness, the cars employed metal bottle caps for wheels, tin cans for the bodies, and aluminum foil or cardboard for decorative elements. Nearby, a group of three women wandered by, balancing full buckets of water on their heads without using their hands. As we pulled back onto the road, another group of women came by with enormous bundles of grass thatching on their heads.

From the car, I waved to children in their school uniforms. Every child seemed interested in our white faces. They would typically wave and excitedly yell, "Wazungu, wazungu," their voices quickly receding as we zoomed by.

Along the road, I noticed local "grocery stores"—nothing more than small open shacks that sold all manner of fresh produce. Doug and Linda stopped at one to pick up some provisions, and I got out of the car to also look. I was most interested in the bananas, which came in different sizes and colors—large bunches of tiny yellow bananas, fat and long green plantains, medium-sized red bananas, and the typical yellow bananas common in America. Linda bought a small bunch of red bananas. I meticulously peeled one expecting it to look different on the inside, but it didn't. It only tasted sweeter than the bananas I was used to.

Every once in a while, Linda turned from the front seat and said, tongue-in-cheek, "There's another public restroom if anybody needs one." We laughed each time she said this, as it became more and more apparent that bushes, trees, and even the wide-open side of the road were all potential restrooms in Tanzania. For as much as we'd been warned that modesty was a virtue here, we'd already seen more exposed flesh than we had expected. Just as I was beginning to wonder if all the fuss about orienting us to proper attire and behavior was more about my own Protestant American roots than about anything truly pervasive about this culture, Doug proclaimed, "Shield your eyes, shield your eyes. Naked men."

A group of three men were bathing in a small pond near the road. Just beyond them, a couple of women washed laundry in the same pond and then hung it to dry on nearby bushes. I noticed, with a chuckle, that underwear seemed nonexistent, or certainly well hidden.

When we arrived at the language school after a half-day's drive, I immediately began to meet other expatriates. I quickly discovered we were as diverse as the causes we sought to address. A tiny

Japanese woman needed to learn Swahili to complete a study on health care. A priest from South America planned to work in central Tanzania at an orphanage. Germans, Brits, and other Americans worked with humanitarian organizations, churches, or universities.

As a group, we sought to improve health care; prevent AIDS, malaria, and other diseases; provide clean water; help orphans; educate the masses; build rural schools and clinics; improve conditions for women; support agriculture; develop community organizations; comfort the sick; and, in some cases, save souls.

Here I first heard the generally accepted truism about expatriates in Africa. Namely that people who come to work in Africa are either running from something or running to something.

After spending three weeks at the language school, I came to believe this was true. We were an odd group of characters. Each of us had come here seeking something—meaning, hope, God, friendship, self-worth—or hoping to leave something behind—dysfunctional families, divorce, abuse, civil unrest, oppression. As I got to know my fellow students, I began to listen for these recurring patterns in their stories, and I found myself once again examining my own reasons for coming here.

I knew I'd come to Tanzania because I wanted to do something that made a difference, that improved the quality of life for the people who needed it most, and that broadened my perspective on the world, but I secretly struggled with self-doubt. While I'd taught writing to undergraduate students at Colorado State University and English to high school students during my student teaching, I worried that I was ill prepared to teach nonnative speakers the complexities of English grammar. Sentence diagrams caused me to break into a cold sweat.

In addition, I wondered how I could possibly teach English to beginners without a working knowledge of Swahili, which, to my disappointment, I found difficult to master. Furthermore, the connection between teaching Maasai girls English and my broader, nobler goal of improving the lives of my students seemed tenuous to me. All these doubts didn't even cover my questions about the impact of education on local traditions and culture.

However, I tried to shelve these concerns while at language school as something to worry about later when my "real" work began. Instead, I filled my days at the language school with limpid, unadulterated discovery. Swahili language lessons took several hours each day, which still left me with plenty of free time to explore the grounds and get to know other expatriates as well as the Tanzanian language teachers, most of whom lived on campus and were about my age.

The teachers existed as a quiet, polite, and gracious presence among a menagerie of expatriates with questions, problems, and demands. After class, Mark and I would sometimes join the teachers in a game of volleyball, and in the evenings, after dinner, we'd gather in the dining hall or somewhere on the language school grounds to hang out with the teachers and with other students. Doug and Linda were often part of these gatherings. They had developed their own pidgin Swahili and purposely played with words and made exaggerated mispronunciations to draw laughs from the teachers who earnestly wanted them to learn the language.

Mark and I made fast friends with Nelson, a teacher whose eagerness to help us understand Tanzania and learn Swahili endeared him to us, as did his warm smile and friendly presence. His parents lived near Arusha, and he invited us several times to visit him there, once we settled in Monduli. He wanted to teach us about farming on his parents' land.

On the sly, Doug and Linda would invite "the cool kids," or the expatriates for whom drinking a beer didn't equal moral destruction, to their "after-hours study group" at a little bar not far from the language school. It felt as if we were sneaking off campus as we crammed too many people into the back of Doug and Linda's Land Rover for a bumpy journey that ended in a lukewarm bottle of Tusker, Safari, or Kilimanjaro beer. This, of course, only increased our solidarity.

When I wasn't studying or getting to know other students and teachers, I could often be found somewhere on the school's grounds examining tropical bushes or flowering plants, hunting for lizards or butterflies, waiting for colorful birds to alight near me, or reading a book in the shade. The landscape seemed alive to me in a way I'd never before experienced, and this both amazed and frightened me.

One afternoon, I sketched a chameleon as it traveled in herky-jerky fashion from brown, to green, to yellow, to orange, to red through a poinsettia bush nearly as tall as me. I captioned my sketch with a Swahili proverb I'd recently learned, "*Haraka, haraka haina baraka.*" Hurrying does not bring blessings. Like most things in Tanzania, this little lizard moved at its own pace, which doggedly tested my ability to sit still and move slowly.

Another day, Mark and I discovered a tarantula the size of my fist resting against a closed classroom door. We backed away slowly and spent the remainder of our time at the language school wondering where it had gone and how many of its relatives were lurking about.

I remained hyper-paranoid about snakes, particularly after a couple of the teachers paraded past my perch one afternoon with a machete and a headless spitting cobra they'd killed near their dormitory. I think my inability to look away, like a spectator at the scene of a crime, inspired them to regale me with other tales of black mambas and puff adders, which I later sincerely wished I had not heard.

"*Mwalimu* Julie, black mambas can travel as fast as a motorcycle, and even without provocation they will chase you," Nelson warned.

"You have to watch for them at your new school, and also spitting cobras. If their venom hits you in the eyes, that's it, you'll be blind for sure," he continued.

Then he paused, taking in what was surely a horrified look on my face, and said a little more gently, "But don't worry. God will protect you."

I also took several "cultural" field trips during my time at the language school. One day, about halfway through my stay, I visited a local sisal farm with Mark, Doug, Linda, and several other students. We learned from our earnest tour guide that German colonists had introduced sisal to East Africa in the nineteenth century, and that it still played a significant role in Tanzania's economy. We saw workers harvesting the sisal, processing its leaves into stiff fibers, and packing the fibers into huge bales. Our tour guide told us the bales would travel to China and India, where the sisal fibers would be woven into twine, rope, rugs, and other products.

When I closed my eyes that night, however, I saw only the bare chest and protruding ribs of a hunched, gray-haired man who'd obviously spent his life breathing sisal dust, bundling its valuable fibers, and moving it from rapidly rotating rollers, past dangerously open conveyor belts, and onto enormous drying racks. When I'd asked our tour guide how much the man earned for his work, he told me seventeen thousand shillings per month, or about twenty-three dollars.

The image of this man haunted me. I had come here to help, but I couldn't even begin to address a global economic system that thrived on the backs of hunched, old men who worked for less than ten cents per hour. The human cost of this system had become real to me in a way that made me feel culpable, helpless, and incredibly naive.

Another day, I decided to visit the local market in Morogoro to pick up some fresh fruit with Doug and Linda, while Mark showed Nelson how to play his guitar at the language school. For a long time, even after Doug and Linda set off on foot to do their errands, I sat in their Land Rover just watching and working up the courage to get out.

An overhead patchwork of thatched roofing, plastic tarps, and burlap sacks shaded the improvised open-air market from the intense midafternoon sun. Neatly stacked piles of tomatoes, avocadoes, oranges, mangoes, and papayas sat in small groups on makeshift tables and in brightly colored plastic buckets of every size and hue. Women, young and old, seemed to share the day's news as they tended to their fruits and vegetables—washing, sorting, and selling—while small children played together underfoot.

At the edge of the market, a sinewy old woman sat on the ground, her legs extended in front of her, a flat round basket in her lap. She was sorting rocks from rice.

Several sun-wrinkled men leaned on their walking sticks in the shade of a nearby mango tree—their silhouettes bent together in quiet, leisurely discussion. They watched as women came and went with easy, careful grace—a basket, a bucket, or a huge tier of bananas balanced upon their heads.

Watching them, I felt foolish in my fear, yet fearful nonetheless. As a mzungu, or white person, I knew that as soon as I left the relative safety of the Land Rover in which I sat I would instantly become the center of attention, something I commonly sought to avoid even in familiar settings. But here, there was no place for me to hide. I stood out—a colorless, brilliant white in a sea of bold color incarnate.

I recited a few basic Swahili phrases to myself with the stifling knowledge that I didn't know nearly enough. I briefly closed my eyes and took a deep breath. As I reluctantly slid out of the Land Rover, I tried to shrink, to become invisible, to blend in, but it was impossible. I felt as if every head was turned, every eye upon me.

I moved through the market haphazardly, looking for nothing in particular while playing my part as the unwilling spectacle. I avoided eye contact. I didn't speak. The smaller children stared wide-eyed, clinging to their mothers a little more tightly. The older children whispered to one another as they cast sideways glances in my direction. A woman stretched toward me, "Sister, sister, I give you good price." Dust and human toil, sunlight and stench, flies amid delight—I was overwhelmed.

It wasn't long before I realized I was being followed. A group of three boys trailed several paces behind me. I glanced at them out of the corner of my eye as I pulled my backpack off my back and held it close to my chest. The youngest looked to be four or five and the oldest maybe eight or nine. They were dressed in dirty, overly roomy blue shorts and ragged colored T-shirts, and they weren't wearing shoes.

In an effort to lose the boys, I avoided the market's interior and began making erratic turns here and there. I didn't look directly at them, worried if I did that they'd ask me for money. I composed my Swahili phrase in my mind. *Samahani sina pesa kwa wewe.* There isn't any money for you. A message, I supposed, they received in many ways.

I looked for Doug and Linda but couldn't spot them anywhere, so I nervously browsed the fruits and vegetables and vacantly nodded in response to any use of Swahili. The small parade of boys persisted.

Just as I started counting the minutes until I could return to the safety of my small, spare room at the language school, Doug and Linda emerged from the crowd walking toward the Land Rover. They didn't see me, even though I stood within dashing distance of them. Though I felt like running to catch them, I didn't. Instead, I turned to face the three boys, prepared with my Swahili phrase.

The smallest boy reached out to me with a wide, juicy smile and quietly offered me half of his peeled orange. He was eating the other half.

I blinked back hot tears as I knelt down to the boy's eye level and smiled back at him. We remained like this for a long moment, as the market's cacophony receded into the background. He'd caught me unprepared, but it didn't matter. We didn't need words, Swahili or otherwise, for this simple yet powerful exchange.

■ ■ ■ ■ ■ ■ ■ ■

The next Sunday, Mark and I hiked about six miles with several of our language school compatriots to what seemed like the very top of the Uluguru Mountains, which rose up sharply just outside Morogoro. We started the hike in a dense tropical forest where monkeys were chattering and swinging through the bright green canopy above us. As we rose higher, the vegetation opened up into steeply terraced fields of maize punctuated by banana trees and cascading water.

At times, the trail felt more like climbing an endless upward staircase than gradually ascending a well-trodden footpath. Our destination was a crudely built one-room whitewashed church. When I arrived in my plain khaki wrinkled dress and dirty hiking shoes, I was dripping with sweat and knew that Morogoro's humidity had once again taken its toll on my curly brown flyaway hair. I tried to corral my curls into a ponytail and shake out my dress as I watched Tanzanian women arrive at the church with neatly woven cornrows; crisp, brightly colored dresses; and smart black sandals. I'd already noticed that the female teachers at the language school seemed immune to the conditions that always had me looking as if I'd just rolled out of bed in my bland, lifeless clothing, and the women at this small, far-removed church seemed no different. They appeared tidy and fresh.

The local Tanzanian evangelist had invited us to join this community for Sunday services. As I sat on a rough wooden bench in the portion of the church reserved for women, the Tanzanians around me began to sing in multipart harmony with a beauty truly unparalleled to anything I'd ever heard in my stiff, Protestant, hymnal-bound past. I closed my eyes and let the rhythmic rise and fall of the music wash over me.

I don't know if it was the exertion of the hike or my growing anxiety about what life would be like in Monduli, but I felt raw and vulnerable in that little church, and the music seemed to crack open my soul. The obviously urgent and steadfast faith of the tiny community gathered at the top of this mountain humbled me. While I'd been nobly plotting out my strategy to make a difference in the world and turning my nose up at the idea that my religion, or any other for that matter, had the corner on truth or the right to impose that truth on another, particularly an underprivileged other, I'd missed the fact that it might just be my soul that required saving.

As if I didn't already look enough of a mess, big tears began to flow down my now ruddy cheeks. Mark gave me a worried look from across the church, and I smiled weakly at him and mouthed, "I'm okay," even though I wasn't so sure I was.

In recent days, I'd begun to regularly experience what I not so fondly referred to as "system overload." It usually began with the sense that my brain was moving several beats slower than the world around me and was followed closely by the feeling that I wanted to do nothing more than sleep, which I'd been doing in abundance—ten to twelve hours a night in addition to a regular hour-long afternoon nap. Often, I still awoke in the clutches of a fog I couldn't seem to escape.

I'd overtly attributed my inability to concentrate and constant drowsiness to Morogoro's muggy, hot temperatures—a big change from the dry, cool mountain air I was accustomed to breathing— or to the on-again, off-again food poisoning I'd experienced since arriving at the language school. I worried, though, that my recurring lethargy went deeper than just a change in climate or an upset stomach. A worry that was compounded by the fact that "system overload" increasingly preceded or followed tears—sometimes big, silent rolling tears and other times torrents of sobs, which I hid well from everyone except for Mark.

There wasn't much opportunity to talk to Mark privately, but we often sat on the stoop of one dormitory or another, or we went for walks around the language school's grounds. He hadn't seen all the tears, but he knew I was struggling with a growing sense of fear that in coming to Tanzania, I'd undertaken more than I was capable of handling. In his typical unflappable, optimistic fashion, he would try to buoy my spirits with a joke, or get my mind off things with some kind of a distraction. Without the usual cadre of options—television, movies, the internet, or even the ability to leave the language school grounds without the color of our skin attracting significant attention—we often played a game of cards.

Between these games, I would sit alone in my room and wonder how I could have prepared myself for the responsibility I felt as a person of relative privilege living in the midst of not just poverty, but of generous, welcoming people like Nelson, who extended friendship and hospitality to me at every turn, even in the midst of their own hardship.

I often told Mark that life would be easier if I just cared less, but I did care, and deeply so, about the problems I saw around me. He told me this was one of the things he loved about me—that I wanted the world to be a kinder, gentler place.

Even so, I now saw just how unkind and rough the world could be, and these problems loomed over me large and complex. I felt paralyzed in their shadows—a bright, idealistic young woman who wanted to help but didn't know how and foresaw a future where the problems would get even more complex and much more personal as we entered our permanent placements in Monduli.

Increasingly, Mark or I received simple requests from the language teachers, or the cooks, or the gardeners, or the people we met on the street.

"Can you find two hundred dollars for school fees so my brother can attend school?"

"My daughter is sick and I need fifty dollars to take her to the hospital. Please, can you help me?"

"I want to build a primary school in my village; can you find me a sponsor in America?"

"I am hungry, sister. Please can you give me money for food?"

The requests usually far exceeded Mark's or my ability to address them. The Lutheran church in America had covered our travel expenses to Tanzania, and they also paid us a small monthly stipend, which was a substantial amount by local standards but certainly didn't live up to the expectations that our white skin aroused in many Tanzanians.

So we found ourselves frequently responding, "Pole sana. We're very sorry, but we can't help you." Then I would quietly retreat to my room to sleep, or to cry, or to simply sit alone with my questions. How much do you really need? How much are you willing to live without? Can you live with putting your needs above the needs of others?

The night before our departure, Mark and I climbed the thirty-foot-tall water tower at the language school to see what we'd heard from others was an amazing starscape. As we began our ascent up the rickety metal ladder attached to the water tower, I realized I wouldn't make it to the top if I looked down, or if I thought too much about the condition of the ladder to which I was clinging. Mark encouraged me from below. When I rose to the top, I stood in the very middle and wondered how I was going to gather the courage to get back down. When Mark stepped off the ladder, we lay next to each other on the flat, round tower top and held hands. Nobody could see us up here. It felt as if we could reach out and touch the stars. We looked for the Southern Cross and then for other constellations more familiar to our eyes. We found the big and little dippers and noticed Scorpio on the very edge of the horizon.

We lay quietly like this for a long time until I whispered, "I'm scared to leave." My time in Morogoro had turned the hypothetical Tanzania I'd heard about from afar into a complex, tangible, real place that Mark and I would now venture into alone.

Mark squeezed my hand and said, "We'll be together. It'll be okay."

I wasn't so sure, and in the days to come, I would find that in some ways I had been right.

CHAPTER 4:

SHOCK AND AWE

As I arrived in Tanzania, Neng'ida and many girls like her were arriving in what to many of them was an equally amazing and disorienting place—the Maasai Secondary School for Girls. Years later, Neng'ida would confess with some embarrassment that her arrival at the school represented her first exposure to running water and flush toilets, among other things, like wazungu. She had never seen a white person before she arrived at the school, let alone spoken to one. No doubt, in the days after our respective departures from home, we both found that the world was a much larger, more diverse, and more complex place than we had realized. Though we probably shared little else, we shared a deep-seated desire to do what we'd come to do, even though we both found it a formidable, even overwhelming challenge.

■■■■■■■

Neng'ida looked down at her hands. She hadn't been aware that her fists were so tightly balled. She opened and closed them several times in an effort to shake off the tension. The journey to her new school had taken little more than a couple of dusty, bumpy hours, but Neng'ida had acutely felt each and every mile as it passed. Since leaving her former primary school, she and her classmate Esupat rode in hesitant silence, leaning against one another in the back of the school's Land Rover.

Neng'ida sat up a little straighter when the vehicle pulled up and stopped in front of an oddly oblong-shaped white building with a green bati roof. Neither traditionally round as a Maasai boma would be, nor square like her primary school and most modern Tanzanian construction, the unusual concrete-block building was unlike anything Neng'ida had ever seen.

In the front window, brightly patterned *kitenge* curtains lightly fluttered behind open louvered jalousie windows. A leafy large-canopy tree shaded the building, and several chickens pecked at the ground near the wide-open front door. On the stoop, a motley collection of recycled plastic jugs and large tin cans overflowed with various flowering plants and leafy cuttings. Behind the parked vehicle, Neng'ida could hear the distant sounds of girls talking and laughing.

As she climbed out of the Land Rover, Neng'ida noticed that a sizeable iron gate and a thorny *michongoma* hedge separated her from the sonorous rise and fall of the chattering girls. The campus and its coffee fields sloped downhill away from Neng'ida, the lush Monduli Mountains rising behind her, and northern Tanzania's arid plains stretching below her for as far as she could see. She knew her *engang* lay on the other side of the mountains, and save for the couple of round boma-like buildings at the school, nothing looked familiar here.

Nonetheless, she'd made this journey, and she knew she needed to see what this place was about, so she took Esupat's hand, and they walked one tenacious step after another past the industrious chickens, up the stoop, and through the open door into the oblong building before them. They soon learned that the building served as both the school's main office and the headmistress's home. The headmistress and her immediate family, like all the teachers at the school, lived on campus in the buildings outside the thorny hedge.

Students, though, rarely left the hedge's confines—sleeping in dormitories, studying in classrooms, and eating in the dining hall—all within the substantial thorny boundary. According to the Maasai elders who had established the school, the hedge was necessary to protect students—less from the threat of wild animals, which were sparse in Monduli, and more from wandering Maasai morani interested in socializing with young Maasai girls, as well as from the handful of begrudging parents with a mind to forcefully remove their daughters from the school. Thus, Neng'ida's world was about to shrink to a spare circle of land about 250 yards in diameter.

Within the school's office, a stout, slightly gray-haired Maasai woman in a loosely tailored, but colorful, matching skirt and suit jacket peered impassively at the girls from behind large round glasses. Though she didn't wear a traditional Maasai *shuka*, her cheeks bore small round "beauty" scars, and her earlobes had once been stretched long but were now surgically made small again—an indicator that she now subscribed to more Western notions of beauty.

Neng'ida's own cheeks reflected the same small round scars, which she'd been given as a very small child, and her own earlobes were already stretched long. Thus, she didn't miss the telltale signs that the woman before her was, in fact, a Maasai and her elder. All this she surmised even before the woman greeted her in Maa.

The two girls approached the woman with their heads down and quietly whispered, "Shikamoo," a common Tanzanian greeting of respect spoken by the girls to someone they recognized as an elder.

"*Marahaba . . . endito, takwenya?*" the woman asked. The girls responded to her greeting in unison, "*Ikuo.*"

The woman then introduced herself as Mama Mkuu, the school's headmistress, and spent several minutes enquiring about Esupat's and then Neng'ida's home and family. The headmistress wanted to know how Neng'ida and Esupat felt about coming to school, and she asked directly about their parents' attitudes toward secondary school.

Neng'ida repeated her answers from the interview, "I want to go to school, but my father does not approve. I respect him, but I still want to attend this school."

Mama Mkuu raised her eyebrows and asked what Neng'ida's mother thought. Neng'ida pondered this for a moment and then quietly responded, "My mother is supportive, but it is difficult for her to disagree with my father. I left today without telling her because I thought this would make it easier for her with my father. He will be furious." As she divulged this, Neng'ida's lower lip began to quiver. She swallowed hard and blinked back her tears.

Mama Mkuu put down the papers she was holding and walked toward Neng'ida and Esupat. She bowed her head slightly and held her hands behind her back as she told the girls that she was also from the Rift Valley, so she understood the difficulty many people had with educating girls. Nevertheless, she said she was glad Neng'ida and Esupat had chosen to come to the Maasai Secondary School for Girls. She believed they were taking an important step for their futures and for the future of the Maasai. All this she said in the Maa language.

Mama Mkuu then walked with the girls out of the building, past the parked Land Rover, and through the iron gate onto the main part of campus. It was time for morning chai, so the head-mistress headed toward the dining hall. As they walked, the sounds of animated conversation and laughter got louder and louder, and Neng'ida's mouth grew drier and drier. Her hands were all knotted up again.

When they arrived, the simple dining hall was packed full of girls sitting at long tables on benches, drinking chai, eating boiled eggs, and speaking Swahili at a breakneck pace, first loudly and then in hushed whispers when the headmistress entered. Neng'ida's stance was reserved and shy. She stood close to Esupat and slightly behind the headmistress. Her Swahili wasn't very good, and she immediately began to worry as she realized that everyone in the dining hall seemed to speak Swahili fluently.

Neng'ida noticed that all the students, except for a few of the youngest ones like her, were wearing school uniforms—khaki-colored skirts with neatly tucked in, brightly colored T-shirts in yellow, blue, green, and purple with the school's logo emblazoned across the back. It appeared that each class wore a different colored T-shirt, and Neng'ida wondered which color she would wear, even as she stood mutely with her eyes cast down.

Mama Mkuu first introduced Neng'ida and Esupat to the school's matron and then to one of the school's founding elders.

In Swahili, the headmistress explained, "This is *Bibi* Neema and Bibi Ruth. They are here to help you. If you have questions, you should ask them."

Neng'ida knew that "bibi" meant "grandmother" in Swahili, and both these women looked the part. Though Neng'ida quickly identified both of the women as Maasai, she guessed they shared little, other than gray hair, cloudy eyes, and weatherworn faces.

The matron, Bibi Neema, was short, very stout, and imposing, if not slightly threatening, in her demeanor. She wore a neatly tailored contemporary dress and assessed Neng'ida and Esupat coolly.

She curtly said, "Report to the dormitory to check in after chai."

Then, without further ado, Bibi Neema turned sharply, marched across the dining hall, and began interrogating a group of students. Eventually, Neng'ida would come to marginally sympathize with the matron. It was her job to keep more than 250 girls in line around the clock. Admittedly, she often had reason to be stern.

Bibi Ruth, on the other hand, was a towering six feet of jovial, grandmotherly affection. Old age had thickened and softened Bibi Ruth so she was less the tall, proud, angular Maasai woman that she had obviously once been, and more a contented, slightly stooped elder. She wore traditional red-and-blue checked mashuka and customary Maasai beads around her neck, wrists, and ankles and through her elongated earlobes. With some curiosity, Neng'ida stared at Bibi Ruth's feet. She didn't wear the typical *raiyo*, or rubber sandals made from old tires. Instead, she wore bright red Converse high-top sneakers—a signature, of sorts. After an exchange of traditional Maa greetings, Bibi Ruth smiled warmly at the girls, shuffled her bright red shoes across the dining hall, and began introducing Neng'ida and Esupat to other students who had also recently arrived at the school.

Bibi Ruth was the school's only female founding elder—a distinction she earned on her knees. Though Bibi Ruth had never been to school, she carefully bent all six feet of her aged frame to the floor and begged on her knees when it looked as if a meeting of male elders might not agree to support the school. The uncommon gesture must have convinced her male counterparts because they agreed with Bibi Ruth—the school would move forward. Once Bibi Ruth had convinced this, her toughest audience, of the school's merits, she set about convincing reticent parents to agree to keep their daughters at the school. If the Maasai Secondary School for Girls had a cheerleader, Bibi Ruth, in her bright red Converse high-top sneakers, was it.

As Neng'ida and Esupat sat with Bibi Ruth and several other students who were also new to the school, two girls dressed in khaki skirts and yellow shirts brought Neng'ida and Esupat each a cup of chai and a boiled egg. Neng'ida had never eaten an egg before. She wasn't quite sure what to do with it, so she overtly stared at a nearby student as the girl peeled the shell off her egg and bit into it. Neng'ida's nose wrinkled and she frowned before she looked away.

After deliberately placing her unpeeled egg on the table in front of her, Neng'ida brought the chai to her lips, but she paused and jerked her head back abruptly when she caught a whiff of something she found suspect. She typically drank chai at home, but this chai smelled different. She warily took a sip, but choked slightly as the tepid liquid rolled over her tongue. She circumspectly put her still-full cup of chai on the table next to her uneaten egg and placed her hands in her lap. The clank of an iron bell signaled the end of teatime, and Neng'ida was grateful to leave behind the new and unusual provisions.

As she left the dining hall, Neng'ida whispered to Esupat, "That tasted awful." Then they both giggled nervously.

Checking in with Bibi Neema at the dormitory turned out to be even more harrowing than the food in the dining hall, not just because the matron was uncompromising in her instructions, but also because Neng'ida was introduced to a bathroom with running water, which she had no idea how to use, and a bedroom with bunk beds, which she'd never seen before. She was used to sleeping huddled with her sisters on a pile of blankets inside her mother's boma.

By the time Neng'ida reached the classroom where the other Form I students had gathered, she was overwhelmed with both trepidation and exhilaration by this strange and wondrous world she'd walked into. Now that she was here, she worried that she wouldn't be able to keep up, despite her eagerness to try.

■ ■ ■ ■ ■ ■ ■ ■

The next day just after breakfast, which Neng'ida also refused to eat, an older student walked up to the table where she was sitting with other Form I students and asked, "Is Neng'ida here?"

Neng'ida shyly stood and walked over to the girl.

"You're wanted by the headmistress. Please go to her office," the girl directed.

Neng'ida walked quickly, with a nervous sense of dread. Had she done something wrong already? Were they sending her home because her Swahili wasn't good enough, or maybe because they thought she didn't fit in at this modern, orderly campus? Her stomach sank at the thought that her weaknesses had so quickly been uncovered.

However, when she arrived in the headmistress's neatly appointed living room, she discovered something far worse than she'd imagined. There, perched on a flowery sofa cushion, sat her obviously beleaguered mother and, in a nearby chair, the intractable-looking man to whom she suspected she'd been promised in marriage.

CHAPTER 5:

NEGOTIATING PROMISES

All eyes were on Neng'ida. In one rapid sweep of the headmistress's silent living room, she took it all in. Her mother's shoulders were bent forward as she systematically twisted and released the already-tattered corner of her shuka. She examined Neng'ida with ambivalent, weary eyes and then glanced sideways at Neng'ida's yet-to-be husband.

He sat bent over, his elbows resting on his knees and his fingers wrapped around the shiny, well-worn wood of his *eng'udi*, the traditional long, thin walking stick carried by most Maasai morani. The man glanced up at Neng'ida with impenetrable eyes, and then he looked at his feet while compulsively spinning the end of his eng'udi against the floor.

Mama Mkuu stood next to Neng'ida. The headmistress's head tilted forward as she peered over her glasses at Neng'ida's mother with uncertain eyes. After a moment's hesitation, the headmistress placed her hand squarely in the center of Neng'ida's back and guided her fully into the room. Neng'ida sat at the far end of the couch near her mother, and away from her would-be husband, a man she hardly knew. Mama Mkuu lowered herself into a chair beside the tense girl.

Neng'ida felt rooted to the sofa. She couldn't bring herself to get up for the customary blessing from her mother, her husband-to-be, or Mama Mkuu. Instead, she murmured, "Shikamooni," to all of them. From her mother and Mama Mkuu came the typical response, "Marahaba," but from the man came nothing. The room fell silent again.

Her mother shifted her position on the sofa to gaze directly at Neng'ida, who was fastidiously studying the woven grass mat that covered the concrete floor in front of the couch. In a controlled voice, her mother asked, "Why did you leave without talking to me?"

Neng'ida was wearing her newly acquired secondary school uniform. She fiddled with the khaki-colored cloth of the skirt and bent her shoulders forward against the stiff fabric of her new T-shirt. As if encouraging her to talk, Mama Mkuu leaned forward in her chair. Neng'ida remained silent.

Her mother took Neng'ida's hand and said with more emotion, "I have been so worried about you. Your cousin came yesterday to tell us that you left the primary school with Esupat . . . that you left to come to this school. We want to know why you would do this. You have no money to pay for school. Your father has made plans for you to marry this man, and he wants you to come home. We are here to take you there."

Neng'ida continued to look at the floor. She left her limp hand in her mother's tight grasp. In little more than a whisper, Neng'ida stammered, "I don't want to go home."

She felt her mother flinch.

Now Neng'ida's husband-to-be fixed her with a firm stare, "I've already moved to your father's engang to help him with his cows and goats until we are married. Why don't you want to return home? Your father will be angry with you. He has told me to bring you home."

Neng'ida still stared at the floor but knew her mother had begun to cry. She swallowed hard and blinked back her own tears.

Mama Mkuu shifted uncomfortably in her chair as she cleared her throat. "This is a special school for students, just like Neng'ida, who come from Maasailand. I am also from the Rift Valley, and I know the difficulties our people face there. Education will give Neng'ida so many opportunities to improve her life and also your lives. We have a scholarship for her. It will cost you nothing. Please, if she wants to stay, let her stay. You will see the benefits. She can still get married later."

With this and the quiet sounds of her mother's weeping, all the tension and uncertainty of the last thirty-six hours softly burst forth. Hot tears ran down Neng'ida's cheeks. She cried because she'd left home—a place where everything was familiar and expected, and where she knew she was loved—to come to a place where everything and everyone was unfamiliar and new. She was struggling to understand Swahili, the food was foreign to her palate, and she felt as if she didn't know how to behave in this strange, new environment. But most of all, she cried because she had left her mother to worry and wonder why she had disappeared without even a word.

Through her tears, though, Neng'ida realized that she had to make her mother understand. Neng'ida knew if she could convince her mother that she wanted to stay, then it might be possible for her to go to school even over her father's objections. With this thought, she squeezed her mother's hand and began, "I didn't know secondary school was possible for me, but I have this opportunity, and I want to know more about what is possible if I stay at this school. I want to stay here. You know I love school. This is my chance. Please, let me stay."

Though neither Neng'ida's tears nor her mother's stopped, Neng'ida felt her mother's posture shift ever so slightly. This gave Neng'ida the courage to look at her mother, who was gazing back at her with a subtle glint of amazement and determination. Her mother understood. She would let Neng'ida stay.

When they both turned to look at the man to whom Neng'ida had been promised, his posture had also changed. He sat upright. His eng'udi rested against his shoulder, his arms crossed around it. His face was drawn and tight.

Her mother took the lead. "I know this was not the plan, but Neng'ida wants to stay. Do you want to take her away and start your marriage with unhappiness? What good will come of this? Do you want a wife who will resent you for what you have taken away from her?"

The man maintained a steely silence. Neng'ida turned her eyes back to the floor.

Mama Mkuu, who had remained quiet through this exchange, added, "Your children will be better off because they have an educated mother. Neng'ida will be able to teach your children. She will be able to manage your household better, and she will have the skills to earn money for your family."

Anger flickered in the man's eyes as he stood and curtly asked, "What good does any of this do me now? None. You have decided. There is nothing I can do to convince you otherwise. I will discuss this with Neng'ida's father. He will have something to say."

With that he turned and walked out the front door, leaving the women in silence.

CHAPTER 6:

THE ARRIVAL OF *WAGENI*

After months of waiting and preparing to start our teaching jobs in Monduli, the final journey to the schools came with a rush. In rapid succession, Mark and I made the daylong trip north with Doug and Linda from Morogoro to their new house in Arusha. The next morning, a Saturday, we whizzed around Arusha in their Land Rover, running errands before making the relatively short trip to Monduli. Though I felt nervous about this final step in what had been a long process, the anticipation associated with the unknown had become tiresome. Come what may, I needed to get settled and get started.

■ ■ ■ ■ ■ ■ ■ ■

Although it was Saturday, Dr. Msinjili had asked the teaching staff to gather for morning chai at ten thirty in the staff building, which sat in the center of Moringe Sokoine Secondary School's scattered, aging campus. He'd told the teaching staff that today they would welcome two new American teachers. One would teach math at Moringe, and the other would teach English farther down the hill at Moringe's new sister school—the Maasai Secondary School for Girls.

As Dr. Msinjili approached the small, worn-out staff building, he walked slowly, as he always did, with intention, as if each step required great thought. Though slight of build and contemplative in demeanor, Dr. Msinjili still drew people's attention most everywhere he went, not because of his physical presence but because of his wisdom and integrity. People sensed this about him even before they experienced it; thus they listened closely when Dr. Msinjili spoke because he was the kind of man who didn't waste words.

As Moringe's headmaster, Dr. Msinjili was a ubiquitous presence on campus—even when he wasn't there, it felt to students and staff as if his essence remained behind to keep watch over the school. Truth be told, he rarely went home, even though he had a wife, a son, and a young daughter. If you asked anybody why Dr. Msinjili spent so many hours at the school, they would tell you he stayed because he would do anything to inspire, cajole, encourage, or badger the more than four hundred students on his campus to learn. He believed education was that important.

Though he certainly had more than enough to do, he sometimes provided advice to the new school down the hill—the Maasai Secondary School for Girls—which hadn't been open long enough to graduate its first class yet. It served a particularly at-risk population, so he knew the staff there faced many challenges. In fact, he'd recently spoken to the headmistress about a girl named Neng'ida, who had chosen to stay at the school even after her family had come to take her home. He knew stories like Neng'ida's were commonplace there, and that the headmistress had a big job educating not just students, but also Maasai families.

Dr. Msinjili had anticipated that we would arrive in the morning, but as two o'clock came and went, he now worried about our whereabouts. He'd already made several announcements after chai, and then the staff had discussed how to discipline two Form III (tenth grade) students, young men who had snuck off campus to visit Monduli town the night before.

The boys wouldn't be sent home, though some of the teachers argued for this. Instead, the errant students would spend their afternoons for the next week clearing grass around several of the school's buildings. The staff had agreed on this course of action, and the teacher on duty would supervise the work while the discipline master would give the boys a stern lecture, and perhaps a few swift licks of a reed across the knuckles. In Tanzania, whether right or wrong, the expedience of corporeal punishment made it common practice at most schools.

Since nearly all the school's students lived on campus, the teachers, even the young ones, knew they were more than just teachers to these students. In many ways, they took on the roles of older siblings, or parents, or even grandparents. The staff taught students more than just history, agriculture, biology, or some other subject matter—they ushered students into adulthood, and because these students were part of Moringe's community, the teachers sought to instill good manners and a sense of responsibility in them, and that required discipline—sometimes with a carrot and sometimes with a stick.

Now that it was midafternoon, most of the staff was sitting quietly on the wooden benches and sofas that lined the staff room. Having finished the discussion of formal school business and having run out of neighborly small talk, a few teachers snoozed, one or two graded tests, another read a book, a small group chatted about local politics, and another one or two milled around outside the staff room answering students' questions.

Two female teachers bustled about in several classrooms just below the staff building as they enlisted students to sweep the floors, tidy up the desks and chairs, and wipe off the chalkboard-painted front walls in each classroom. The women led the school's joint staff and student committee on school cleanliness. The committee wanted the school to look well-ordered for our arrival and had spent the week hounding students to pick up trash around the campus.

As the hours wore on, though, everyone became increasingly restless and hungry for an overdue afternoon meal. On a typical Saturday, the teachers should have been busy at their homes, which surrounded the main part of campus, or in the nearby fields harvesting maize and beans. For many of them, May represented a busy time of year. They needed to harvest the food that would sustain their families for the rest of the year, but they all respected Dr. Msinjili, and they would remain here as he had asked.

Dr. Msinjili felt he couldn't expect the staff to wait around much longer, so he decided to walk down to the administrative building to see if anyone had sent a message. Most of Monduli lacked telephone service, so the staff and students typically sent or received messages by mail or messenger. However, the school had recently installed a somewhat unreliable telephone that required operator assistance. Dr. Msinjili used it strictly for school business. He thought maybe his secretary, who was waiting at his office in case we came there first, might have a message.

As he walked down the hill, the headmaster noticed several students washing their clothing in buckets around a nearby dormitory. He greeted them with a wave. Water was flowing today. He worried about many things, but this issue particularly concerned him. How could he house thirty teachers and their families and provide for four hundred students without water? He'd already convened a staff committee on the issue so that when the dry season came in August and September, they would be better prepared this year.

Down the hill, just above the administration building, a soccer game was underway on the large dirt field that separated the administrative building from the upper part of campus where most of the dormitories, classrooms, the staff building, and teachers' houses resided. When he arrived at his office, all was quiet. No one had sent word.

As Moringe's headmaster, Dr. Msinjili had spent months coordinating our work permits and completing the necessary paperwork to make our arrival possible, and he'd hoped we would finally arrive today. Dr. Msinjili knew all too well that the schools in Monduli could always use more teachers, particularly well-trained volunteer teachers in two subjects that proved particularly difficult to fill with qualified local candidates.

Over the years, Dr. Msinjili had hosted several American volunteer teachers, either through the Peace Corps or through the Lutheran church in America. Though the initial paperwork was cumbersome, he'd found value in the diversity, resources, and new perspectives that they brought to his Tanzanian staff and to Moringe's students. He knew that at least initially the students would be thrilled with the novelty of a new white teacher, and, truth be told, having even one or two foreign teachers provided the school with a status symbol that could help attract more students whose school fees kept the school running.

Usually everyone—Tanzanians and Americans—benefited from working together, and Dr. Msinjili felt eager to meet the new teachers, particularly Mark, who would be living and working at Moringe. Dr. Msinjili had closely reviewed his resume with Mr. Panga, the head of the math department, and they were impressed— other than Dr. Msinjili, Moringe had never had a PhD-educated teacher on staff. Though Mark had taught mathematics to high school students in Washington, DC, for several years, he'd more recently gone back to school to complete a PhD in operations research, or mathematical modeling for business. Dr. Msinjili and Mr. Panga felt the students would benefit from Mark's knowledge of how to apply math in the real world.

Dr. Msinjili struggled, though, with the pronunciation of those difficult nasally American "r" sounds, which littered both our last names. Mr. Panga and the headmaster had agreed, after a peel of laughter at each other's pronunciation of "Cutler" and "Rehrig," to simply call us Dr. Mark and Mwalimu Julie.

Dr. Msinjili had been told we were a couple but that we hadn't set a wedding date yet. He had met several Americans and even remembered from his university work in Russia so many years ago that different cultures approached courtship in different ways. He wasn't sure what to expect from us, but he wasn't worried about it either.

Just as the headmaster was about to walk back up the hill to dismiss the teachers for the day, he heard a Land Rover approaching.

■ ■ ■ ■ ■ ■ ■ ■

The pothole-riddled road into Monduli had at one time been fresh, smooth tarmac, but that was difficult to imagine now. Left to its own devices, the treacherous stretch of road had me firmly grasping the handle above my window and earnestly wishing I had skipped lunch in Arusha. In fact, I'd overeaten at breakfast and lunch thinking the meals might represent the last vestiges of Western food. I imagined the grocery situation in Monduli would be limited to staples—beans, rice, flour, tea, eggs, and whatever fruits and vegetables I could find at an open-air market.

Before we'd left Arusha, Linda had insisted that there were a handful of items that we couldn't leave without, including fresh pillows and basic groceries, so we'd explored Arusha's bustling central shopping district and added several plastic bags of purchases to our already substantial load of luggage.

At each stop, Doug stayed in the Land Rover to guard our luggage and purchases. In Arusha, wazungu often served as targets of convenience—an unwatched bag could disappear out of an open car window, even if the car was moving, and a backpack set down in a restaurant could be off and running on someone else's back in seconds.

I knew the word for "thief" in Swahili was "*mwizi.*" At language school, one of the teachers had advised me that I could stop a would-be thief by yelling this pejorative, explaining with disdain that Tanzanians viewed thieves as the lowest of low. Afterward, another student who had overheard this exchange pulled me aside and mentioned that I needed to reconsider the teacher's advice. He explained that mob justice often prevailed in these situations because people lacked confidence in Tanzania's justice system, which had a reputation for inefficiency, corruption, and delay. Recently, an angry mob had caught an accused thief, bound him inside a car tire, covered him in gasoline, and lit him on fire in Dar es Salaam. With horror, I quickly relegated "mwizi" into the category of words I would never, ever utter.

No doubt, our every move was closely watched in Arusha, and this made me nervous, not just because I feared someone would steal something from me, but because the color of my skin also attracted the attention of beggars and street kids. I tried not to stare at more than one beggar with leprosy, something I thought had been erad-icated shortly after biblical times, but the street kids troubled me most. Linda told me that many of Arusha's street kids had lost their parents to AIDS. They ranged in age from toddlers to teenagers, and they took care of each other on Arusha's streets.

I couldn't help but hand the smallest children the coins in my pockets when they grabbed my hand or hung on my skirt asking for money. What I didn't know was that this would make me even more of a target in the future because these children would remember me every time I came to Arusha.

When we stopped at an Indian-owned grocery store fre-quented by many of the city's expatriates, Mark and I were surprised that we could buy pasta, peanut butter, bread, jam, and even highly processed and thus unrefrigerated cheese. It seemed fresh cheese, or most anything that required refrigeration, was still a pipe dream.

Mark made sure to buy coffee, though all the store had was Africafé —a highly potent, instant powder that we'd encountered at language school as the strongest, blackest coffee we'd ever drunk. As Mark picked up the instant coffee, I said, "Isn't it ironic that I'll be teaching at a school on a coffee plantation, and we can't buy anything but instant coffee in this country?" He laughed, not so much because he thought this was funny, but because he'd been living in Seattle, the home of the modern coffee movement, prior to our departure, and the state of coffee in Tanzania had left him underwhelmed.

I, on the other hand, felt enthusiastic about finding the simple ingredients to make a plain peanut butter and jelly sandwich. I'd spent much of my time at language school with various forms of intestinal distress, so even though at home I was unaccustomed to eating processed foods, anything from a jar or package had become a high-value commodity to me because it represented "safe" food. The language school's kitchen staff, though apparently trained in food safety, still managed to prepare meals that disagreed with my system. I'd left language school five to ten pounds lighter than I'd arrived, and I didn't particularly need to lose weight.

After an already-thin fellow language-school student's fight with a particularly virulent form of food poisoning, which required medical intervention and intravenous fluids, I watched with sympathetic and fearful eyes as her skeletal frame and sunken eyes emerged after a week in bed. As my own clothes got looser, I began to worry that it wouldn't take too much to push me over a similar precipice, which often left me picking at my food wondering what unwelcome guests might lurk within.

Arusha's shopping excursion had taken longer than expected, and the road into Monduli required, to put it mildly, care and patience, which delayed us further. As we approached Monduli, a dilapidated, overloaded dala dala, or minibus, appeared on the horizon moving at a surprisingly rapid rate. A great cloud of dust followed the bus, making it difficult to miss. Even so, Doug veered into the ditch, unwilling to play a game of chicken for the smoothest stretch of road. The idea that this road had at any time in recent history contained lanes seemed absurd, and even if it had, I'd already learned from my hair-raising time on Tanzanian roadways that most Tanzanian drivers viewed the generally accepted rules of the road, such as don't pass when there is oncoming traffic, as not applicable to them.

The dala dala driver, who obviously took passengers between Monduli and Arusha regularly, knew precisely where to swerve off the road and into the ditch to avoid the biggest potholes. Even when the embankment pitched the bus at alarming angles, the driver pressed on as if this were just another humdrum trip to Arusha. For him, it probably was.

As the bus passed, several dozen eyes turned toward us with curiosity—a car full of wazungu obviously attracted attention in these parts. I peered back with equal interest, but for a different reason. People hung off the back of the bus and out its open door and seemed to be stacked on top of one another inside. I realized with a sense of dread that this would soon be our primary mode of transportation if we wanted to leave Monduli. I felt secure in knowing that Doug and Linda lived in Arusha, only about two hours away, but I hadn't anticipated that my mode of transportation to get to them would be quite so primitive.

Some of my anxiety about what the coming days would hold had subsided, or at least taken a backseat to my growing excitement about finally getting to the girls' school. Even as I bumped along the rough road into Monduli, I sensed there was something to love about this place. The landscape around me looked every bit the mythical Africa of my daydreams. To the east, Mount Meru, the little sister of Mount Kilimanjaro, rose up from flat, acacia-dotted grasslands, still green from the long rains. Though I knew there were no longer many wild animals around Monduli, I imagined a graceful giraffe floating across this landscape amid a herd of zebras.

To the north, the densely forested Monduli Mountains, which I knew marked the edge of the Great Rift Valley, sloped upward where the sun glinted off the buildings of what could only be Monduli town.

To the west, a dust cloud trailed a large herd of cattle. It was then that I saw them—the Maasai—two upright red dots in a landscape etched in neutral browns and greens. Their angular bodies, long strides, and thin walking sticks kept time to the movement of their cattle. I gazed at them as if they'd walked out of some other world—an enigma I could solve if I stared long and hard enough.

As we entered Monduli, we bypassed the main part of town. It looked to contain a handful of quiet, dirt-packed streets lined with a range of brightly colored simple structures, small shops perhaps. A few people milled about, but Monduli seemed downright sleepy compared to Arusha. As we skirted town, I noticed a hand-painted sign indicating the direction to Moringe Sokoine Secondary School and the Maasai Secondary School for Girls, both to the east of Monduli town.

About one mile down a dusty dirt road that obviously saw more foot than vehicle traffic, we pulled up to a long, stout auburn-colored building fronted with airy, open windows, some of them missing their glass. A handful of students sat at desks inside the building, and a Tanzanian flag fluttered lightly on a flagpole near the building's entrance. Block letters neatly painted on the building's eaves indicated, "Moringe Sokoine Secondary School Administration Block."

I quickly squeezed and released Mark's hand in the back seat and took a deep breath.

We clambered out of the Land Rover, tossing aside plastic bags of purchases as we went. A short Tanzanian man with close-cut, slightly graying hair and kind-but-penetrating eyes came out of the building. He wore comfortable-looking shoes, neat slacks, and a button-down short-sleeve shirt with a pair of reading glasses in the breast pocket. As we walked up to him, he stood with his hands behind his back and his head slightly cocked to one side, as if he was closely considering the scene before him.

Mark and I both greeted him with, "Shikamoo." He responded with the customary "marahaba" and then followed that with a quick string of Swahili phrases: "*Karibuni sana. Naitwa Dr. Msinjili; ni mkuu wa shule. Nimefurahi sana kukuona. Habari ya safari?*"

Doug, Linda, Mark, and I all stared blankly at one another and then fumbled around for an appropriate Swahili response until Doug laughed and said, "As you can see, we're still learning Swahili." The man smiled sympathetically and rephrased in English, "You are very welcome here. I am Dr. Msinjili, the headmaster. I am so glad you are here. How was your trip?"

Doug took the lead and said, "We're glad to be here too. I was a little worried we might fall into a pothole on that road and never be heard from again."

Dr. Msinjili chuckled gently. "Yes. That road reminds us that in Tanzania things move *polepole,* or slowly, whether we want them to or not."

After brief introductions with Doug and then Linda, Dr. Msinjili reached out to shake first Mark's hand and then mine, as he concluded, "You must be Mark and Julie. The staff is eager to meet you. We've been waiting for your arrival all day. Please, let's go up to the staff room now so you can meet your new colleagues."

At Dr. Msinjili's direction, Doug and Linda drove the Land Rover up a rough dirt road that bisected the campus. At a row of modest, crudely constructed square houses, they cut off the road and into the grass to reach a small white house in the middle of the row. From a distance, we could see tall grass surrounding the humble structure, though a path had been cut through the grass to the home's blue wood-plank front door, now held shut with a durable padlock. On either side of the front door, similarly fashioned blue wood-plank shutters stood slightly ajar over glassless window openings.

A lanky, colorful plant bloomed bright orange near one window, and a broad-leafed banana tree shaded the other. Dr. Msinjili indicated Mark would share the house with a Peace Corps volunteer, which took both Mark and me by surprise. We didn't know the school had a Peace Corps volunteer, let alone that Mark would be living with him. We had been under the false impression that Mark would be living alone.

Dr. Msinjili, Mark, and I followed Doug and Linda up the hill on foot. At first, we walked quietly, Mark and I on either side of Dr. Msinjili. The headmaster seemed almost shy, but in an assertive, time-tested kind of way, as if he knew more than he was willing to say. Dr. Msinjili moved deliberately and pointed out various structures along the way, trying to orient us to our new surroundings.

When we arrived at the staff building, the headmaster led the way inside. The large room was lined with couches and benches now filled with a sea of Tanzanian faces. On one wall a colorful poster read, "Dare to dream it. Work to achieve it," and a bulletin board contained several snapshots of students, teachers, and visitors along with a few announcements, the school's timetable, and a handwritten letter or two. Above the door, a color photo of President Mkapa smiled down at us, and on the opposite wall a photo of the first president of Tanzania, Mwalimu Julius Nyerere, gazed back.

A hush came over the room as those who'd been standing took their seats. Off to the side, we noticed two young, white faces, presumably the Peace Corps volunteer and another American volunteer we'd been communicating with through email. We knew her tenure would soon be ending, and our arrival had been timed to overlap with her for several months before she returned to the United States.

When he had everyone's attention, Dr. Msinjili stood with us at the front of the room and spoke for several minutes in Swahili before switching to English and saying, "... but our visitors are still learning Swahili, so now I will introduce them in English." By this time, Doug and Linda had entered the room and were sitting at the back.

"This is Dr. Mark and Mwalimu Julie, our long-awaited new teachers." With this, several of the female teachers ululated with joyful trills while other teachers clapped and smiled broadly at us. Even though I felt as if I wanted to hide in a corner, I smiled back and waved. Mark shuffled uncomfortably next to me. Neither one of us enjoyed being the center of attention.

Dr. Msinjili continued, "We are so glad they have come to help us here in Monduli. Doug and Linda, who are sitting back there, have brought them. Doug and Linda help American volunteers in Tanzania, and they live in Arusha.

"Dr. Mark will teach math, a very unpopular and difficult subject for our students here at Moringe," the headmaster teased, "but I know he is quite experienced at helping students love math, so we expect a lot from him. I know Mr. Panga, the head of the math department, is very happy you're here." With this, Dr. Msinjili referred to a broadly smiling man who peered at us through large square glasses, clasped his hands together over his heart, and tilted his head toward Mark in a sign of appreciation and esteem.

Dr. Msinjili continued, "I think you will also see Mwalimu Julie around because she will be teaching with our friends at the Maasai Secondary School for Girls. Her specialty is English, and hopefully she won't grade us too hard for our mispronunciations. Mwalimu Julie, you are always welcome here at Moringe too.

"We appreciate so much that you have come to work with us, and we are looking forward to getting to know you. Now I will ask the second master, Mr. Kwayu, to also say a few words."

At this, a jovial, slightly aging man stood and walked toward us. He also smiled warmly, and he said, "You are most welcome," as he took Mark's hands in his and then did the same to me. "Colleagues, let us welcome these new teachers," he declared as he began to clap. All the other teachers followed suit and then the meeting broke up. Several people came up to us and introduced themselves as they exited the staff building. I could tell Mark felt overwhelmed as I watched him shake hand after hand while smiling and nodding. Neither of us had expected such a welcome.

As we left the staff building, Dr. Msinjili led Mark toward his new house. I trailed behind and watched Mark talking quietly to the headmaster, who once again moved with the same slow, deliberate walk I'd observed earlier. His head was bent toward Mark and his hands clasped behind his back as he listened closely to whatever Mark was saying.

Several other teachers ran ahead to help Doug and Linda unload the Land Rover. A female teacher already had one of Mark's trunks balanced on her head as she carried it into his new house. I felt embarrassed by all the bags and luggage the teachers were now examining in Doug and Linda's Land Rover.

Before I knew it, Mr. Kwayu took one of my hands and Mr. Panga took the other. We gradually walked toward all the activity in front of Mark's house. They spoke softly to me, as if they knew I felt like a scared animal that needed reassurance. I don't remember exactly what they said to me, but I remember I felt enveloped in this welcoming community, as if Dr. Msinjili, Mr. Kwayu, and Mr. Panga, along with all their colleagues and neighbors, would shepherd us through fire if they had to.

CHAPTER 7:

LIKE A STRANGER IN THE NIGHT

While Mark remained at his house to unpack, Doug and Linda drove me a mile beyond Moringe to the school I would now call home. As we approached the campus, I wondered with eagerness and a somewhat inflated sense of self-importance what kind of welcome would await me here, but a stop at the school's office, which doubled as the headmistress's house, revealed everything was shut tight. Doug, Linda, and I stood near the Land Rover wondering what to do for several minutes until a lone young girl, who appeared to be cleaning, emerged from the front door.

After some machinations in broken Swahili, she understood I was the new mzungu teacher. With this understanding, she quickly walked back into the house, returned with a key, and directed us down the hill to a house that looked exactly like that of the head-mistress—a one-story, whitewashed concrete-block building with a green bati roof. The house fit into a series of similar-looking oblong buildings that resided in the coffee fields just outside a tall thorny hedge that delineated the main part of campus. The eight-foot-tall imposing hedge made a big loop, about 250 yards in diameter, around numerous other buildings that I assumed were classrooms and dormitories. I noted immediately that all the buildings here were newer and in much better condition than those at Moringe.

As we approached my new place of residence, I studied the coffee trees with interest. I'd always pictured the school's coffee fields as vast croplands filled with small bean-bearing plants, such as those that grew in my father's arid Montana garden. I'd never imagined that coffee grew on trees in groves and looked more like berries than beans.

The lush, cool greenness of the place jarred my preconceived ideas about what living near the equator might be like. Monduli sat on the side of a mountain at about five thousand feet above sea level, which made it much more temperate, even slightly chillier than I'd expected. This was not the first time since arriving in Tanzania that I realized about half of what I'd packed would be useless.

I knew I would be sharing the house with another American volunteer, Susan, who had been teaching at the school for more than a year. She and I had communicated a time or two by email prior to my arrival in Tanzania.

She didn't answer when Doug knocked, so I tentatively unlocked and opened the front door feeling wary about entering her territory when she wasn't around. Doug and Linda helped me pile my now somewhat impractical belongings inside the front door, and then they quickly bade me good luck and farewell, eager to get back to Arusha before dark. My rather anticlimactic arrival, and Doug and Linda's abrupt departure, left me feeling alarmingly alone after months of handholding. Rather than dwell on this, though, I floated from room to room surveying the contents of the house.

In the living room, a bookshelf held several random paperback novels, teaching resources, and books about Tanzania. I pulled *Where There Is No Doctor* off one of the shelves and leafed through it before gingerly returning it to its slot with the urgent hope that I would never need to reopen it. Before coming to Tanzania, I'd completed an EMT course. Even though I'd gained the certification, my practicum hours in an emergency room had persuaded me that my constitution favored debilitating panic over calming presence when faced with disaster; thus emergency medicine was probably best left to others.

Near the bookshelf, I paused to sit on a wooden bench-like couch made more comfortable by wide rectangular cushions covered in traditional Maasai fabric. I ran my hand over the red-and-blue checkered fabric as if touching it might provide some clues into the Maasai culture. Two matching chairs sat on either end of the couch, and a rectangular coffee table stood in front. A dingy round woven-grass mat covered the bare concrete floor under the coffee table. Near the front door, which I could see from my perch on the couch, several pairs of dirty utilitarian black rubber boots stood guard, and two broken umbrellas leaned against the wall.

Down the hall from the living room, the door to what appeared to be a vacant bedroom, and thus the likely candidate for my room, stood ajar. The room's closet contained a handful of used dresses that looked like they might fit me. A lonely single bed sported a handmade quilt, and a tent-like mosquito net hung from the ceiling and surrounded the entire bed. A bare light bulb dimly lit the room, and a louvered jalousie window that overlooked the front of the house provided a few faint rays of natural light. Like much of the rest of the house, the bedroom smelled dusty and felt shadowy and cold even in the late-afternoon sun.

To give the room a bit of warmth, I wandered back into the living room and grabbed the brand-new pillow I'd gotten in Arusha. I returned to the vacant bedroom, and, pushing past the mosquito net, I gently placed the pillow at the head of the bed, silently thanking Linda that tonight when my tired, overwrought head hit the pillow something would smell bright, clean, and new.

I then examined the relatively bare kitchen, which had an operational gas stovetop and oven, a working refrigerator, and an electric kettle and toaster perched on a utilitarian cement counter-top. A handful of mismatched dishes were neatly stacked on a shelf under the counter, and a simple wooden table and chairs stood just outside the kitchen in the living room.

About this time, a growing rumble in the distance caught my attention. I'd already gathered from my short time in Monduli that its soundtrack consisted almost solely of pastoral notes—cow bells clanked somewhere up the hill, active bursts of Swahili floated across the coffee fields as a pair of children alternately walked and ran past the campus, a light breeze rustled tree branches against the roof, and the sighing, intermittent bleat of a goat drifted from behind a nearby house. Thus, the unexpected thunder of mecha-nized sound drew me to the front window.

I pulled back the curtains and watched as a fussy-sounding, antiquated open-air Land Rover bounded toward my house and shuddered to a stop out front. A dark-haired mzungu woman in sunglasses, a flannel shirt, and blue jeans swung open the vehicle's squeaky door and jumped out. I took a deep breath and prepared to meet Susan.

She walked swiftly toward the house, warmly greeted me, and then took to immediately showing me around as we engaged in the back-and-forth small talk of people who'd been tossed together and were assessing each other, measuring whether we thought we could successfully inhabit the same space.

Susan had grown up in Oregon, which meant I immediately felt a certain kinship with her because I'd also grown up in the American West, in Montana. I hoped that our similar upbringings would translate into common ground on which we might build a friendship.

I learned right away that if I asked Susan a question, I got a straightforward, honest answer. She didn't mask responses in nice-ties or say what she thought I wanted to hear. Susan obviously didn't suffer fools, she didn't mince words, and she didn't feel she needed to impress me or anyone else. For all these reasons, I immediately liked her and knew we would get along just fine.

One of Susan's first self-appointed tasks was to purposefully march me to the darkest back corner of the house as she said, "I'll give you the 'bathroom for dummies' lesson."

Nonchalantly noting the acrid smell, Susan explained it was best to keep the small louvered window at the back of the dank space open since, even though she kept the bathroom clean, "It always smells in here because the toilet doesn't flush all the way. To get it to flush completely, you have to heave a full bucket of water into the bowl."

To my chagrin, Susan proceeded to explain that water was a relatively unreliable resource at the school, so it was best to flush "only when necessary," and to use the bucket-flush method only for "big jobs."

I'd just met the woman and already we were discussing bowel movements, something that I'd admittedly become desensitized to at language school where the daily report was less about the weather and more about everyone's intestinal status after the previous night's meal.

Susan further explained, "The house doesn't have hot water, but the bathroom sink sometimes has cold water that you should not drink. You can't drink any water that comes out of a faucet in this house without first boiling it unless you want to be heaving a lot of buckets into that toilet."

She then told me that the rectangular concrete slab with the drain served as the shower. "It has a faucet that has been hooked up to water, but it mysteriously lacks the pressure required for water to move up and out the showerhead. I've had it looked at, but nobody seems to be able to fix it." She turned on the faucet and we both watched as the showerhead dripped a few drops of water.

In the face of this, I asked Susan how she bathed, a rather personal question for someone I'd just met but something I needed to know if I was going to keep my rising panic at bay.

Susan related her bathing process with matter-of-fact precision. "I heat a pot of water in the electric kettle in the kitchen if there is electricity, or I use the gas cooker if there isn't. I mix the boiling water with cold water in a wide-mouthed bucket and haul it into the bathroom. I stand in an empty bucket on the concrete slab, and I use a plastic cup to dump warm water from the other bucket over my head. I soap up, rinse off, and try to be done with it before I freeze to death. Oh, and I save the bathwater to flush the toilet later."

Susan's nonchalance about nearly everything kept me surprisingly calm. If she could do this, then I could do this.

Take bucket baths? "No problem."

Teach Maasai girls English? "Just get up there and do it. They'll love whatever you do."

Fix three meals a day without access to a grocery store and many of the staples of my diet? "Eat simply. You'll be fine."

When I asked Susan about the run-down Land Rover in front of the house, she said, "The charming piece of junk belongs to the Snake Park." I responded with a look of horror as I enquired, "The Snake Park?"

Susan explained that at the turnoff from the main road onto the pothole-riddled road into Monduli, there was a small establishment that served as a campground and stopping-off point for overland trucks carrying tourists from Arusha out to Ngorongoro Crater, the Serengeti, and other game parks in northwest Tanzania. Known as the Snake Park, the place was run by a South African family with an unusual love for reptiles and a vast knowledge of the way things worked in this part of Tanzania. Susan was dating their youngest son, Wade.

I quickly learned this meant several very important things. One, we had access to relatively clean water in large jerry cans that Susan or Wade regularly hauled up to our house from the Snake Park. The water came from a pipeline that supplied a nearby Tanzanian military base. Two, Susan spent most of her free time down at the Snake Park, particularly on the weekends, so I would be spending a lot of time by myself in Monduli unless I wanted to go with her to the Snake Park. And, three, the Snake Park traded in cold beer and spit-fired barbeque, which seemed like a very good reason to visit the place, even if they did have snakes.

After our introduction, Susan left me to unpack and further assess my surroundings, but not before handing off two books—an English book for Form I and another for Form IV, which Susan casually told me I'd be teaching beginning Monday morning. A knot immediately formed in my stomach.

"I'd hoped to have a few days to get oriented before starting to teach, maybe observe a class or two, meet the other teachers and staff, discuss the curriculum, and become familiar with the campus and its students," I said as calmly as possible.

Susan responded, "You'll be fine. We've been waiting forever for you to arrive, so it's best to just get started. You've only got a couple of weeks before the June break anyway, so this will give you a good start, and then you'll have some time to organize yourself."

I quickly glanced through the books Susan had just handed me. I'd already heard about these books. They'd been written by a previous American volunteer who had taught English as a second language for nearly twenty years in a range of settings. She'd written the books during her tenure at the Maasai Secondary School for Girls and then sent the manuscripts back to the United States to be copied, spiral bound, and shipped back to Tanzania for future use by teachers and students. Local books were in short supply and generally not up to the standards she'd expected, and importing textbooks written for an American or European context meant explaining culture and vocabulary that simply wasn't relevant in Tanzania.

Susan also handed me a slip of paper noting the times each of my classes met and the pages in the books where I should begin teaching. I didn't know it yet, but this would prove to be my sole guidance into what to expect come Monday morning and beyond.

When I asked Susan about a curriculum, she directed me to the *United Republic of Tanzania's English Curriculum for Secondary Schools*, a thin paperback leaflet on the bookshelf in the living room, which Susan described as "not particularly useful." Nonetheless, I added it to the books she'd given me and dug out several English-as-a-second-language books I'd brought from the United States and neatly stacked them on the wooden desk in my bedroom for further review later.

That evening, Mark and I met every other mzungu living in Monduli because Susan had invited them all to our house for spaghetti dinner. Mark and his new, unexpected roommate arrived first, and I immediately realized the pairing might not be the best match. Mark's hair looked muddled as if he'd been running his hands through the top, something he only did when worried. He looked uncharacteristically rattled and wasn't making eye contact with anyone, all bad signs, I thought. While Mark's character tended toward careful thought and quiet introspection, his roommate's seemed to tend toward outspokenness and exuberance.

After a couple of minutes, Laura, the other American volunteer teacher I'd seen at Moringe, showed up bearing a bag of ripe mangos, which she handed to me with a warm welcome while offering to show me around Monduli. When everyone headed toward the kitchen to help Susan with last-minute food preparations, I excused myself to give Mark a tour of the rest of the house.

When we stepped away from the group, Mark uttered under his breath, "My house is much more 'rustic' than yours." He proceeded to enumerate the problems: there was no place to shower, so bucket baths were in his future too; the house's inside toilet didn't really work, so he had to use an outhouse; there wasn't a refrigerator or a stove, so to cook, he'd have to use an outdoor *jiko* similar to the ones we used while camping; and the final straw was that he had nothing more than a simple bed for furniture. "I don't know what I'm going to do," Mark said glumly.

Before we'd left the United States, we'd received a list of the items we could expect to find in our housing at the schools, which included most of the things Mark had just named as missing. I lightly touched him on the arm and whispered, "Maybe we can talk to Doug and Linda and figure something out. Meantime, why don't you at least plan to come down here for dinner for the next few nights." Mark rarely complained about anything, so the fact that he'd said something had me concerned.

"Don't worry. I'll manage," he said, trying to be stoic. "It just isn't what I expected."

As we slowly walked toward the living room, Mark informed me that Mr. Kwayu, the second master at Moringe, had invited us to dinner at his home the following night.

"Great," I said with an easy smile.

"How about if I walk up around six o'clock tomorrow so you can show me your house? Maybe we can find some ways to improve things," I suggested as brightly as I could.

"All right," Mark responded more hopefully. "Have you met any of the teaching staff here yet?"

I looked down at my shoes and answered, "No, other than Susan, it's been quiet." In truth, I felt disappointed that my arrival had gone unnoticed, at least by all but the Americans, who had come out in full force. There were already half a dozen sitting in my living room.

Mark quickly squeezed my hand in a gesture of encouragement and whispered, "Before you know it, you'll know everyone down here."

Just as we stepped into the living room, a broad Hagrid-like man walked through the front door. He smiled and scooped up Susan in a hug.

"Hi, Marvin," she said and then turned to present us. "Meet our new volunteers, Julie and Mark."

"Hey, guys. It's great to see you. Isn't Monduli wonderful?" Marvin asked as he shuffled over in his Birkenstocks, shorts, and cut-off red T-shirt. "I'm Marvin, but you can call me Marv, or Marvin, whatever you like. I'm only one half of the equation, though. Jean is on her way." Marv shook Mark's hand and put his other oversized hand on my shoulder as if we were old friends. "It's great you guys are here," he declared, and I knew he meant it.

Just then, the front door flew open and in walked Jean, a sturdy-looking middle-aged woman with short, slightly salty brown hair and deep brown eyes. She peered at the group over a pair of reading glasses, which perched on the end of her nose. She wore a long brown leopard-print muumuu with white socks and sneakers, and she had a wide, colorful Maasai-beaded bracelet on her right wrist.

"Hiya, friends. I brought cookies with real chocolate chips. Anybody want some? They can be an appetizer," she said with a smile. "You must be Mark and Julie. Welcome! I have to tell you, I don't really cook. Rebecca made these. You'll meet her. Marvin loves her because she is the best cook. She helps us out around the house. We live just down the hill in the round house. Come by tomorrow for coffee. We have hot coffee all the time down there. Good Seattle coffee too. You're always welcome. Hey, Susan. What can I do? Anything?" Jean said without taking a breath as she walked past us toward the kitchen.

Jean and Marv's reputation had preceded them. Whenever we'd talked to American supporters of the school, we'd heard, "Oh, you'll just love Jean and Marv. They are such characters. That place just wouldn't run without them." We knew Jean and Marv hailed from Seattle and that they'd married later in life.

From first impressions, they couldn't have seemed more different. Jean was like nearly every school administrator I'd ever met—friendly, talkative, direct, in-charge, and, truth be told, a little bossy. At the other end of the spectrum was Marv, an enormous teddy bear of a man with a tendency toward scattered genius, an affable go-with-the-flow attitude, and virtually no ego. He was quick to tell us in easygoing, forthright fashion that he was a recovering alcoholic and was setting up Alcoholics Anonymous groups in Tanzania.

Classified as long-term missionaries, Jean and Marv's placement at the school was indefinite. Jean served as the school's chaplain and helped whenever she could with administrative tasks, which I would later learn was no small job. The relatively new school was struggling to implement the stringent, often unclear, and regularly changing government requirements for curriculum, testing, and reporting. As well, the school's at-risk population required constant attention—girls needed to be recruited, parents needed to be persuaded and sometimes managed, and students needed advice and encouragement beyond that of ordinary pupils. And all of this needed to be accomplished while raising money for the school and navigating the sometimes-tumultuous relationships between predominantly white, American donors and local leaders who often didn't see eye to eye. However, Jean had spent most of her career as an administrator and theology teacher at a Bible college in Seattle, and she gave every impression that she was up to whatever task came before her.

As the self-described resident writer and fixer of the broken, Marv made it clear he mostly followed Jean around, but that he had come to the school with the hope of teaching English. The school had a policy that all teachers should be female, so for the time being Marv's teaching career was on hold. Meantime, he told us, he went to Arusha once a week in an effort to get his AA group off the ground there, and he'd also organized a weekly meeting in Monduli.

By the end of the evening, I was slumped in my chair, unable to make any more small talk. Jean noticed, corralled everyone to clear the table, and then offered Mark and the others from Moringe a ride up the hill in the Land Cruiser she and Marv shared.

I wanted to say goodnight to Mark, so I rode along in the front seat squeezed between Jean, who drove, and Mark, who sat in the passenger's seat. All the others, including Marv, piled in the back. As we bumped along toward Moringe and dropped people off one by one, I thought about how long the day had felt while Jean chatted about her family in Minnesota, the expatriate church she sometimes attended with Marv in Arusha, and her duties at the school.

Mark and I both feigned attention, though admittedly we had reason to be inattentive. Today, we'd met some of Arusha's street kids, encountered Moringe's overwhelmingly warm welcome, said goodbye to Doug and Linda and the safety net they'd provided us since we'd arrived in Tanzania, and met more Americans than we'd imagined would be within walking distance of our new homes.

I knew come Monday I'd be standing in front of a group of Maasai girls whether I was ready for it or not, but for now, all I could think of was sleep.

When I returned to the house, Susan had already left for the Snake Park. Though overwhelmed by exhaustion, I lay awake and alone in the pitch black of my new bedroom listening to the rustling of trees, the unusual creak of the roof, and the chirping stridulation of hundreds of crickets.

Susan had warned me that the school's night guard sometimes liked to crouch below my bedroom window or even snooze there for part of the night. Nonetheless, I quickly sat up in bed sometime in the middle of the night having heard a shuffling noise outside my window.

I pulled the quilt up around my chin and sat completely still, listening as the shuffling got closer to the house and then stopped. I took a moment to gather my courage, and then I crept over to the window, pulled back a corner of the curtain, and strained to see any movement in the coffee fields in front of the house.

I rapidly covered my mouth to muffle my gasp when I heard a man clear his throat below the window and then say, "*Niwie radhi, mwalimu. Niko hapa. Habari za usiku?*" I slowly translated his words in my head. Forgive me, teacher. I'm here. How is the night?

I carefully thought through the English to Swahili translation before I spoke. The night is good. I'm sorry for your work, sir. Then I squeaked, "*Usiku ni nzuri. Pole kwa kazi, bwana.*"

"*Asante sana, mwalimu. Karibu sana,*" he said as I translated. Thank you, teacher. You are very welcome here.

"*Asante, bwana. Nahitaji kulala sasa. . . . Usiku mwema,*" I stuttered hesitantly. Thank you, sir. I need to sleep now. . . . Good night.

"*Lala salama,*" he said. Sleep well.

I crawled back in bed, proud that I'd just communicated with my first Maasai morani, but unsure if I felt better or worse knowing that he slept under my window. I curled up tightly under the covers and considered this for a long time before finally drifting off with visions of tall, thin, mashuka-clad men dancing in my head.

Sunday morning, I awoke late to the winsome sounds of singing in the distance. Surfacing from sleep as if still in a dream, I roused as one song rolled into another. I listened as unaccompanied voices set the beat and multiplied the pitches, tones, and notes into ethereal harmonies. A chant preceded a fulsome response.

I pattered to my now light-filled window, pulled back the curtains, and listened as a bewitching chorus floated up over the thorny hedge that separated my house from the rest of the school. It was the students. I was sure of it. They were singing. I stood there and listened for as long as the songs went on. Just as when I'd visited the tiny church in the mountains near Morogoro, I felt the spirit of the place wash over me in those songs.

For the remainder of the day, the mundane intruded on the sacred. I knocked around the lonesome house, unpacked my belongings, reviewed several teaching books, and prepared my lesson plans for Monday. Three times, I walked up to the headmistress's house and knocked while lightly calling, "*Hodi, hodi,*" a common way of saying, "I'm here." Her house and the school office remained silent and shuttered, and with each unsuccessful attempt to find her, I became increasingly anxious.

By evening, a stir craze had set in, and I found myself thankful when it was time to walk up to Moringe to see Mark and to have dinner with Mr. Kwayu and his family. When I arrived at Mark's house, his roommate was away and Mark seemed less frazzled, his face now set with determination. In a matter of less than twenty-four hours, he'd accepted his lot as he came to realize his house was no different from those of his neighbors and fellow teachers. He'd organized his room with precision, cleverly turning his trunks into furniture and hobbling broken pieces of furniture together to create a bedroom space that felt like him, remarkably ingenious and peaceful.

He explained with enthusiasm all he had done, swung the door shut, and embraced me in the quiet privacy of his bedroom. "I miss you," he confided.

"I miss you too," I replied. I felt better in his embrace but still apprehensive that I hadn't met anybody on campus other than the wazungu.

He lightly brushed the hair off my forehead and then leaned forward and whispered in my ear, "Stop furrowing. I can tell you're worrying."

"I can't help it," I said lightly. "It's like asking me to stop breathing."

"I know, I know, but I can always hope," he teased.

Mark then looked over my shoulder through his bedroom window and stiffened slightly before he released me and swung the bedroom door back open. I turned to follow his gaze and saw Mr. Kwayu walking up the path to the house. Mark immediately walked to the front door, opened it, and greeted Mr. Kwayu with "shikamoo." Mr. Kwayu smiled, bowed slightly, and responded, "Marahaba, Dr. Mark. *Habari za jioni?*"

"Nzuri. We are doing well," Mark offered as I joined him at the front door.

"Oh, Mwalimu Julie. Habari?" Mr. Kwayu said with a warm smile when he saw me.

"Shikamoo," I responded as it occurred to me that Mr. Kwayu's voice boomed with the same tenor as that of James Earl Jones. I smile to myself at the thought that, appropriately, Mr. Kwayu spoke with the voice of *The Lion King*'s Mufasa.

"Marahaba, mwalimu. How are you? Is everything going fine down at the girls' school? I think you have been very busy today. I can tell, and probably this guy too. He has been busy too," he stated with a smile.

"We are getting settled in," I said as I walked down the front steps to where Mr. Kwayu stood while Mark locked the door behind me.

Mr. Kwayu took both my hands in his and shook them slightly as he bent forward and said again, "Karibu, mwalimu. Karibu sana. You are most welcome at Moringe. Right, Dr. Mark, she is welcome?" Mr. Kwayu's eyes sparkled and several warm, deep chuckles accompanied his smile as he watched Mark walk toward us and nod. "Yes. I think he agrees that you are welcome," Mr. Kwayu stated conspiratorially.

"Please, let us go to my house so you can rest and meet my wife. You know we call her Mama Conrad, because Conrad is our eldest child. Mama Conrad, she is there waiting for us," he said as he directed us up the hill from Mark's house. "I think you will also meet my three children."

As we walked, Mr. Kwayu laughed and smiled slyly as he said to Mark, "You know, sir, you are now the *kiazi kikubwa* here. You know what that means?" He paused a beat and then continued, "It means 'big potato.' You are Dr. Mark. No other teachers are doctors, so I think we will call you kiazi kikubwa." Mr. Kwayu laughed heartily at his own joke. "What do you think of that, doctor?"

Mark laughed lightly and countered, "Well, I am not *mzee*, so old and wise, like you. I think I am only kiazi *kidogo* sana . . . 'a very little potato' compared to you."

At this, Mr. Kwayu stopped walking and doubled over with a peel of deep laughter. "Oh, Dr. Mark. You are very clever. I can tell, Mwalimu Julie. He is so clever. You are going to marry a very clever man."

Mark and I exchanged a glance, and then I felt my cheeks turn pink. Neither of us knew how to respond to this. We'd talked about marriage in the hypothetical future, but Mr. Kwayu had just made it sound like invitations were already in the mail.

To mask my embarrassment, I laughed and declared, "Yes. He is very smart, Mr. Kwayu, and to me he will always be a kiazi kikubwa." At this, Mr. Kwayu tipped his head back and chuckled with amusement; then he linked one arm in mine and the other in Mark's and led us onward.

CHAPTER 8:

LIFE INSIDE THE BELL JAR

I awoke before sunrise to the strident crowing of roosters—many, many roosters. My austere bedroom with its cold, bare concrete walls and floor had already lightened from pitch black to soft gray, but it still felt too early to get up, so I lay ensconced in the mosquito net that hung over my bed listening to the sounds outside and wondering if there would be electricity this morning. A lone dog barked in the distance, a dove cooed softly in the large-canopy tree outside my bedroom window, a yet-to-be identified animal scampered across the metal roof above my head, and the pervasive roosters continued their calls and responses from one side of campus to the other.

I'd slept fitfully, and I felt taut everywhere, as if my body had drawn itself in overnight and now threatened to uncoil starting with my stomach. It seemed breakfast might be out of the question today.

From my bed, I looked across the room at the dress that hung from the hook on the back of my bedroom door. The school year was well underway for my students, but today was my first day, so I'd carefully looked through all my dresses as I'd unpacked them yesterday and settled on the long brown one with delicate yellow flowers, my favorite, as my first-day-of-school outfit. Even though it felt a little superstitious, I'd chosen all my clothes right down to my underwear as if I were once again an insecure elementary school student who thought my school year would go better if only I could dress right on that first day. The stakes felt higher today, so I'd even polished my sandals for good measure.

I climbed out of bed and pattered in my bare feet across the cool concrete to my simple wooden desk. I grabbed my notebook, skittered back across the room, ducked under the mosquito net, and climbed back in bed. I began leafing through my lesson plans, written and rewritten several times before being transcribed in my neatest handwriting into this brand-new notebook.

I read, "Form I. Introduce yourself. Ask each student to introduce herself and to mention where she comes from. Practice greeting one another in English. Turn to page 27 and go over vocabulary. . . ."

I methodically studied each word on the page even though I'd already gone over the lesson plans so many times I'd nearly memorized them word-for-word. During my student teaching, I'd marveled at my supervising teacher, who rarely wrote more than a couple of words in her planner and still managed to teach an entire day with ease. I didn't think I'd ever feel that comfortable in front of a classroom. Even with three semesters of experience teaching writing at Colorado State University, I still lived in constant fear of standing before a group of students with absolutely nothing to say. Thus, I continually spent far more time preparing to teach than actually teaching.

After making my bed, I washed my hair with cold water in the kitchen sink while I heated water for a bucket bath in the electric kettle. I quickly bathed, dressed methodically, and then pilfered a slice of bread from Susan's stash. I toasted it and then ate it plain with a cup of instant coffee while making a flexible, yet hopeful, grocery list. I needed to walk to Monduli after school to investigate my options for food. Mark was coming over for dinner so we could compare notes on our first days of school, and though I'd purchased several items in Arusha with Doug and Linda, I needed to find some fresh fruits and vegetables, and I wanted to get a better sense of what was available in Monduli.

When Mr. Kwayu and Mark had walked me home after dinner last night, I'd noticed Susan's Land Rover in front of the house, so I'd known she was home, but she'd already gone to bed by the time I'd arrived. Now I heard her moving around in her bedroom as I stood gazing out the louvered windows above the kitchen sink mindlessly washing my dishes. I studied the coffee trees and maize fields divided by a network of dirt footpaths. I caught the smell of wood-fire smoke and once again heard the call of a nearby rooster. A mangy dog trotted along one of the paths through the coffee fields, his ribs etched in sharp relief, his ears askew, and his shoulders hunched in permanent meekness. I wondered if I had that same look of wary fear in my eyes as I wandered around this strange new setting. I rolled my shoulders back and shook my arms in an effort to reduce the tension I felt.

When Susan emerged from her room, she was dressed in a purple batik sheath dress that came well below her knees, and she'd pulled her hair back into a neat ponytail. She had a pile of books in her arms. "You ready for today?" she asked.

"I'm not sure. I think so. When are you going up there?"

"I don't usually go to morning chapel, but I thought I'd walk up there with you today and show you the classrooms you'll be teaching in," she offered.

"Great. Let me get my things."

I rushed off to gather my stack of books and lesson plans, a hard lump forming in my throat. I took a few deep breaths before I walked from my bedroom back into the living room. I didn't want Susan to know how nervous I felt.

As we walked up the hill past the headmistress's house and school office, I noticed with concern that the building still appeared lifeless, though a Land Rover was now parked out front. When we reached the main gate onto campus, singing similar to what I'd heard the day before began. Today, however, I felt determined not to let the music affect me the way it had yesterday. There was no room for being weepy and more vulnerable today. I told Susan I'd heard the same singing yesterday, and she informed me that the school had a Sunday-morning church service, which I'd probably heard.

As we crossed the threshold onto campus, I tried to focus on Susan's words and keep pace with her confident, long strides. She told me that the school day started and ended with a fifteen- to twenty-minute chapel service that mostly consisted of singing. As the school's chaplain, Jean, the spunky woman I'd met on the night of my arrival, usually led Sunday services or organized a guest preacher. During the week, she typically offered a short message at the morning or evening chapel, unless she managed to coerce another teacher into giving one of the daily devotionals.

As we walked toward the singing, I quickly took in my surroundings. The school had been built in a circular configuration. Dormitory buildings extended down the hill to my right, and classrooms dotted the hill to my left. Ahead and across the circular campus, I could see smoke coming from an open-air kitchen. Susan pointed out the dining hall uphill and adjacent to the kitchen and then more dormitories below the kitchen. She indicated the classroom nearest to the main gate as the place where I'd teach Form IV, and another classroom nearer to the dining hall as the place where Form I met. Susan explained that the teachers moved from building to building, and the students stayed in the same classrooms all day.

I noticed all the buildings had the same architectural character as my house—single-story whitewashed oblong structures with green bati roofs and small front porches. Even though large sections of louvered windows fronted and backed the buildings, the classrooms still looked dark and barren inside. I clutched my books and lesson plans a little tighter as I tried to picture myself standing in one of these classrooms.

Three thin Maasai girls in white knee socks, black shoes, pleated khaki skirts, and red sweatshirts scampered from the dining hall toward the center of campus. As Susan and I got nearer to the place they had gone, the singing grew louder. A broad, open-air amphitheater held well over 250 similar-looking students, all of whom were singing in multipart harmony.

The students sat tightly packed together on long, tiered benches, and several of them turned to watch as Susan and I tried to tiptoe into the back. We sat down on a bench as I smiled and nodded at what appeared to be several other Tanzanian teachers who sat on a bench opposite Susan and me.

A young woman who looked about my age appeared solemn and resolute with her hair wrapped in a tight bun at the nape of her neck and a neatly tailored matching-shirt-and-skirt outfit. Next to her sat a slightly older and heavier-set woman who smiled benevolently at me and then looked back down at her book as if remembering that somber focus was required in this space. She seemed like an older version of the students; her hair was clipped close to her head, and she wore a bulky brown sweater over a white blouse and a pleated khaki skirt.

Farther down the bench sat two more senior-looking women. The shorter and stouter one, who I would later learn was the matron Bibi Neema, looked over her reading glasses at the students as if scouting for outliers and miscreants. She set her jaw and squinted her eyes under a tightly scarfed head, and her expression changed little when she saw Susan and me walk in after the singing had already begun. Next to her sat a woman who looked to be about the same age, if not a little younger. She wore large round glasses and had pulled her slightly graying hair neatly away from her face. She smoothed her skirt and kept her eyes down when we came in. I noticed she wore Maasai beads around her wrists and ankles and that her cheeks bore small round circular scars that I recognized as typically Maasai.

Once Susan and I were seated, a student walked up and handed me a small red book to share with Susan. Before returning to her seat, the girl smiled bashfully at me as she flipped the book open and pointed to the place where we could find the words to the song they were singing. The page contained only Swahili words, and very difficult Swahili words at that. I flipped quickly through the book looking for musical notations and realized that not only did they sing unaccompanied, but they also knew all the melodies by heart because there were neither staffs nor notes to guide the music. I flipped back to the page the student had showed me and tried to follow along while surreptitiously studying the students.

In terms of dress, they were indistinguishable, but they clearly varied in age. There were girls who hadn't gone through puberty yet and still looked like small children. They seemed to stick together, all sitting nearly on top of each other on the same two benches. These youngest students also seemed to be the most curious about me. They kept looking over their shoulders in my direction. When they caught me looking back, they covered their giggles with a quickly placed hand and whispered through their fingers to each other. I couldn't help but smile as I watched them.

In the middle of this bunch, her round bald skull sticking head and shoulders above the rest, sat a robust elderly woman, known to everyone on campus as Bibi Ruth, though most simply called her Grandma. Her traditional checkered Maasai mashuka stood out against a sea of school uniforms. As the young girls continued their quiet tittering, she turned to see what had caused the commotion and spotted me. Her hazy pale eyes stared out of a timeworn ebony face, as colorful beaded earrings swung from her ears. She tilted her head slightly as if in curiosity and then fixed me with a lopsided, somewhat toothless grin. Turning back to the girls, she gathered them closer with one sweep of her long, bead-bedecked arms, and suddenly they were still and quiet.

I then turned my gaze to the other side of the amphitheater and noted with nervousness that the students looked older, taller, and more imposing than I expected. Most of them exceeded me in both height and weight. A few of the older students regarded me with what I perceived as aloof indifference, which immediately made me shrink in my seat and avoid eye contact with anyone for several minutes while I focused on following along in the book and got lost in my own thoughts.

Although I found the idea of starting and closing each day in reflection and song a welcome ritual, I didn't know how I felt about the religious education associated with not just the Maasai Secondary School for Girls, but with most secondary schools in Tanzania, well more than half of which were Christian, Muslim, or some other religion. I knew that when the students arrived at the Maasai Secondary School for Girls, the majority of them had not yet been exposed to traditional, organized religions. I'd read that the Maasai believed in God, but that their God was more akin to the fire-and-brimstone, law-bound God of the Old Testament than to the forgiving father figure of the New Testament.[1] If the school provided its students with a progressive, safe place to explore their spirituality, their identities, and their futures—the very same things most girls the world over crave, in fact the very things I'd found myself unexpectedly seeking in Tanzania—then I would remain open-minded about the school's approach to spiritual education.

My reservations came largely from growing up in Montana, where in the 1800s many Native American families were forced to send their children to parochial schools. Once at school, these children were forbidden to speak their native languages and forced to assimilate to Western ways.[2] I'd done enough investigating to know that wasn't directly happening at this school, but I also knew a fine line separated education for empowerment from education for assimilation. In this case, Maasai leadership remained central to the school, so I hoped for the best, though already I could see the ways colonialism's legacy remained strong—in school uniforms, in standardized curriculums, in teaching materials, and, perhaps, even in my presence.

I knew the school would expose the girls to many new ideas. Since arriving in Tanzania, I'd spent a fair amount of time wondering what I hoped to achieve by teaching at the school. My time in Morogoro had relegated my "I've come to make a difference" mantra to the realm of naive visions of grandeur. Already, I realized it was far more complex than that.

While I believed providing equal access to education for all girls, particularly disadvantaged girls, a just and worthy cause, I still grappled with questions about whether the benefits of education always outweighed the potential downsides. I wondered how education would change these girls and what this would mean for their families and their culture. I wondered if some of the students would eventually feel alienated from their own culture because of the education they'd received, or if they would find that education empowered them to be leaders within their culture. I knew part of the reason the school had been established was to cultivate leaders who could guide the Maasai into the twenty-first century, a place where water and land would increasingly have limits and boundaries, and where survival would often require shillings instead of cattle.

When the singing ended, all remained quiet for what felt like several minutes. I breathed shallowly, kept my eyes on my feet, and clasped the songbook to prevent myself from fidgeting. Eventually, one of the women on the bench opposite Susan and me stood. From the back of the amphitheater, she spoke in hushed Swahili to the students who remained facing forward. From time to time a student would stand and respond to the woman in a nearly whispered response. I strained to hear even while knowing that my chances of understanding were slim. I couldn't believe more than 250 people could communicate with each other across an amphitheater in murmurs and sighs. It felt as if they were passing secret messages right before me.

After another long moment of silence, the woman walked to the front of the amphitheater, paused, looked at me, and then spoke in quiet, yet audible, English.

"Today, we welcome a new teacher. Please, can you come forward and introduce yourself?" she said as nearly every face in the amphitheater turned toward me.

I felt frozen to the bench as I picked up my books and the notebook that contained my lesson plans, stood, and then carefully placed them on my now empty seat. I hadn't prepared an outline for this. I stiffly walked down the sloped path toward the front of the amphitheater as I tried to smile. When I reached the woman, I turned, and there they sat, more than 250 Maasai girls earnestly awaiting me. All I had to do was start.

I cleared my throat and turned to look at the woman who had called me forward. She peered at me through her round glasses and then whispered under her breath as she shook my hand, "I am the headmistress, Mama Mkuu."

"Shikamoo," I said quietly, and the girls erupted with a mixture of laughter, gasps, and lightning-quick Swahili.

I didn't understand what I'd said or done to provoke the outburst, so I looked at the headmistress in puzzled distress.

She gave the students a withering look, and they immediately quieted. "They're surprised you know Swahili," she explained. "Please. You are welcome. Go ahead and introduce yourself."

"My Swahili isn't that good, so I will introduce myself in English," I said nervously to the group as several students murmured something I couldn't understand. I felt like a specimen under a bell jar, all of them looking in at me, judging my peculiarities and examining my inadequacies.

"My name is Julie Rehrig," I continued. Many of them giggled and guffawed as they tried to say my last name with exaggerated nasally sounds.

"Rrrrehrrrrig. Raregg. Ririg."

The laughing continued as my cheeks began to burn. I noticed two of the younger students looking at me with what appeared to be bewildered confusion, a look I recognized from my recent struggles with Swahili. I realized they didn't yet know enough English to understand me.

Once again, the headmistress quieted the amphitheater with only a look and encouraged me to continue with a nod.

"I'm from the United States, and I understand I'll be teaching forms I and IV," I said, almost as a question, as I looked at the headmistress for confirmation.

She nodded as another wave of murmurs swept through the students. I couldn't tell if they were happy or disappointed about this.

"I'm very glad to be here. I've heard a lot about you, and I'm excited to get to know you. I'm not sure what else I can tell you about myself," I continued.

"How old are you?" came from the vicinity of the older students.

"I'm twenty-five years old," I responded to more giggles and guffaws.

I would later learn that the Maasai understand and relate to one another based on age-sets. Maasai girls, as well as boys, of approximately the same age form an age-set at the time of circumcision, the ceremony that marks the transition from childhood to adulthood. The age-set lasts throughout life, as its members move through a hierarchy of levels, each lasting approximately fifteen years. The age-set level determines a person's power and influence within the tribe. Those at the oldest age-set level are the elders, and they are responsible for making decisions that affect their whole community.[3]

Since an age-set can span five to seven years, I didn't know it, but I'd just indicated to some of my oldest students—those I'd be teaching in Form IV—that I belonged to their same age-set.

Suddenly, Bibi Neema, the severe-looking woman I'd noticed when Susan and I walked into the amphitheater, stood and let out a torrent of stern Swahili. The amphitheater fell silent, and several students ducked as if they thought they could avoid the onslaught of words.

As the woman's voice got louder and louder, I stood at the front of the amphitheater in mute, horrified confusion. Then she firmly clapped her hands together, and with that, all the students began to rapidly move out of the amphitheater and up toward the classrooms. The teachers huddled around the severe woman at the back of the amphitheater as the students scuttled by.

I turned toward the headmistress but didn't know what to say. I felt as if I'd done something wrong, but I didn't know what.

The headmistress smiled meekly and shuffled her feet slightly as she fiddled with a piece of paper in the book bag she was carrying. Her eyes remained focused on some point in the distance as she quietly said, "That's the matron. She works hard to teach them respect, and she felt they weren't showing you enough." With that, the headmistress slung her book bag over her shoulder, lowered her head, and started walking toward the huddled teachers.

CHAPTER 9:

MWALIMU MGENI

Several tidy rows of black shoes stood like little soldiers on the classroom's front porch—probably more than thirty distinctive pairs. Neatly balled-up white socks poked out of a pair of loafers, one or two silver buckles winked in the sunlight, loose laces drooped about several sets of Oxfords, and a pair or two of Mary Janes sat with straps askew. From where I stood, I couldn't see inside the classroom, so I studied the well-worn but neatly polished shoes and listened.

Through the louvered windows just above eye level, I could hear the students scurrying around. They spoke to each other in sharp flashes of words I couldn't decipher as Swahili or Maa. The tones sounded hurried, irked, and bossy, the way I remembered my sister and I often speaking to one another in our adolescence. As I waited for the classroom to quiet, I heard books slam on hard surfaces and furniture abrasively shift from place to place.

I closed my eyes for a moment and squeezed the bridge of my nose between my thumb and forefinger. Then I nervously glanced down at my watch as I noticed a student dashing from a neighboring classroom to one of the few substantial trees to be found in the campus's center. Once there, she picked up a metal rod and forcefully struck it against an iron wheel rim mounted to the tree's trunk. The loud clank marked the start of the day's first period. The time had finally come for me to teach.

When I didn't immediately enter the classroom, first one, then two, then three sets of brown eyes peered around the doorjamb at me. When I waved at them, the eyes quickly disappeared amid squeals and laughter. I giggled inwardly and started to feel slightly more at ease after my turbulent introduction to the entire school only a handful of minutes earlier.

Then, from the windows, came a timid voice: "Karibu, mwalimu. Please, come inside now. You are welcome." I turned toward the windows and looked up to see a small, shiny face and an eager smile beaming down at me.

"Thank you. I'm coming," I responded with a grin as I bent to remove my sandals. This set off an unexpected flurry of activity. Two students immediately came flying around the corner and out the door. They both wore brightly colored flip-flops with white socks, the rubber and fabric wedged between the first two toes on each foot. The girls vigorously insisted that my sandals stay on my feet, mostly through gestures and by saying over and again, "No, mwalimu. No." One of them took my books and notebook, while the other one guided me inside the classroom, as if she were herding an errant goat.

As I walked through the door, the jarring, dissonant sound of furniture legs scraping across concrete greeted me as each and every student rose from where she was seated and in a more or less uniform chorus pronounced, "Good morning, madam."

Even though caught off guard by this unexpected formal greeting, I replied, "Good morning. How are you?"

This seemed to be an atypical response because the students began to murmur to one another as I walked toward the front of the classroom. Then one student, among the tallest and most robust of the bunch, shushed the room with a short, harsh-sounding imperative that I didn't fully understand.

When I reached the front of the classroom, I walked behind a simple wooden table where my books and notebook had been placed, and I turned to face the students. The tall, robust girl who seemed to be in charge—I wasn't sure if by default, size, self-appointment, or strength of English-language skills—then responded to my question with, "We are fine, madam." Many of the other students then followed her lead by saying the same thing, until she rolled her eyes and once again quieted them.

Uncomfortable that the students were still standing, I exclaimed, "Oh, good. I think you can sit down now." This, the tall girl translated into Swahili, and then the scraping and scuffling began again as everyone took their seats.

As they sat, I studied them and the classroom before me.

Along the two walls to my right and left, louvered windows stood open at various incongruent angles, some missing the small rectangular panes from their metal frames. Even with the building's many windows, the classroom felt shadowy and dim. The handful of bare light bulbs that hung from the ceiling remained off, which I wrongly attributed to a lack of electricity. However, I'd soon learn that the students couldn't abide electrical lighting during daylight hours. For the first several weeks of teaching, I'd switch the lights on as I walked into the classroom, and within minutes one or another of the students would switch the lights back off. Eventually, I came to accept that teaching in the shadows would be my plight.

Though the building couldn't have been more than a couple of years old, the classroom's pastel yellow walls, probably once bright and cheery, appeared unevenly faded and dingy. In a few places, floor-to-ceiling cracks zigzagged up the walls leaving crumbling concrete in their wake. Behind me, a large rectangular patch of concrete wall had been painted black, which I assumed to be the chalkboard. It had been wiped clean with a wet sponge, but I could still see chalk dust lining the edges of the bare concrete floor and clinging to the wall.

Near the door, a simple wooden cabinet stood with its doors padlocked shut as if to say that school supplies and books had to be kept under lock and key. Otherwise, the room was devoid of any accoutrements—no bookshelves, colorful bulletin boards, student artwork, or inspirational posters.

Six long rectangular tables stood before me in two rows. The students sat on one side of each table facing me, seven or eight wide-eyed girls per long wooden bench. The students overlapped one another, shoulder to collar bone, elbows askew, crunched together nearly on top of one another. Most of them wore khaki-colored skirts and purple T-shirts with the school's logo printed on the front and back, but a few of the smallest girls wore red plaid skirts with oversized red sweatshirts. As they settled in, they melded together with relative ease, only a little pushing, wiggling, and one or two uncomfortable winces.

Each of them seemed to have the same olive green notebook and blue pen, which resulted in a series of brief, grabby disagreements as more than one student reached for the wrong pen or notebook. Scattered about the tables, I felt relieved to see numerous copies of the English book Susan had given me. My hands trembled slightly as I flipped my own book open and laid my lesson plan across its pages.

I noticed the students seemed to be arranged in the room by size—the smallest in front to the largest in back—thus the smallest girl in the room sat in the front row gaping at me out of a petite round child's face. When I looked more directly at her, at first I thought I saw fear, but then her eyes began to sparkle before her face broke into a wide, earnest smile. I couldn't help but grin back at her. I soon learned her name was Dinah, and every time I looked at her this same smile would light her face and then the trembling in my hands would calm.

From the back of the room, however, the tall, robust girl studied me as if I were some kind of science experiment. She, like most other girls in the room, appraised me with a serious gaze, as I said slowly and deliberately, "I am glad to be here. Let's begin with introductions."

I looked around the room for a piece of chalk, and when I couldn't find one, I asked, "Does anyone know where the chalk is?" In response, the tall, robust girl rose from her seat and walked toward me, and when she arrived, she handed me a piece of brand-new chalk with a curtsy and said, "I am Gladness, the class monitor." Then she turned on her heels and walked back to her seat.

I thanked her and thought to myself, *So I have a class monitor, whatever that means.* My own public school experience hadn't included class monitors, curtsies, school uniforms, standing in the presence of teachers, or addressing them with "sir" or "madam." And none of this seemed to match up with the feeling I'd had in the amphitheater that I'd been the butt of an unpleasant joke.

I turned and carefully wrote on the blackboard, "My name is Mwalimu Julie, and I come from Billings, Montana, in the United States of America." The rough surface of the wall made the chalk crumble in my hand and meant I had to go back over several letters to make them dark enough to see. While I did this, the girls behind me remained silent, and I considered whether my first name was the correct way to introduce myself in this setting. *Too late to change it now,* I thought with chagrin.

When I finished tracing and retracing the letters, I walked to the edge of the blackboard and noticed many of the students were copying what I'd written into their notebooks. Others sat with furrowed brows and stared at the words. I stated the sentence aloud: "My name is Mwalimu Julie, and I come from Billings, Montana, in the United States of America."

I watched as a bright-eyed girl in the middle of the room whispered the words to herself as I pointed to each word and said it again. Under the sentence, I wrote the words, "Name. City. Region. Country," to denote the meanings of different words. By now, nearly every student had her notebook out and was writing exactly what I'd written.

I repeated the sentence and then said in Swahili, "*Jina langu ni Mwalimu* Julie," as I pointed to the word "name."

"What is the Swahili word for 'city'?" I asked as I pointed to the word. Three hands shot in the air almost simultaneously. I smiled at the nearest girl and encouraged her to answer. To my surprise, she stood, neatened her skirt, and said, "*Mji.*" I wrote the word "mji" next to the word "city."

I repeated this process for the words "region" and "country," since I didn't know these words in Swahili. Each time I asked a question, more students raised their hands, some with unfettered enthusiasm, as if getting called on was very nearly a matter of life and death.

I said the entire sentence again and then asked the students to introduce themselves in the same manner. Several tittered with eagerness as I invited a quiet, cautious-looking girl on my right to begin with what I hoped was an assuring smile.

She stood hesitantly and almost in a whisper haltingly began to read exactly what was on the blackboard: "My name is Mwalimu Julie and I come from . . ." At this, several students addressed her in sharp Swahili. She stopped, covered her mouth with her hand, looked away from me, and then stood silently.

I asked if another student could demonstrate the introduction. At this, several hands shot up. I called on the small girl I had noticed earlier who now enthusiastically squirmed in her seat and fixed me with a glowing smile.

She shot out of her seat and said, "My name is Dinah. I come from Arusha Town in the Arusha Region of Tanzania."

I then turned to the first girl, who was still standing, and asked her if she could introduce herself. She looked at the girl sitting next to her, who whispered something to her in Swahili or Maa, I wasn't sure which, and then she slowly began, "My name is Neng'ida. I come from . . . Monduli Juu . . . Tanzania."

Her words sounded so unusual to my ear that I wasn't sure exactly what she'd said, but I nonetheless smiled wildly at her and exclaimed, "Good, very good."

She sat down immediately with a look of restrained happiness as the next girl began.

We went through this routine with varying forms of accuracy and confidence some thirty times—once for each student. I realized I would never remember most of the places the students came from and probably wouldn't be able to find many of their villages on a map even if I did remember. I also feared I wouldn't be able to remember, let alone pronounce, many of their names. I made a mental note to find a class roster as soon as possible.

After the introductions, we opened the books to the place Susan had indicated I should begin teaching and started on some vocabulary exercises. As we entered the terrain of rote learning, the students seemed to gain confidence and eagerness. It seemed that even if they didn't know the answers to the questions in the book, their arms shot up anyway. They simply wanted a chance to stand up and try to answer. Whether they got the answer correct or not seemed inconsequential.

I quickly surmised that the students' English-language skills ran the gamut from Gladness, the class monitor, who seemed nearly fluent and bored by the slow pace of the class, to Neng'ida, the shy student in the front of the room, who seemed confused and, at times, even frustrated because she didn't understand. It surprised me that no matter their skills, they helped each other to understand by translating for each other and sometimes by whispering the correct answers under their breaths to each other, which secretly made me smile. They seemed to operate under the philosophy that no one should be left behind.

After the oral exercises, I gave the students some written exercises to work on and began to circulate to answer questions and check on their progress. To my surprise, they were all diligently working—some individually, some in pairs, and others in small groups. I realized that in this setting, my job wasn't going to be to keep them on task. It was going to be to keep them challenged no matter their language levels.

I stopped at Neng'ida's table to assess her work since I'd already identified her as someone who would need extra help. As I bent over to read what she'd written, her hand came up and she timidly touched my hair. When I turned my head, she snatched her hand back and giggled nervously.

I smiled warmly at her and said, "It's a little different from yours, isn't it? You can touch it if you want to." I turned my head to indicate she could touch it again.

She reached up and took one curly lock and rolled it between her fingers. As she did this, the girl sitting next to her lightly touched my arm and then quickly drew her hand away.

I grinned at them both as I sighed, "It's okay. You'll see; I'm not *so* different from you," even though I sensed neither one of them understood a word I'd said.

In the coming weeks, I continued to build relationships with these, my youngest, students. I first came to learn each of their names by taking photographs and then studying the images at night. Mark and I had brought a first-generation digital camera with us, so I had the girls stand at the back of the classroom in alphabetical order, a small feat in and of itself, and then I snapped their pictures in groups of three. After each snapshot, the featured girls would huddle around me for a look at their picture and, I suspected, a chance to sling their arms across my shoulder, hold my hand, or just lean against me—all uncomfortable gestures to me, but quite natural, I'd already learned, to most Tanzanians.

For many of my Form I students, the photographs represented the only image ever recorded of them, and their reactions varied from silly smiles and giggles to gasps of amazement. They all wanted a copy of their photograph, so the next time I went to Arusha I had each image printed three times, one for each girl featured in it. The day I handed them out, the excitement in the classroom became palpable; it took nearly half the class period to corral them back into a frame of mind for learning.

As a class, my relationship with them blossomed. I knew they loved the rhyming activities from the book, so we often repeated these lessons several times. We'd recite the short rhythmic sections together—they using their most boisterous voices, and me laughing aloud at their enthusiasm.

Even though I now knew them as a group, I still couldn't recount much about them individually beyond their names, and I found this disheartening. For the most part, we still couldn't communicate with one another well enough to do more than share niceties and cursory details. I'd heard some of their stories from Jean, who had helped recruit a few of them, but otherwise I didn't know much about them.

Gradually, though, I started to learn. I knew, for example, that Paulina and Endesh remained ever serious and studious, wanting to get everything right; Riziki and Dinah lit up the room when encouraged or praised; Elisipha had a penchant for mischievous yet harmless teasing; and Neng'ida struggled against being left behind with considerable determination and perpetually curious eyes. I didn't yet know that she was already promised in marriage, as were several others of my students.

My hours with Form I flew by, and I found myself wanting to spend even more time with them. Form IV, however, was a different story.

A formidable class, they numbered more than forty, and their presence rippled across campus. Anointed as the pioneers of the now relatively famous Maasai Secondary School for Girls, they'd grown up with the school, experiencing the rough early days with only a handful of teachers and cramped accommodations at the nearby teachers' college before the first classrooms and dormitories were completed.

Always the oldest at the school, they'd never had to answer to girls who went before them. These Maasai girls had blazed their own trails, and they expected to be treated accordingly. As they paraded around campus, the proud Maasai that they were, other girls made way for them. Smaller, younger students would skitter out of the way as a group of Form IV students approached, the young girls scattering like scared dogs, and the Form IV students barely acknowledging those they'd displaced, heads held high while floating by with aloof disinterest.

To them, I was not only a newcomer who hadn't experienced the early days of the school as they had, but I was also young, even in their same age-set, and not nearly as polished as their previous English teacher, whom they'd adored. She'd literally written the English books for the school and had nearly twenty years of teaching experience even before she arrived. For so many reasons, I simply didn't measure up. I knew it, and, more importantly, they knew it.

CHAPTER 10:

LEADING FROM BEHIND

Abandon a week after my arrival at the school, the headmistress summoned me to her office early one morning, even before chapel. I'd already learned that most days started before sunrise here, but still the last-minute early morning summons seemed somewhat unusual given that I'd heard little else from the headmistress since I'd arrived at the school. I immediately wondered if something was wrong.

When I hesitantly walked into the office, Mama Mkuu shuffled about the room, restlessly gathering papers into a large canvas bag. At first, she didn't speak, but looked at me sideways, as if my presence made her nervous.

Then she stammered, "The Lutheran diocese in Arusha called this morning . . . umm . . . you know they run this school. Well . . . umm . . . they've called us to their office . . . for a greeting, I think."

I felt somewhat relieved as I wondered if this might be the welcome I'd been hoping for since my arrival at the school. After our initial welcome at Moringe, Mark had told me that he'd been building relationships with Moringe's staff, and that Mr. Panga, the head of the math department, had been orienting him to the school. Because I'd received no such orientation at the Maasai Secondary School for Girls, I continued to feel unsure of my responsibilities and an outsider among the Tanzanian staff. I harbored hope that my trip to the diocese might be a start toward the type of interaction I sought.

"Perhaps Mark should join us?" I asked, thinking that he was also a new teacher at a diocese school, but the headmistress quickly indicated only my attendance was required, which I found odd. Nonetheless, I silently acquiesced, not wanting to make Mama Mkuu more uncomfortable than she already appeared and wondering if Mark's and my relationship should not be acknowledged in some settings, such as at the diocese.

However, I soon surmised why Mark might not have been invited on the journey as the headmistress and I bounced our way out of Monduli in the school truck, which had a single bench seat. Mama Mkuu sat in the passenger's seat, the school driver behind the wheel, and I squished between the two trying to avoid hitting my knees on the gearshift.

I quickly ran out of small talk, and the headmistress did too. The driver didn't speak English and probably surmised that my poor Swahili made communication difficult, so we rode together in silence. Even if most Tanzanians seemed comfortable with long stretches of mute repose, in this context, my inability to make conversation made me feel inept, if not rude. I wanted to get to know Mama Mkuu, and I felt as if I was missing my chance.

When we arrived in Arusha, the headmistress led me into a simply constructed office block before disappearing down a hallway without any indication of where she was going or what I should do. Now I waited, unsure of myself and apprehensive about the headmistress's demeanor upon our arrival. She'd seemed agitated and even quieter than usual. I'd expected a cup of chai and a friendly conversation when we arrived here. Instead, I sat alone worrying about why I was really here.

■ ■ ■ ■ ■ ■ ■ ■

Mama Mkuu slumped in the chair in front of Mr. Langoi's desk and looked at her well-worn black pumps. The portly Maasai man in a rumpled black suit bellowed forth in Maa from behind his desk. In her relatively short tenure as headmistress of the Maasai Secondary School for Girls, she'd seen him do this before. For this reason, she feigned attention.

Earlier that day, the headmistress had received word that she was to report to Mr. Langoi's office in Arusha, about two hours away from the school, with me, the new American teacher. Even though she'd been told that Mr. Langoi wanted to meet me, Mama Mkuu suspected the summons meant a *shida*, or problem, was brewing, and her suspicion had proven true. Mr. Langoi, who managed the church's worldly affairs, while the bishop managed its spiritual affairs, was known for being brusque most of the time.

As Mr. Langoi continued his lecture in short, abrupt bursts, Mama Mkuu became increasingly concerned about me, the subject of today's meeting. She knew I was sitting just down the hall waiting for what I believed would be a welcome. Now she felt certain this would not be the greeting I anticipated.

Today, Mr. Langoi took issue with a letter Mama Mkuu had written for me. I was finishing my graduate degree in the United States and hoped to write my final paper on my teaching experiences in Tanzania. The university required a letter of permission from the headmistress before I could write the paper. Mama Mkuu had already given me permission even before I'd left the United States, and the letter had already been submitted to the university, but now Mr. Langoi wanted to reverse her decision, and he was rather forcefully explaining his reasons.

"We can't have just anyone coming into the school. This woman is supposed to be teaching. We didn't ask her to do research. Why would you agree to this?" he forcefully asked.

Mama Mkuu shrugged and kept her eyes on her shoes. Arguing with the man would certainly not turn out well. She knew this from experience. Mr. Langoi had little patience for diplomacy.

The headmistress could understand, in part, Mr. Langoi's difficulty with the notion of Maasai girls being the subjects of a study. There were plenty of examples of outsiders "studying the natives" in less than respectful ways. She and the Lutheran church in Tanzania took seriously their promise to parents to protect the girls while they went to school. This was the only way some parents agreed to leave their daughters at the school.

At this point, though, Mama Mkuu couldn't unsend the letter even if she wanted to, and she knew from my proposal that I would be writing about my own teaching practice, which seemed harmless enough. In fact, Mama Mkuu thought that good teachers ought to be reflecting on their work. As someone who had attended university and written her own final paper, she could see both sides of the issue. Even though she felt that my paper posed little threat to the students, she felt unsure how to navigate the issue with Mr. Langoi. When he'd made up his mind, changing it seemed nearly impossible.

Mama Mkuu was no stranger to this type of controversy. She knew everybody had an opinion about how things should be done at her school, and it often felt as if she could do nothing right and today was no different. If she wasn't managing the constant intervention of local officials, such as Mr. Langoi, in the work of the school, then she was appeasing American sponsors or talking to concerned parents.

Sometimes she wondered if she'd been chosen for this work because local leaders thought of her first as a Maasai woman who would inevitably bend to the will of men, and second as a woman who cared deeply about the girls in her charge. While she would admit that she still adhered to many Maasai traditions and that, as a woman, she had to pick her battles carefully, she also had a stubborn streak. By nature, she avoided direct confrontation, but from time to time, she ignored requests or purposefully did the opposite of what she'd been asked to do, just to make a point—her own subtle form of resistance.

In truth, Mama Mkuu had hoped to avoid taking this very visible and very political job. Though she had a house at the school, her true home—her engang—was hundreds of miles away from the school, and her children preferred to stay there, where they had friends and relatives. Her kids and even her husband thought of the Maasai Secondary School for Girls as a lonely place, and they couldn't abide staying there more than a day or two at a time, which left Mama Mkuu torn between two worlds, two sets of responsibilities.

She'd been appointed to the headmistress's job, not because she'd sought it out, but because she was a Maasai woman in the right age-set with a higher education and connections at the highest levels of the Lutheran church in Tanzania. She couldn't say no when they'd asked her. In fact, the Maasai elders on the school board hadn't really asked her so much as told her.

Even so, Mama Mkuu wanted to do right by the students. She saw a former version of herself in many of them. They were the part she felt equipped to effectively handle and the part she most enjoyed, but the regular influx of white visitors to the school, mostly sponsors and donors, took a lot of her time and energy. Making small talk didn't come naturally to her, whether in Maa, Swahili, or English; thus she found talking to foreign visitors particularly challenging and avoided it whenever she could. Just managing the steady flow of parents who needed constant reassurance and convincing of the school's merits often required her full attention. When she wasn't dealing with visiting American sponsors or concerned Maasai parents, then her staff, local church leaders, and even government officials demanded her attention.

In addition to balancing the often competing agendas of these various groups, she had to ensure the proper implementation of the government's ever-changing requirements for curriculum, testing, and reporting, and run a boarding school where everything had to be provided for the students based on donations coming predominantly from the United States. In all, her responsibilities weighed heavily on her, but she felt she had no choice other than to do the best she could under the circumstances.

As someone who'd witnessed the dawn of postcolonialism in Tanzania, she'd known the relationship between the Tanzanian Lutheran diocese which managed the school, American missionaries and volunteers who built the school, and sponsors in the United States who funded the school would be fraught even before she'd experienced the reality of this in the school's day-to-day operation. Today was one of those days when she got to experience it firsthand.

Though Mama Mkuu had just met me the previous week, she already liked me. She found me polite, eager to please, and someone who paid careful attention to pleasantries, in my own reserved way. To her, my motives seemed pure, as if I truly wanted to help, even though I was obviously intimidated by my new surroundings and somewhat unsure of myself. Truth be told, Mama Mkuu identified with me because of these character traits. Clearly, she felt the same way often enough.

She wondered if this might be another opportunity for quiet resistance. Mr. Langoi could tell her to deny me permission. Meanwhile, she would "forget" to do anything about the situation, and I could quietly go about finishing my paper. However, the headmistress knew there was no way for her to shelter me from what was about to happen in this office.

■ ■ ■ ■ ■ ■ ■ ■

I waited in a dimly lit, bustling hallway as I watched various Tanzanians come and go and listened to one or two Swahili conversations drift down the hallway. It had been almost half an hour, but I was getting used to the reality that everything in Tanzania seemed to take more time than I expected.

I looked at my watch again and noted that I should be standing in front of Form IV giving a lesson on the use of the past participle, something I'd spent numerous hours studying myself over the last couple of days. I'd wanted to make sure I could explain a language concept that came naturally to me. It felt like trying to explain how to swallow or blink—I used English verb tenses without thinking, but now I needed to explain how to think through something that I just knew. Instead of teaching today, though, I'd given the students some independent work on yesterday's lesson because I'd been summoned to Arusha.

Just as I began to wonder if my entire day would be spent sitting on a hard metal chair in a dark hallway, Mama Mkuu emerged from behind a closed door. She angled toward me and then stammered that Mr. Langoi, a diocese official, wanted to see me. I stood and walked toward the now open door as I heard the headmistress shuffle along behind me.

When I entered, a substantial Maasai man was sitting behind a wooden desk. He wore a dark suit with a red tie. Though well dressed, he appeared slightly disheveled, as if he'd gotten too hot under that heavy suit. Patches of gray hair framed his fleshy face, and his stern eyes made him look as if he was angry.

I smiled, though, and immediately greeted him with a deferent "shikamoo" as I extended my hand to shake his.

He remained silent and stared at me impassively from behind a pair of fingerprint-smudged glasses. Rather than take my extended hand, he gestured to the single wooden chair in front of his desk. My pulse quickened. Why had he just ignored my greeting? This was rude in any culture, but particularly in Tanzanian culture.

I looked over my shoulder at Mama Mkuu, whose eyes seemed tied to the floor. She stood just inside the door leaning slightly against the jamb, her arms crossed over her stomach, as if she felt sick. I sat heavily in the chair, waiting for him to begin.

He loudly cleared his throat, his lips parting to reveal a set of stained, crooked teeth. He leaned toward me and snapped, "I've just told Mama Mkuu that you are not welcome here if you intend to do research for your university degree. We will send you home because this is not acceptable and we did not agree to this."

I felt my face flush and bile rise in my throat. I swallowed hard as I searched for an appropriate response. "I wrote to Mama Mkuu many months ago," I cautiously volunteered, "when I first considered coming to Tanzania, to ask if I could complete my thesis at the girls' school. She agreed, and I've already submitted her letter of permission to the university. I have come here with the understanding—"

At this, the man slapped his hand on his desk and barked, "Well, you don't have permission. If you persist in this, you must go home."

Even though tears threatened to burst forth, I refused to cry in front of this man. It seemed clear that there would be no reasoning with him, so I quietly responded, "I understand. I want to teach, and that is the most important thing."

"Good," he stated as he leaned back in his chair. "Stay focused on doing a good job as a teacher."

He then turned his gaze to Mama Mkuu and spoke to her in rapid, direct Swahili or Maa, I wasn't sure which. She mumbled one or two responses that I could barely hear. As this exchange took place, my mind raced along the long path that I'd taken to get to the girls' school, and a deep resentment settled over me.

For three months prior to our arrival in Tanzania, Mark's and my work permits had been delayed. With growing impatience, we'd remained in a holding pattern in the United States, knowing that we should already be in Tanzania. We knew the longer we were delayed, the later we would arrive in the school term, and though there seemed little we could do about the situation, we increasingly felt unsettled by the difficulties with our work permits, wondering when and if they would ever come through. Distastefully, we began to wonder if this was an instance where a bribe was required to move things along, as Tanzania's reputation for corruption had reached us even while we were still on American soil.

However, we soon learned the problem resided not with the government, but with the church. In order to legally work in Tanzania, as in many countries, we required local sponsorship from our employer. Since both schools were under the auspice of the Lutheran church in Tanzania, the local diocese was our sponsor. As time continued to pass, we received various, often conflicting explanations for the holdup.

"We haven't received the correct paperwork from the schools."

"The government is slow in processing the permits and they can't be rushed."

"This is just how things work in Tanzania. You have to be patient."

"There is missing information on your applications."

Meantime, Doug and Linda arrived in Tanzania, and one of their first jobs was to sort out the problem with our work permits. We quickly received word from them that the applications hadn't even left the diocese office. After several days of sitting in the diocese office, Doug and Linda finally received our work permit applications with the requisite diocese signatures. They hand-carried the applications to the correct government office, and our work permits were processed in a matter of less than a week.

We felt our delayed work permits might be the first indicator that not everyone in Tanzania welcomed our presence. At the time, we didn't know we would be walking into a very complex set of politics. The push and pull of competing tribal, racial, national, religious, and cultural interests, as well as the struggle over who controls donor money and who sets the priorities for this money, all caused nearly constant friction and tension between different interest groups. In short, years of white intervention in Tanzania meant we found ourselves in a hotbed of issues we didn't fully understand

and perhaps never would. And yet, these issues defined us even before we set foot in the country.

Today, I realized my nationality, gender, race, and age defined my role in ways I'd never before experienced. In the eyes of this man, I had many strikes against me—I was a foreigner; I was a woman; I was white; and I was young. It was the first time in my life I felt absolutely powerless to change my circumstance.

As I watched Mr. Langoi finish his stern conversation with Mama Mkuu, I realized that I wasn't the only one in the room with a few strikes against her. As a middle-aged Maasai woman, Mama Mkuu had certainly faced and would continue to face more challenges than I could fathom. If I felt small and powerless for the first time today, I knew she probably felt this way regularly, and this made me feel ashamed of my own indignation.

Without another word, for fear I might lose my composure, I rose from my chair and followed the headmistress out the door.

CHAPTER 11:

WOMANHOOD

B efore the June break, Neng'ida's biology teacher and the school matron rounded up the Form I girls for a lesson on female genital cutting, something still commonly practiced among the Maasai. In direct language, the matron warned the girls that they might face circumcision during the upcoming school break. In her usual no-nonsense manner, she advised them to refuse the procedure, though as a Maasai woman, she certainly knew refusing circumcision was no simple matter. Thus, she told the girls they could stay at the school over the break, if they felt at risk.

Due to the complex nature of the subject, the matron and the biology teacher gave the lesson in Maa and Swahili. Many of the teacher's words haunted Neng'ida. "Infections, hemorrhage, increased risk of sexually transmitted diseases, lifelong pain, scarring, prolonged labor, fetal distress, maternal death, incontinence." Neng'ida now knew what most of these words meant, though others still confused her.

After the lesson, Neng'ida retreated to the dormitory, where she discussed the issue at length with some of her classmates. A few of her friends had already been circumcised, though none of them were eager to admit it after the lesson. Most of the girls seemed to believe what the matron and biology teacher had said, while others discounted them by saying that their mothers, sisters, and aunts didn't have any of these problems, even though they'd been circumcised. One of the girls, Paulina, wondered aloud how it would be possible to get married without being circumcised, and another, Riziki, said her family would despise her if she refused.

During this discussion, Neng'ida kept quiet, uncertain how she felt. To refuse circumcision meant her family and her entire community would forever view her as a child, never as a woman. Refusal would surely bring public disgrace not just to her, but also to her family. How could she possibly refuse the procedure?

Though Neng'ida considered staying at school during the break, she hadn't anticipated that her mother would come to collect her. When Neng'ida saw her mother at the school gate, she almost started crying, not really realizing until that moment how homesick she had been. In fact, now that her mother was there, she couldn't wait to tell her about all she had seen and learned in the few short months she'd been away.

Before she could leave the school, though, Neng'ida's mother needed to sign her out, and this involved a pointed conversation with the headmistress.

"What happened with Neng'ida's father after you left her at school?" the headmistress questioned.

"He was angry. He threatened to come to the school himself, but I told him what you said about school and how it can help Neng'ida and all of us," Neng'ida's mother explained.

"Is he still angry?" asked the headmistress.

"He is, but I have convinced him to allow her to stay at least for the first year."

"So you promise you will bring Neng'ida back after this break? You must absolutely promise this, or I cannot allow her to leave school," the headmistress warned.

With an earnest promise from Neng'ida's mother that she would ensure the girl's return at the end of the break, the headmistress allowed Neng'ida to pack her bag.

■ ■ ▪ ▪ ▪ ▪ ▪ ▪

As Neng'ida walked the last few miles to her engang with her mother, an unusual silence fell over them. Up to that point, Neng'ida had been telling her mother about her new friends and all she was learning. Her mother had asked many questions. They'd laughed together as Neng'ida had recounted her experiences watching other girls eat eggs, something Neng'ida still found disgusting.

Her mother had been reserved with news from home. Initially, Neng'ida attributed her mother's taciturn behavior to the problems her mother had certainly encountered with Neng'ida's father after she'd allowed Neng'ida to stay in school. Neng'ida felt guilty that her mother had faced this alone and nervous about how her father would behave once they both arrived at the engang. She hoped her mother's silence didn't mean it would be too difficult.

Soon, however, Neng'ida realized the true reason for her mother's reserved behavior. As they approached the engang, Neng'ida saw an *oloileti* tree placed prominently outside her home. This tree symbolized that the engang was preparing for a circumcision. Neng'ida's stomach knotted as she realized what this meant. Unbeknownst to Neng'ida, her family had been planning for her circumcision while she was at school. As she and her mother entered the engang, a stream of relatives and neighbors greeted Neng'ida confirming her suspicions. They'd all come to celebrate Neng'ida's coming of age.

That evening as Neng'ida quietly sat among her relatives, she listened as her father told everyone that he didn't think Neng'ida would remain in school for long. He felt so confident of this that he'd invited her husband-to-be to live in the engang until Neng'ida finished school and they could be wed. Though Neng'ida hesitated to look directly at her future husband, she kept track of his every move and purposefully avoided him.

Everyone knew circumcision was the logical next step on Neng'ida's path to marriage, since according to Maasai culture she could not be married without it. Neng'ida's mother and father, like most Maasai, believed that to marry without circumcision would be to invite infidelity and even infection. Many years later, Neng'ida would convince her mother that this was mere folklore.

Initially, Neng'ida seriously considered returning to the school. She knew running away to attend school was one thing, but running away from this, she felt, would mean she could never return home. Her father, already unhappy that she was still in school, would perceive her refusal of circumcision as evidence that she'd entirely turned away from her culture and her family—an unforgivable offense and one that would deeply embarrass him in front of his entire family and community, so Neng'ida remained even though she kept thinking about the words of her science teacher: "infection, bleeding, pain."

Over the next several days more people gathered at Neng'ida's engang. Two other girls, who would also go through the ceremony with Neng'ida, and their relatives arrived. Her father slaughtered an ox, and her mother and sisters cooked nearly continuously. Neng'ida, for the first time in her life, did none of the cooking and was offered as much meat as she could consume.

That night as the sun slipped below the horizon, the gathered morani, or young Maasai warriors, began to sing and dance, their red and blue mashuka a colorful moving patchwork of rhythmic bounces and lanky, quivering jumps. A few bore spears; most carried their eng'udi, or long wooden walking sticks that served as extensions of their trim bodies—the men and their staffs all lines and hard edges. And yet, laughter and smiles remained in their midst as the young men goaded each other to jump higher and higher.

Neng'ida and the two other initiates, as well as all the other young girls attending the ritual, participated in the singing and dancing. Neng'ida knew the calls and responses by heart. She loved the low, hypnotic hum of Maasai songs punctuated by high-pitched yips and drone-like horn bleats.

Everyone had gathered here for Neng'ida and the other two initiates—to honor their coming of age. Though she felt conflicted and anxious about what was to come, as she sang and danced with her family and friends, it was difficult not to feel the special honor of this ceremony. For the first time in her life, Neng'ida was the focus of her entire community. They were celebrating her. As the night wore on, she received several gifts—her aunt gave her a baby goat, and her grandmother presented her with a large, colorful ilturesh she'd beaded for Neng'ida. The rigid, saucer-like necklace encircled Neng'ida's throat and lay over her chest. She no longer wore small, child-like necklaces; this was the ilturesh of a woman.

After many guests fell asleep under the stars, Neng'ida and the other initiates moved into a dimly lit boma. From the packed earthen floor where Neng'ida sat, she tried to pay attention even under the hazy fog of half sleep. Throughout the night, different women—her mother, the mothers of the other initiates, her older sisters, some of her father's other wives, and several aunts—had entered the boma to contribute their voices to the process. The many important women in Neng'ida's life came to give her encouragement and advice, as did the *engamuratani*—the elderly Maasai woman who would perform the circumcision.

"Stay strong."

"When the cutting happens, you must be still and you cannot cry. It's a sign of weakness."

"Now you will be a woman, and with that comes responsibilities—"

Some conveyed their messages through traditional Maasai songs; others quietly offered their advice as they held Neng'ida's hands.

For Neng'ida, these voices resonated with her heritage. She had participated in these traditional Maasai events for as long as she could remember, probably attending more than half a dozen circumcision ceremonies in the mere fourteen years she'd been alive, and actively participating in both her sisters' coming-of-age rituals. However, this time it was different. As she listened to the women of her family give advice, other more troubling and less familiar voices echoed through her memory. She remembered the words of her science teacher and the matron: "hemorrhage, scarring, even death."

As dawn approached, Neng'ida knew the final steps of the ritual would soon begin, and a persistent fear kept her fully alert even though her body felt heavy and sluggish. She looked at the two other girls who would share this experience with her. Like them, she wore a thin black shuka, known as an *enanga*, across her shoulders. In the days leading up to the circumcision, she'd worn only this black shuka, as an outward sign that she was preparing herself for womanhood. Though she already wore her hair closely clipped at school, her sister had shaved Neng'ida's head clean—another outward sign of her preparation.

Now Neng'ida shivered slightly, whether from the cool predawn air or from apprehension she wasn't sure. As sunrise approached, she and the other two girls were brought buckets of cold water and were instructed to bathe. Afterward, they lay side by side on a clean Maasai blanket. The engamuratani opened her circumcision kit and extracted three new razor blades, one for each girl.

As the sun rose, her mother sat silently behind Neng'ida, who turned the side of her face into her mother's lap. They clenched each other's hands as the engamuratani parted Neng'ida's legs. She closed her eyes. A scream gurgled in her throat, but never escaped her mouth, and then it was done. Neng'ida's body instinctively convulsed, and then everything went black.

CHAPTER 12:

DIAMONDS IN THE DARKNESS

"But do you think the Maasai will ever change?" asked the Tanzanian man in standard-issue khaki-colored national park attire.

He stood behind a counter in the welcome center at Tarangire National Park, about a two-hour drive from Monduli. Two of his colleagues had now joined the conversation—one leaning against the counter with his chin resting on his hand and the other one wandering over from where he'd been stationed near the door to listen.

It surprised me that they would be interested in this topic. I hadn't imagined educating Maasai girls would intrigue national park rangers, but these men, Tanzanians who were clearly not Maasai, seemed keen for a debate, perhaps because there was a lull in activity at the park's entrance.

Jean and I had simply walked in to pay our park fees and to get our entrance permits. When we'd greeted the man behind the counter in Swahili, he'd wanted to know where we'd come from, since white, Swahili-speaking national park visitors came in small numbers. Jean, in her usual friendly, outgoing fashion, had immediately switched to "Swa-English," as we'd come to call it, and explained to the man that we worked at the Maasai Secondary School for Girls in Monduli.

This began what was turning into a lengthy conversation about the school, its population, and its vision. I'd mostly listened, as had Marv and Mark after they'd strolled in, wondering what had happened to us. Though ready to move on, Marv, Mark, and I all knew steering Jean away from an interesting conversation was like trying to find hot running water in Monduli—nearly impossible. And hot running water was exactly what we all sought. Marv had already regaled Mark and me with tales of hot showers, plentiful Western-style food, laundry service, and amazing views from the Tarangire Safari Lodge. My dusty body and dirty hair felt ready to get there, but instead I hovered with Marv and Mark just behind Jean, close enough to listen but far enough away not to have to participate in the conversation.

"We are trying to uplift girls from the Maasai culture, which, as you know, is quite marginalized. These girls don't have much chance for secondary education outside of our school. We want to empower them to adapt to a changing world. Change is coming to the Maasai, whether they're ready for it or not," Jean explained.

"Yes, but what do you think? Will they change with the world?" replied the man behind the counter.

"I don't think they will," responded the man leaning on his arm. "Change is too hard for them. They don't want to educate their daughters. They don't want to give up their cows."

"There are signs of hope," Jean explained with a smile. "You know the saying 'Give a man a fish and you feed him for a day. Teach a man to fish and he'll eat for a lifetime'? Well, we're teaching these girls to fish."

"That's good. You have a good heart. I hope they will change, but I think it will be difficult," said the park ranger behind the counter.

I had remained silent during the conversation because I'd felt unsure about how to respond to the men. Their skeptical, almost prejudiced attitudes toward the Maasai made me realize that even among their own countrymen, the Maasai are often viewed unfavorably. I'd naively assumed that Tanzanians put country above tribe, but this obviously wasn't always true.

"Here's an example of the challenges we face here," he continued. He explained that Tarangire National Park rangers regularly interact with the Maasai villagers who live on land adjacent to the park. When protected wildlife crosses national park boundaries and threatens Maasai livestock and communities, park rangers and the local people find themselves in conflict over appropriate wildlife management strategies. Likewise, during the dry season, as water and green grass dry up outside the park, the local Maasai seek to graze their herds inside the boundaries of the park, creating ongoing tension and frustration on both sides around land and water rights.

"This is a difficult situation," another of the rangers explained. "The Maasai can be very stubborn, but I understand this is their way of life. There is not a good solution, but maybe education will help them."

I was learning that, like nearly everywhere else in the world, Tanzania's network of tribal politics is layered and complex, based on a history of competing interests and ongoing struggles for limited resources. Though the country had worked hard to provide equal access to an integrated education system, the Maasai remained slow to embrace education and modern ways of living. For this reason, many Tanzanians, including these park rangers, viewed the Maasai as clinging to a "stubbornly backward" way of life.

Truth be told, I found it difficult to argue with the men. In my mere month at the school, I'd wondered if Westerners, namely me, and their ways were not altogether welcome in Maasailand. I'd certainly been asking myself if the Maasai would change and, even more importantly, what stake I should or shouldn't have in that change.

Ultimately, for my own self-preservation, I'd told myself that I would remain as neutral as possible on the Maasai and their culture, even on the difficult issue of female genital cutting. I'd taken this stance mostly because I recognized my own ignorance. There was so much I simply didn't understand about the Maasai, perhaps so much that I would never understand. I felt the Maasai to be unknowable and mysterious because of the vast gap between their culture and my own, and yet, in more ways than one, I admired the Maasai for their love of family and their desire to maintain social cohesion. I wished I could claim a culture in which I felt as much pride and to which I felt as much allegiance, so I'd decided that instead of espousing my own opinions, I would work to give my students the knowledge and critical thinking skills necessary to decide for themselves how they and their culture should or should not change. However, in practice, I wasn't yet sure if this would be possible.

I'd intended to come to Tanzania to help people who, I'd perceived from afar, needed my help. What I was learning up close is that helping people is a tricky business. I couldn't escape the next part of the equation—helping people *to what end* and *in whose interest?* I thought my motives pure, but was that enough? When faced with the vast complexity of my students' needs, could my meager contribution amount to much?

These were the questions that haunted me at night when I lay cocooned inside my mosquito net listening to the voices of my students drifting from the dormitories into my window. What would these girls gain and lose because they'd been educated?

But here, at the entrance to Tarangire National Park, I selfishly and honestly only wanted to escape the questions for a few brief days during the June break from school. However, it seemed the questions would follow me no matter where I went.

"What type of education are you giving them?" the ranger behind the desk asked Jean. "Do you focus on agriculture?"

"As you know, in Tanzania, there is a standardized curriculum for secondary schools. We are teaching this curriculum, and the students must pass the national exams just like at any other school," Jean replied.

In truth, this curriculum, like most inherited, postcolonial educations, prepared the girls to enter a thriving capitalist economy, which didn't yet exist in Maasailand. Furthermore, all Tanzanian students were required to take a national exam starting at the end of primary school and then continuing every other year during secondary school in order to continue further with their schooling. Already, I'd seen the tremendous stress this evoked in students, who understood that in order to advance to the next level they must pass these exams. To me, the system seemed designed to eliminate students rather than advance them, I presumed because the country simply didn't have the resources to educate all children.

Only the brightest and most determined students found success in Tanzanian schools, and this scared me. Where would my students who failed the national exams go? What jobs could they get with only a partial education? Would they be able to safely return home if they didn't yet have the means to support themselves?

"You have a long road ahead of you, but I wish you a good journey on that hard road," said the man behind the counter as he handed Jean our permits. He continued, "'*Safari njema*,' we say in Swahili. We wish you a good journey in our park and beyond."

■ ■ ■ ■ ■ ■ ■

The next morning, Mark and I rose before dawn. We sat on folding camp chairs in front of our canvas tent—a full-sized safari-style affair large enough to stand upright in and to contain two twin beds and a small desk in the front half and a toilet and shower in the back, all on a rectangular concrete slab. To say we were roughing it would have been an exaggeration. I'd already taken three hot showers in less than twenty-four hours and stuffed myself full of barbequed meat and fresh fruits and salads the night before. Piping hot coffee had been delivered to our tent and to Jean and Marv's just next door as our predawn wake-up call.

As the horizon turned pink, Jean and Marv emerged from their tent. We all sat in watchful silence sipping our coffee as the atmosphere began to hum with life. Our tents, like all those at the Tarangire Safari Lodge, overlooked the Tarangire River, and though we couldn't yet see it in the opaque morning light, we knew it flowed in the valley below us and drew animals of every color and stripe.

The afternoon before, we'd watched as three giraffes floated across the landscape like mirages. In this, their natural habitat, they became stunningly graceful and beautiful, fluid in a way I'd never imagined. Later, we watched a herd of elephants bathe in the river, kneeling, rolling, and wallowing in the river's waters, trunks lolling over each other and ears flapping languidly. As the sun set, the enormous, gentle beasts leisurely marched onward, ripping up mouthfuls of grass along the way and passing within throwing distance of our tent as I peeked through the door, captivated by their movements and sounds and yet anxious about their proximity. In their wake, a troupe of baboons invaded the riverbank, noisily taking up residence in the tops of the palm trees—a place where even hungry leopards couldn't follow them.

In the night, I'd awakened to the guttural grunts and moans of what I'd correctly assumed were lions. Their powerful rumbles reverberated through the valley and right through the thin walls of our tent in a way that left me shuddering and wondering if a lion could actually drag me out from under my bed if I crawled down there and curled up in a tight ball. It was just after this thought that I ended up in Mark's single bed, the two of us entwined together listening to the lions roar around us.

Though I basked in this short return to my own culture where public and private displays of affection seemed normal, I recognized the safari lodge as an island of Western excess in the midst of great need. I couldn't quite rid myself of these thoughts as we toured the park in the back of Jean and Marv's Land Cruiser, swam in the lodge's pool, and ate candlelit dinners along with other white tourists. Guilt gurgled in my belly.

Most of the Tanzanian teachers with whom I now worked had never visited one of their own country's national parks. Many of them had never seen the elephants, zebras, and giraffes that had now become almost commonplace to me, and the swimming pool contained enough water to meet the needs of a Maasai family for weeks. I had no idea how to live with this new knowledge—how to come to terms with the cold, hard fact that I enjoyed access to vast wealth only because I'd been born with white skin in an affluent country with plentiful resources and opportunities, just as those I now called colleagues, friends, and students struggled because they'd been born with black skin in a country burdened by deep poverty.

I turned a critical eye not only on myself, but also on those around me. More and more, I found myself watching other tourists as if I were now Tanzanian. "Oh, you are looking so fat," I whispered to myself as two obese Americans waddled by, a phrase I'd learned from Mr. Kwayu, who'd told me that in Tanzania telling someone they're fat is a compliment because extra weight is an outward sign of good health and wealth.

In my best Swa-English, I snarked quietly to myself in a way no Tanzanian ever would because already I knew them to be courteous to a fault. Nonetheless, I couldn't help myself.

As I listened to a man complaining at the bar, an unwieldy voice in my head responded: *I'm sorry, sir, that there is only electricity until midnight, but there are no power lines here, only a generator. The bar is closing, and by the way, you've already spent more than most Tanzanian's monthly salaries on a single night's drinks.*

Over breakfast, the voice returned. *I'm sorry, ma'am, that you don't like anything on the breakfast buffet, but did you know that just*

outside the boundaries of this national park, there are children who won't
have enough to eat today?

The internal monologue went on and on as I watched and listened to those around me, and the guilt and shame continued to tug
at me. These people were part of my culture—one that was beginning to seem hopelessly self-centered, oblivious to the difference
between wants and needs, entitled beyond hope, and unaware of the
way 80 percent of the world's population lived.[1] I realized most of
us no longer remembered, or we never knew, hunger, deprivation, or
longing without hope of fulfillment. I recognized these failings in
myself, and it disconcerted me. This was the first of many times I felt
trapped inside my own culture without a clear path to redemption.

■ ■ ■ ■ ■ ■ ■ ■

Our last night at Tarangire, Mark and I sat in front of our tent
quietly discussing our growing uneasiness with our own cultural
identity and the many issues we faced back in Monduli. How
could we live responsibly as people of relative wealth in the midst
of poverty? How could we best serve our students and colleagues
recognizing that we would always be outsiders? How could we help
our students find success in an education system rife with shortcomings? As young people who had grown up in the Lutheran
church, what did our Christian faith call us to do? Were we like the
rich man to whom Jesus said, "Go sell your possessions and give to
the poor. Then come and follow me"?

Were we literally to give up all we had to address the needs we
saw around us? We stared and we stared at the miniscule eye of the
proverbial needle and wondered just how we might pass through
it.[2] We felt in a way we never had before that much was required of
us because much had been given to us.

We sat in silence for long stretches between these questions.
We watched the moon rise over the Tarangire River and listened

to the yips of jackals in the distance. We figuratively and literally clung to each other in a new way now. In the weeks since we'd left Morogoro, we'd become careful and gentle with each other as we formed our own culture of two. We knew we now had an unspoken knowledge and way of seeing the world that bound us together irrevocably.

Though we'd talked about it on and off since early in our relationship, in recent weeks our conversations about marriage had become more serious and urgent. That night, as a grand and extravagant African panorama stretched before us, the moonlight glinting like diamonds off the surface of the Tarangire River, and the outlines of baobab and acacia trees majestically defining the landscape, we decided the time was right to announce our culture of two to the rest of the world. In six months, we would return to the United States to get married, formalizing the bond we already knew would stand up to some of life's most urgent and pressing questions. Together, we believed we just might be able to face them.

CHAPTER 13:

THROUGH MAASAI EYES

After only a few days in Tarangire, I returned to the school to diligently spend the remainder of the school break preparing for the return of my students. In a month's time, I carefully reviewed every word of the *United Republic of Tanzania's English Curriculum for Secondary Schools* and several previous national exam samples. I devised a content outline for the remainder of the school year, which ended in early December, and developed lesson plans for the first few weeks of the second semester. I rounded up books and other supporting materials from the library to help with my plans. I'd come here to teach, and regardless of my questions and doubts, I'd decided that is what I would do to the best of my ability. I realized Susan's advice was correct. I couldn't wait for someone to tell me how to do this. I just had to do it.

During this time, I also took it upon myself to learn as much as I could about my surroundings. I assigned myself field trips, like those I'd experienced at language school, except this time self-directed. I regularly walked into Monduli and began forging relationships with the women and children who worked in the open-air market there. Now that I knew what to expect in this setting, it didn't feel nearly as intimidating as it had in Morogoro, and besides, I had to eat.

I wrote letters home and walked to the post office to mail them—one way that Mark and I began slowly preparing for our wedding from afar. And I regularly saw Mark. For the most part, he and I undertook these self-appointed field trips together, and, to our great relief, nobody cared how much time we spent together. Regardless of local customs, we were wazungu. While this attracted attention everywhere, it also meant that people expected us to be different and to relate to each other in ways that local couples might not. Without pause or reservation, everyone expressed delight that we would soon be wed.

As I went about all this, the campus seemed desolate and abandoned, so as students began filtering back to school at the beginning of July, I eagerly awaited them. I'd learned that home was not a safe place for some of them. In fact, a few had stayed on campus during the break because they feared forced marriages, circumcision, and even rape. I had no idea what it might feel like to be without home or family at the age of thirteen or fourteen, or at any age for that matter. I knew it would take considerable courage, probably mixed with desperation, to leave home permanently, and that it would likely feel profoundly sad and lonesome to know that your family still existed in a place you could no longer safely return.

Before the break, my Form I students had remained every teacher's dream—eager to learn, enthusiastic to participate, enamored with everything I presented, thankful for each and every learning opportunity, and curious about our differences. However, most of my Form IV students remained aloof and impenetrable. They sat impassively in their neat rows of slightly-too-small desks donated from some faraway primary school in the United States. A few showed hints of having once been as uninhibited as my Form

I students, though I had to look hard to see this beneath a tough veneer of teenage pseudo-indifference.

My Form IV students did not think of themselves as girls. They thought of themselves as notable women who had achieved something few other Maasai women had—an education. Within their culture, they should already have been wives and mothers, but instead they had grappled, clawed, and fought their way through school, and they were on the cusp of graduating from O-level, which would happen in only a few short months. They carried themselves as the Maasai warriors they'd become. The only chink in their tough facades came at the mention of the upcoming national exam. This instilled great fear in many of them.

I'd quickly learned that their sole focus and quest to pass the national exam meant that they barely tolerated anything that wasn't directly relevant to this goal. For these young women, passing the national exam meant the difference between staying at school to continue to A-level, or some other, as-yet-unknown future. So, even before the school break, I had begun to couch all my lessons in these terms, even while I looked for opportunities to insert other types of engagement, beyond rote learning and memorization, into my lessons.

For the first week of the second term, I devised a plan to have my Form IV students brainstorm and write about various topics in what I called their writing journals. After they'd written about a topic, we would discuss it in class. I'd taken some prompts from previous national exams, but I'd also inserted some of my own.

"Learning English is important because . . ."
"Animals in national parks are protected because . . ."
"Women and girls should be educated because . . ."
"The best things about Maasai culture are . . ."

When they turned in their first drafts, the last prompt was the most popular and had produced some of the most interesting responses. Many students wrote about the importance of family to the Maasai—about how the Maasai love children and view them as a blessing. A few students wrote about life in their engang, and a few more about the importance of cattle to the Maasai, but more than half of the students' essays started, "The best thing about Maasai culture is circumcision." This stopped me cold, long before I knew what had happened to Neng'ida.

■ ■ ■ ■ ■ ■ ■ ■

Neng'ida stood in the bathroom, a pain low and sharp between her legs. She couldn't stand fully upright, but rather hunched forward, bracing herself against a sink, her complexion sallow and sweaty. She didn't want anyone to know what had happened to her. In this setting, she felt ashamed and worried that the matron might not help her since she'd warned the girls against this very thing just before the school break.

Neng'ida had told two of her friends, Esupat and Nashipai, about the circumcision ceremony because she knew they had both already been circumcised and thought they would understand. The two girls now stood with Neng'ida holding her cold hands and speaking softly to her. They glanced at each other with furrowed brows. Based on their circumcision experiences, this seemed abnormal.

After the ceremony, Neng'ida's wound had been dressed with fermented milk, but she'd continued to bleed profusely for several days. During that time, she felt neither like eating the fatty meats nor drinking the cow's blood that her mother encouraged her to take in order to regain her strength. In addition, Neng'ida refused to drink chai, water, or anything else in an effort to avoid having to urinate, which she'd learned only a few hours after her circumcision felt like caustic acid flowing out of her body.

Normally, Neng'ida would have spent at least two months in relative seclusion, resting and healing, but her school break was only one month. This left little more than three weeks for Neng'ida to recover before she had to return to school—something her mother insisted on since she'd promised the headmistress she would return Neng'ida to the school.

Even in her weakened state, Neng'ida had agreed with her mother. She'd felt compelled to return to school on time, knowing she was already behind many of the students and not wanting to miss any of the lessons. She also knew the longer she stayed at home, the higher the risk that the man to whom she was promised in marriage might declare her healed from the circumcision and forcibly take her as his wife, something she thought about with an increasing sense of dread.

Neng'ida had already overheard some of the older girls at school conspiratorially whispering and giggling in the dormitories about falling in love with boys their own ages. One of the Form IV students had defiantly wagged her head from side to side, pointed a finger urgently upward, and declared she would choose her own husband. This had resulted in peals of nervous laughter and several murmurs of assent from other girls.

Before the school break, Neng'ida had remained ever watchful of all the girls at the school, but particularly the older ones. She tried to emulate their behaviors—studying when they studied, doing laundry when they did, and behaving as they did—but now she felt too weak for this.

While she had stopped bleeding in the days before she left home, once she arrived at school, the bleeding had returned. As she left the bathroom and tried to walk toward the Form I classroom, the edges of Neng'ida's vision turned black, and she reeled dangerously to one side. Esupat ran to find the matron, even against Neng'ida's wishes. Truthfully, Neng'ida wasn't in any shape to object. She sat on the ground with her head in her hands while Nashipai sat with her and quietly cried, something Neng'ida was too disoriented to even notice.

The matron tottered down the path toward the girls with Esupat in tow. Her look of stern disapproval softened when she saw Neng'ida. The girl was obviously suffering, and even the matron knew now wasn't the time for reproach. Now was the time for action.

After a cursory assessment, she sent Esupat running back up the hill to the headmistress's house to report the situation and request that the school truck be prepared immediately for a trip to the Monduli Clinic—a rough-and-tumble outpost where sometimes a doctor was present and sometimes not.

Neng'ida sat inertly in the front seat squeezed between the school driver and the matron. Though Esupat and Nashipai wanted to accompany Neng'ida to the clinic, the matron forbade it. She operated under the policy that only the sick and infirm belonged at the clinic, and since the girls were perfectly healthy, she told them in a manner that left little room for debate that their time was best spent in the classroom. The girls watched as the school truck pulled away, and then they turned toward the classroom, their heads hung low.

■ ■ ■ ■ ■ ■ ■

Meantime, as I read one essay after another that started the same way, I first recoiled and then became increasingly puzzled. I realized that many of the students worked together after class to complete the essays, and I recognized that for those who struggled with English, copying someone else's essay proved to be a simple way to get the work done. However, there were enough differences in the essays that I realized that many, even most, of my students did, in fact, view circumcision as the best thing about their culture. Though I wanted to keep an open mind, I couldn't help but wonder how a culture could possibly survive if the act of circumcising young girls and boys was its most redeeming quality. Even more troubling, this conclusion—that circumcision was the best thing about their culture—came from a group of educated young Maasai women. I wanted to understand, but I simply didn't.

My knowledge of the practice told a bleak story. Prior to coming to Tanzania I'd sought to understand the implications of female genital cutting, and since arriving I'd heard a number of informal reports about the Maasai. I knew that, officially, approximately 18 percent of Tanzanian women and girls under the age of fifty were circumcised.[1] Of the more than 120 cultural groups in Tanzania, the Maasai were among only fourteen that continued the practice. Unofficially, I'd heard the rate of circumcision among the Maasai varied from about 60 percent to nearly 100 percent. The number seemed difficult for anyone to accurately capture, as Maasai women often fail to report what has happened to them, fearing social stigma, retribution, or even prosecution.[2]

I also knew that the Maasai practice Type I circumcision, entirely or partially removing the clitoris. Though Type I circumcision is the least destructive form of female genital cutting, the health implications can still be profound and include increased risk of contracting sexually transmitted diseases, recurrent bladder and urinary tract infections, infertility, cysts, and increased risk of childbirth complications. Beyond this, the practice is a violation of girls' and women's basic human rights as established by numerous international treaties and declarations, including the United Nations' *Convention against Torture and Other Cruel, Inhuman, or Degrading Treatment or Punishment*.[3]

In 1998, just before I arrived at the girls' school, the Tanzanian government prohibited female circumcision for girls eighteen years of age and younger. Unfortunately, I'd heard one of the alarming side effects of the prohibition was that the practice had gone underground in many parts of the country. There was an emerging trend in cutting girls at an early age, many before their first birthdays. And when there were complications, parents often didn't take girls of any age to the hospital for fear of prosecution.

I'd surmised that the vast majority of the girls in attendance at the Maasai Secondary School for Girls had either been circumcised before they arrived at the school or underwent the procedure during school breaks. I also kept most of my feelings about this to myself, as I understood the complicated history of colonists, missionaries, NGOs, Westerners, and now the Tanzanian government intervening to discourage the practice among the Maasai. For some Maasai, this had resulted in a perception that attacks on circumcision were attacks on Maasai culture. I certainly wanted to appreciate the Maasai culture. I wanted to be respectful of it, but reading the girls' essays celebrating circumcision tested my limits. How could I appropriately and sensitively respond to these essays as a woman who was not Maasai?

I began by looking a bit deeper, rereading each essay. Not one of the essays focused on the physical act—the actual cutting of flesh. Most of the essays discussed the gathering of family and friends, the singing and dancing, the special food, and the exchange of gifts—the same types of things I would describe if I were writing about Christmas or my birthday. In sometimes fluent, sometimes broken English, the essays described the ceremony—the love and the laughter, the importance of tradition, the hallmark Maasai bravery, and the celebration of adulthood—and then they would end with a single sentence: "Nevertheless, for girls circumcision is bad." One or two of the more articulate essays included a sentence or two about how the coming-of-age celebrations should continue, but the physical act of cutting should stop.

I could almost feel the internal conflict of these young women. They valued their culture and their families, even beyond what they could express in any language, and yet whether by education or by their own circumstances, they recognized the need for change. Though a few of the girls' essays expressed a sense of helplessness that they would personally be able to change anything, a few of the students were advocating for a Maasai concept called *engisaisai*, which recognizes that Maasai culture is not static but dynamic and that positive change is possible through the adaptation of traditions.

As if seeing the future, I realized that, of anyone, these girls might become the leaders and drivers of that change. Though most of them had likely been circumcised, they would be among the young women responsible for redefining what it means to be a Maasai woman in the twenty-first century. I didn't have to do anything but ask the question. They already had the answer.

The day after I read these essays, Neng'ida returned to my Form I classroom thinner and gaunter than I had remembered. At the time, I thought she'd arrived at school a week late, and I felt disappointed that she'd missed so many lessons, particularly since I knew she already struggled to keep up. What I didn't know is that she'd returned to school on time but had spent a week at the Monduli Clinic recovering from complications associated with her own circumcision. A blood clot that had initially stopped the bleeding broke loose when Neng'ida arrived at school. Once again, she began to bleed profusely. Neng'ida had arrived at the Monduli Clinic in the early stages of shock, and with a severe urinary tract infection brought on by her inability to urinate after her circumcision.

But I didn't know this. All I knew was her hand no longer shot into the air to answer every question. She no longer smiled at me before shyly hiding her face behind her hands. She sometimes seemed distracted. All this made me wonder if Neng'ida marked the beginning of a transition in my Form I students—a shift toward the reserved and distant behavior that dominated my Form IV classroom.

When I offhandedly asked the matron about Neng'ida a few days later, I received a tightlipped response. "She was sick and had to be admitted to the Monduli Clinic. She stayed there for a week."

When I asked what was wrong and if Neng'ida had recovered, I received a vague, "She'll be okay."

The matron was right—like many young women who underwent circumcision, Neng'ida would be okay—but more than a decade later, Neng'ida would tell me this story, her internal conflict still etched on her face. She would end the story with the same conviction I'd seen in those essays so many years earlier. "This will never happen to my daughters."

CHAPTER 14:

A GRANDMOTHER'S TOUCH

Since the start of the second term in July, I'd found myself getting into a more or less comfortable routine, even if parts of the
day still remained challenging. My days started early. I usually rose
by six in order to take my bucket bath, dress for the day, prepare
breakfast, and review my lesson plans—all before morning chapel
at seven thirty. Right after chapel, I taught Form I, which remained
the highlight of my day.

Afterward, I spent a little over an hour back at the house
bracing myself for Form IV, which began around eleven, just after
morning chai, which I'd taken to having with Susan at our house
or down at Jean and Marv's instead of up at school. Seldom did
more than one or two other teachers gather in the staff room for
tea. Even when they did, they typically drank their tea in silence, or
they engaged in Swahili conversations from which I felt excluded. I
remained disappointed that I had yet to meaningfully connect with
anyone on staff except for the other wazungu.

Most of the Tanzanian teachers were outwardly friendly to
me, but our interactions failed to go beyond cursory exchanges. I

wasn't sure if language, culture, or some other factors created what seemed to me a deep, almost impenetrable barrier. I suspected the persistent awkwardness had something to do with my own limitations, such as my inability to master Swahili, or my propensity for introversion when faced with uncomfortable situations, or my ongoing aversion to situations where I believed I might be asked for something—predominantly money to meet a range of sometimes valid, sometimes questionable needs.

I'd also gotten the sense that my mere presence made some of the teachers, even the headmistress, slightly wary, as if they believed judgment followed me around whispering in my ear about poor English-language skills, the shortcomings of Tanzania's education system, or the need for more thoughtful planning, and admittedly, it sometimes did.

I remained envious that Mark seemed to be finding more collegiality in his setting, though even he felt similarly uncomfortable around many of Moringe's staff. The difference was he had a handful of colleagues who went out of their way to make him feel he belonged—that his contributions and opinions were valued and that he was a respected member of Moringe's team.

While Moringe didn't escape the circumstances of education in Tanzania—few resources, inherited curricula, inadequate teacher training programs, and ill-conceived national exams—it did seem to stand outside the politics that frequently plagued the Maasai Secondary School for Girls, including tribal politics, church politics on not one but two continents, and sponsor politics. It was no wonder I felt as if I was tiptoeing through a field of land mines, because, in fact, I was, and so were all the other staff members, which I believed hindered forming relationships, not just for me, but for everyone.

In the midst of this, my relationships with Jean, Marv, and Susan flourished. Along with Mark, they became my support system even as I gradually began to find unexpected mentors among a handful of Tanzanians. As my need for local advice and guidance increased, Mark encouraged me to maximize his connections at Moringe, so I began to walk up to his school in the late afternoons to visit with him, headmaster Dr. Msinjili, second master Mr. Kwayu, and sometimes the head of math department, Mr. Panga.

Gradually, I came to develop a deep trust in these men, enough so that I began to discuss some of the challenges I faced down the hill at "the other school" in town. As they patiently listened to me and gently taught me about Tanzania and its many cultures, I began to observe that race, gender, age, and economics played a significant role in how and why things happened as they did.

While Dr. Msinjili, Mr. Kwayu, and Mr. Panga were not Maasai, they were all older Tanzanian men who had extensive experience working with and among the Maasai. They helped me, in ever so subtle and indirect ways, to understand that my skin color, age, gender, and relative wealth—all things over which I had little to no control—defined me and my relationships within the Maasai community more so than my education, work ethic, intentions, leadership skills, or talents—all things I'd carefully honed and managed so as to gain high value and respect within my own culture. While I intellectually began to understand this new reality, I nonetheless found it abrasive and unpalatable, and I regularly bristled against it. My place in this reality seemed a lesson I would have to learn over and again the hard way.

After a time, I even felt brave enough to share what had happened at the diocese office with Dr. Msinjili, who listened attentively. After I was through, he sat for a long moment in thoughtful silence before he said, "Well, Julie, pole sana. I'm sorry this has happened, but don't feel alone. This is something we all endure. Know that you are welcome to teach at Moringe and to write your paper on the teaching you do here."

By this time, I'd already quietly come to an agreement with Mama Mkuu and the diocese; I could write the paper so long as I did it discreetly. This news came not from the headmistress, but from Doug and Linda, who had facilitated a follow-up meeting between Mr. Langoi and an American professor who had been working closely with the diocese for years on education-related programs. Without doubt, I felt grateful not to be in attendance, but I did wish I'd been a gecko on the wall of his office during the meeting. I never knew how a deal was struck; only that I was to keep my head down, do a good job teaching, and write the paper without another word to anyone about it, and so that is exactly what I did.

While I remained friendly with the staff of the Maasai Secondary School for Girls, I avoided any significant emotional investment and remained guarded and unsure of myself. I thought it best to stay focused on the students with whom I felt I had a better chance of making uninhibited, apolitical connections, though even with them race, gender, age, and economics played their roles.

▪▪▪▪▪▪▪▪

One dusty morning in September, I wandered back to the house at teatime to take a quick break before I had to teach Form IV. As I walked through the coffee fields, my shoes picked up a fine coating of brown silt. Everyone hoped the short rains would come early this year because the long rains had failed to bring the usual downpours. Lately, we'd had little water at our house, and I'd begun hoarding it—storing bucketfuls under the sink when the water came, so that we'd have some when it didn't. I spent an unusual amount of time worrying about water. How often should I bathe? How many times could I get by with wearing something before it really needed to be washed? What would I do if the buckets under the sink became empty? The constant feeling of grit and grime wore on me.

This day I felt particularly grubby and my mood reflected this, so I thought some quiet time might do me good. Just as I sat down on the couch, put my feet up on the coffee table, and took my first sip of hot tea, the typical "hodi, hodi . . . hodi" rang out at my door.

Someone had come for a visit, and I guessed from the pitch and cadence that it was a Tanzanian woman.

I considered ignoring the call as I quietly took another sip of my tea, held my breath, and rolled my eyes. The call came again as the doorknob rattled. Though the door was locked, it seemed my visitor wasn't likely to give up as I heard her walking toward the front window for a peek inside. She called again, "Hodi, hodi," more tentatively now.

She'd probably seen me walking down from the school and knew I was here.

"Karibu," I called, trying to sound welcoming.

I grabbed my still-full cup of tea and thrust it onto the kitchen counter before calling out again, "Karibu," as I walked toward the front door to unlock it.

All six feet of Bibi Ruth, the school's elderly Maasai matriarch, beamed at me with an aged radiance that immediately lifted my mood. She smiled broadly at me as she fiddled with the *kanga* knotted around her shoulders with one hand and swung a heavily laden plastic bag with the other.

"Shikamoo, Bibi," I said as I gestured for her to come inside. She nodded and shuffled past me in her red Converse high-top sneakers. I smiled despite myself. Ruth's choice of shoes cracked me up. No old sandals for her. Bibi Ruth rolled in style, even if she didn't know it.

"*Endito takwenya,*" she replied in Maa, which I didn't really understand. Bibi Ruth was easily the friendliest person on campus. However, I found communicating with her particularly difficult because neither of us felt comfortable using Swahili, though this didn't seem to dissuade or bother Ruth in the slightest. Bibi Ruth preferred Maa, and I certainly preferred English. *This should be interesting,* I thought, and not just because of the language challenges.

I felt pretty certain Ruth had seen me walking down here. She'd been stalking me around campus the last several days, and now she'd cornered me. Susan had warned me that Bibi Ruth, like most Maasai, felt there was simply no harm in asking—asking for money, food, the shirt off my back if she liked it, and all manner of other things. I imagined this tactic was how the Converse sneakers had ended up on her feet. Fortunately, she was a lot bigger than me, so neither my clothing nor my shoes would readily fit her.

I politely offered her some tea while she settled into one of the chairs in the living room. By now, my own tea had grown cold.

As we sat together sipping our tea in silence, having exhausted the handful of Swahili greetings and phrases we jointly knew, Ruth opened up her plastic bag and began spreading all manner of beaded objects onto the coffee table in front of me as she spoke to herself in Maa.

No doubt, her work was beautiful. She had beaded bracelets in red, green, blue, and orange, and several long, multicolored strands of necklaces. Two traditional ilturesh stood out: large and rigid as dinner plates, the outermost ring of beads alternated between white and black followed by wide rings of orange, blue, white, and red; a narrow yellow ring finished the circular beaded collar at the hole for the wearer's throat.

I picked up several of the pieces and admired them as Bibi Ruth began unrolling something she'd obviously squirreled away in the kanga tied at her waist. From the folds of fabric emerged two beaded wire loops with a series of small, reflective metal disks dangling from them. Ruth held them up with one hand and pointed at my ears with the other. I nodded and smiled as if to say, *Yes, those are earrings.*

With some effort, she pushed herself up off the chair and came over to me with the earrings as she said, "*Zawadi,*" or "gift" in Swahili, and smiled at me. She bent at the waist and began fiddling with one of my earlobes, her face right next to mine as she strained to see if I had holes in my ears. When she discovered that I did, she began poking at my ear with one of the earrings in an attempt to loop it through. Though breaking into a cold sweat from both her proximity and the relative ease with which she touched me, I sat still until she eventually found the hole in my ear and repeated the process on the other side.

"*Umependeza sana*," she said as she stood back and admired her handiwork, which I understood to mean, "You look so beautiful."

"*Asante sana, Bibi Ruth. Asante. Sasa mimi ni Maasai.*" Thank you so much, Bibi Ruth. Thank you. Now I am Maasai.

She giggled, covered her mouth with one hand, and slapped her thigh with the other. Then she grabbed one of the ilturesh and carefully bent it around my neck. I stood next to her and began to move my shoulders up and down to make the collar quiver back and forth as I'd seen some of the girls do on campus one afternoon. We both laughed, her cloudy eyes filled with mirth, as she said something to me in Maa that I didn't understand.

Bibi Ruth remained a ubiquitous, traditional presence on campus. Most afternoons, I'd see her near one of the classrooms, one or more students sitting next to her. Most of the time, they seemed to just be sitting together enjoying one another's company without words. Sometimes they sat with their legs extended straight in front of them, a pile of small beads in their laps, and strings of shredded grain sacks hanging from their lips as they quickly slid the beads onto the twine. Some of them worked with wire instead of twine, but only when Bibi Ruth had found a way to buy some. Often she did her handiwork alone because she didn't always want to share her limited supply of beads with the girls.

As she was my elder, I felt I ought to be respectful and friendly to Bibi Ruth—feelings I knew were rooted in my own culture and also in hers—though, inexplicably, I also felt like keeping her at arm's length. I'd complained that it was difficult to build relationships with my Tanzanian and Maasai colleagues at the school, and yet here was one extending friendship to me, and I hesitated to accept it. I wondered if the problem was more mine than theirs—if they sensed my hesitation and perceived me as guarded and unfriendly.

Truth be told, I was still unsure about how to cope with the differences in our socioeconomic status—unsure about how to live in their midst, to understand their needs, to become their friends, to care for them, and yet tell them that I couldn't give them money, send their children to school, take them to America, or, in this case, buy all their beadwork.

It felt to me as if this issue—of wants and needs and haves and have-nots—was the current that ran beneath nearly all my relationships with Tanzanians. I felt, and I think they did too, that we didn't come to the relationship on equal footing. Though I loathed being perceived and treated as a wealthy white patron, that is exactly what I was in many of their eyes. I wanted to be like them, just another teacher at the school doing my job, but this seemed impossible. Too much history preceded my arrival.

Bibi Ruth and I settled on the sale of one ilturesh—the one she'd put on me—after a bit of haggling over the price, something I'd learned was both expected and necessary in any business transaction in Tanzania, even if I found it awkward. Though obviously pleased with the sale of one of the most expensive items she'd brought over, that didn't stop Ruth from encouraging me several times to buy more, even as I graciously refused each advance. Truth be told, with a wedding back in the United States planned for January, Bibi Ruth had tapped whatever extra bit of money I had for the month.

After several minutes of polite back-and-forth over the potential sale of additional jewelry, Ruth finished her tea, packed up her beadwork, and headed back toward the school with my spare money folded into her kanga where the earrings she'd given me had been. I smiled to myself as I watched her amble away. Perhaps I ought to just accept Ruth's grandmotherly presence at face value. In friendship, we had everything to gain and nothing to lose. There was no harm in asking.

CHAPTER 15:

THE FIRST GRADUATION

As the graduates processed past me, I couldn't help myself. I had to swallow hard several times and blink fast. I stood along the pathway into the chapel in a blue batik sheath dress, camera in hand, snapping pictures. Mark stood beside me in khaki pants and a white shirt. Emotions that seemed difficult to discern pricked my senses as they vibrated around me, blew through the jacaranda trees and down into the chapel, rustling my dress and fluttering through my hair. I sensed them even though I couldn't name them.

Like a battalion marching to war, the graduates kept their eyes steadfastly forward, their chins high, and their spines straight. It occurred to me, not for the first time, that many of these young women had done battle, though like many veterans they remained mostly tight-lipped about their seen and unseen wounds. Today, they appeared regal, in traditional Maasai dress, for this, their victory parade.

It was late October, and though I'd only taught them for a small portion of their time at the school, I felt a tremendous sense of pride, not in what I had done, but in what they had achieved.

Though most of them remained reserved and withdrawn around me, I still felt I was bearing witness to a momentous change in their lives, the implications of which none of us yet fully understood.

The caboose on the long procession came in the form of two imposing, almost startling, men—Bishop Laiser, the Maasai man responsible for convincing reticent tribal leaders of the need to educate girls, and David Simonson, the American missionary who'd spent more than forty years living and working among the Maasai and had spearheaded fundraising for the school. Though I'd not met either man personally, their reputations as strong leaders intimidated me and led me to believe that I'd rather stay safely amid the anonymous flock than to be noticed, so I found myself shrinking slightly and avoiding eye contact as they walked by.

The bishop wore brilliant, Maasai-red vestments. From his tall pointed cleft cap to his papal shoes, the man radiated authority both in this world and the next, it seemed to me. In contrast, David Simonson wore what I'd seen him wear nearly every time he'd been on campus—sturdy work boots, blue jeans, a button-up Western-style shirt, and his trademark brown leather outback hat. Though he gave off an air of nonchalance, I knew Dave was no man to trifle with as he lumbered into the chapel behind the formal procession.

In fact, I'd heard much of the lore that surrounded the man locals called "The Great White Maasai," and I was duly impressed. One of the most widespread tales about Dave was set in 1950s Tanganyika—the pre-independence version of Tanzania—just after the then-young preacher had arrived in the country. As the story went, local Maasai morani, or warriors, had approached Simonson about a rogue lion that had jumped through an open window in pursuit of two terrified schoolteachers. The morani believed the animal's increasingly erratic behavior needed to be addressed before someone got hurt. They knew the new preacher had arrived in their village with not only a direct line to God but, even more importantly, with several guns.

Not wanting to catch anyone in the crossfire, Simonson had insisted on setting out on his own to kill the lion. Though the morani quietly questioned the seemingly inexperienced lion hunter's sanity, they had a certain respect for the *kichaa*, or crazy, white man's unflagging bravery and a strange, even morbid, curiosity about how this would turn out. In a single night, Simonson, an avid hunter of deer and other small game in America, killed his first African lion, and within three days of the animal's demise, the tale of the young white preacher who'd single-handedly killed a marauding lion had spread across all of Maasailand, and so a legend was born.[1]

More than forty years later, Simonson had established primary schools and health clinics throughout Maasailand, thereby gaining wide respect among the Maasai not only as a fearless lion slayer, but also as a fiercely determined, sometimes demanding, but always dedicated partner.

In fact, Simonson and Bishop Laiser, who had known each other since shortly after the days of the marauding lion, had together envisioned and built the Maasai Secondary School for Girls. Simonson raised funds for construction, supplies, and scholarships from American donors, and Bishop Laiser, with the help of the local Member of Parliament Edward Lowassa, Bibi Ruth, and many others inside and outside the Lutheran church in Tanzania, convinced reticent Maasai fathers and leaders to educate girls. Individually, they were forces to be reckoned with; together, little could stand in their way. Though they sometimes disagreed on the details, Simonson and the bishop found common ground in their belief that the Maasai would face many challenges in the twenty-first century, including dramatic changes to their nomadic way of life, as land and water rights increasingly restricted their ability to move cattle across areas of historical migration.

Simonson and the bishop believed these challenges required new approaches to education and leadership, including the education of Maasai girls and women, which was becoming an increasingly popular area of focus in Africa from the mid-1980s onward as the United Nations, the World Bank, governments, and NGOs began conducting research on gender inequality and developing strategies to address it. In the early 1990s, just as the idea for the Maasai Secondary School for Girls began to gain traction, the World Bank sponsored a number of studies in Africa that showed several significant social and economic benefits from investing in girls' education, and these ideas began to strongly influence Tanzania's political and religious leaders alike.[2]

The Maasai Secondary School for Girls became the right idea at the right time, not just internationally, but also locally. The founders of the Maasai Secondary School for Girls had witnessed the school's impact already. They knew the stories of many of its students. Students like Neng'ida, and like Miriam.

■ ■ ■ ■ ■ ■ ■ ■

As she waited for the processional to begin, Miriam recalled how her route to graduation had been circuitous and fraught with danger. The likelihood that she'd be among the first Form IV Maasai girls to graduate had seemed like nothing more than the glimmer of a distant star when she'd first arrived at the school. Though she didn't expect to see them, Miriam couldn't help but wonder what would happen if her mother and her brother showed up to see her graduate. She wished, particularly today, that she could see her father again. The hole he'd left in her life had remained deep and wide. She didn't know for sure, but she imagined that her path to secondary school and this graduation day would have been much different had he still been living.

Miriam remembered vividly the morning her father found her standing alone on one of the main roads near her engang. At the time, only six years old, she was supposed to be looking for firewood with her sisters, but instead she was watching other children in their school uniforms walk to primary school. When Miriam's father caught her, she started crying not because she thought she might be punished, but because she wanted to attend school like the others. Her tears must have moved him because rather than sending her home, he walked with her directly to the school, spoke to the head teacher, and enrolled his youngest child in primary school. This in itself was an unusual act for a Maasai father.

During that first year, Miriam came home from school in the afternoons and used pieces of charcoal to write on the mud walls of her boma to show her father what she was learning. He listened attentively, and she believed that he had a special affinity for her because of her position as the youngest of his more than twenty children from three different wives. By the time she'd come around, he'd had a lot of practice at fatherhood and behaved more like a grandfather to Miriam.

Much younger than her father, Miriam's mother had married him in her adolescence, though by the time Miriam arrived on the scene, her mother was no longer young. By that time, she'd already spent years raising children, milking cows, hauling water, cooking, cleaning, and otherwise facilitating the daily routine of the engang. Her mother's relationship with her father seemed one of mutual tolerance rather than affection, and at the time of Miriam's earliest memories, her mother had already seemed wrung out, as if she'd given away all her love to Miriam's older siblings—four brothers and three sisters. Miriam cared deeply for her mother, but she'd always felt removed from her, as if they somehow existed on different planes.

Before the end of Miriam's third year of primary school, her father died and then her life began to change, slowly at first, and then more dramatically. Her eldest brother, who took over as head of the household after her father's death, initially supported Miriam's education, perhaps because he'd attended a few years of school himself. However, when Miriam finished primary school, he saw more value in the traditional Maasai ways and began to make arrangements for her marriage as he'd done for some of her elder sisters.

Miriam cried when she heard this news from her mother, who seemed befuddled by her response. Miriam begged her brother to let her continue in school, and he considered it briefly, but then her mother began complaining bitterly that if Miriam went to secondary school, they would have to forego the six cows that had already been negotiated as a bride price. Even though Miriam wept and wept, her brother held firm to his decision. At the age of thirteen, she would be married to the thirty-year-old man he'd found for her.

Miriam had other plans though. She waited until her husband-to-be paid the dowry for her, his cows joining her family's herd. Then, in the dead of night, she packed a few belongings and hid them just outside the engang. The next day, she told her mother she was going to get water. Instead, she retrieved her things and immediately walked several miles on foot to find one of her primary school teachers. She told him about the situation and her plan, which was to go to Dodoma, the capitol of Tanzania, to see a Maasai member of parliament, Mr. Edward Lowassa, whom she'd heard speak on the radio about the importance of education.

Considering her age and the circumstances, Miriam's determination was nothing short of inspirational, so her teacher gave her a small amount of money for the half-day bus ride to Dodoma and agreed to talk to her brother and her mother about Miriam's situation. When she reached the city many hours later, Miriam began walking around asking people where to find Mr. Lowassa, until a kind woman took pity on her, gave her some additional money, and put her on a dala dala to his office.

As it turned out, Mr. Lowassa wasn't there. He wasn't even in Tanzania. He'd gone to Europe, a distant place Miriam knew nothing about at the time. As Miriam began to cry, Mr. Lowassa's receptionist asked Miriam why she had come. Disheartened and tired, Miriam wept as she told the woman that she wanted to go to secondary school, but there was no hope for her because she was already promised in marriage. Through her tears, Miriam explained she'd come to see Mr. Lowassa to beg him for help because she had nowhere else to turn. Moved by Miriam's brave tenacity, the receptionist offered Miriam a place to stay until Mr. Lowassa returned. Two weeks later, she was called back to his office.

When Miriam met Mr. Lowassa, she addressed him in Maa in an extremely timid voice, but she told him her story as he thoughtfully watched her from behind gold-rimmed glasses, his fingers steepled under his chin, his gray hair forming a soft halo around his head. When she finished, he sighed deeply, smiled at her, and called her courageous. From the knowing look in his eyes, Miriam knew he understood the challenges she and many other Maasai girls faced.

Though he made no promises, Mr. Lowassa told her about a new Lutheran secondary school for Maasai girls near Arusha where he thought she might find a place. He wrote a letter on her behalf to Bishop Laiser. Both men were Maasai, as well as long-time friends and age mates, who'd worked on behalf of their tribe in their different, but intersecting, circles of influence.

Mr. Lowassa gave Miriam bus fare to Arusha, another full-day's journey away, along with the letter, and so it came to pass that Miriam met the bishop, and he too understood and found a place for her at the school that today she would graduate from—the Maasai Secondary School for Girls.

Despite all this, Miriam still missed her family, especially today. However, she knew this school represented an opportunity few Maasai girls received, and the students and teachers here had become like family. She loved them, and she thanked God every day for the chance to go to school. She tried not to think about what might happen after graduation. She hadn't been home in recent years because her brother still owed her husband-to-be either a bride or his six cows. If she went home, she'd soon be a wife. For now, she resolved to do her best on the upcoming national exam and hoped that her performance would allow her to continue to Form V in the next year.

Now, like the other girls in her Form IV class, she wore full Maasai regalia even though she'd borrowed most of the beadwork from other girls. One small ilturesh hung around her neck, a simple wide band of white beads encircled her head, and a narrow belt girded her thin waist. Only her earrings and a singular bracelet belonged to her; everything else she would return to others after the graduation.

She hadn't spoken to her mother in over two years, so while the other graduates had received beadwork from their mothers, grandmothers, aunts, and sisters, Miriam had come up short, but this wasn't a new experience for her. She'd spent the last several years feeling exiled. When others had gone home for school breaks, she'd stayed at school. On Sundays, when some parents had visited their daughters, she'd remained alone. When some of her classmates had received spending money from their families, she'd had none.

Luckily, the headmistress had paid several local Maasai women to sew and bead the straight floor-length sheath dresses Miriam and all the graduates wore. Made of brownish-red cloth instead of a more traditional cowhide because the cloth was cheaper, each dress was fashioned in the same way even though the beadwork appeared slightly different.

Walking two by two in a pair of long lines, Miriam and the other graduates paraded into the open-air, amphitheater-like chapel led by the school's choir, which announced the procession with drums and singing. The campus had literally been whitewashed in preparation for this day. The small rocks that lined walking paths had been painted white. The classrooms had been scrubbed from floor to ceiling. Several plants had appeared in new plastic buckets around the chapel, sparkling streamers hung from the rafters, and fresh flowers sat atop the altar.

Monduli's citizens had lined the road from town out to the school to wave at the passing motorcades. Many special guests were attending the ceremony, the most prominent being Tanzania's first lady, who would give the commencement address. Besides the first lady, hundreds of other dignitaries and sponsors were expected, including two people who'd made today possible for Miriam—Mr. Lowassa and Bishop Laiser.

Though her stomach felt unsettled and she preferred to remain quietly on the periphery of today's important crowd, she knew this was impossible, so she held her head high and walked into the chapel with the same air of confidence those around her displayed. As a group, the young women commanded attention and the audience seemed rapt; a few even shed tears, Miriam noticed, something that made her own eyes water as if the emotions were contagious.

As First Lady Mkapa, a striking woman in an amethyst suit, began to speak, Miriam realized that she was about to graduate from what, in a very short period of time, had become one of the most famous schools in Tanzania. While the first lady congratulated the students, she also left little doubt that the eyes of the nation and, even more importantly, of the Maasai people rested upon Miriam and her classmates.

The first lady reminded the graduates that the school's effectiveness and its long-term viability would be measured by the actions of all the girls who today walked proudly before dignitaries, donors, parents, and teachers. Though she was young, this responsibility was not lost on Miriam. When she walked up to collect her diploma, Miriam felt the weight of this responsibility upon her shoulders and its harsh gaze upon her face. Only then did Miriam glance at the large crowd, and, lo and behold, from the rear of the chapel, her mother and her brother stared back at her. Though their faces remained unreadable, Miriam smiled to herself. They'd come. She couldn't believe it, and then a single tear escaped from the corner of her eye before she surreptitiously wiped it away.

....

The presence of so many important people and such a large crowd on campus meant that, as introverts, Mark and I found it more comfortable to remain outside the open-air chapel looking in, rather than to actually sit inside where the action was taking place. And, as the hours wore on, we felt grateful that we'd chosen to sit in the soft grass outside the chapel with the rest of the overflow crowd. We'd heard about, but not yet fully experienced, the epic nature of Tanzanian ceremonies. If a church service typically lasted for two or three hours, a graduation ceremony required a good four or five, and we simply couldn't imagine sitting on the chapel's hard, bleacher-like planks squeezed between Tanzanians who had a different understanding of personal space than we did for that length of time.

Those of us outside could still hear, and mostly see, but we were clearly of a different ilk than most of those inside the chapel. Nearly all of us were women, mostly Maasai women dressed in traditional Maasai mashuka. In my father's Montana terms, we were the "nothing fancy, ordinary people." Out here, there were no airs to put on or people to impress. As the smell of roasting meat floated from the kitchen toward the chapel, I realized we were also probably the group as likely to have shown up for the food as for the ceremony.

Through most of the ceremony, the women sat together in small groups fiddling with blades of grass, whispering to one another from time to time, and passing small children from lap to lap. Since the entire graduation ceremony took place in Swahili, and often difficult, ceremonial Swahili at that, I found it more interesting to watch these women than to try to understand what was going on, and I think the feeling was mutual. They were as interested in Mark and me as we were in them. We soon found ourselves wandering around, whispering greetings to them, and occasionally asking if we could take their pictures. Most of the women responded with shy, eager grins, or solemn nods, but it seemed important to all of them that the image they presented to the camera was one of self-possessed poise—no silly grins or photobombing for this bunch.

As the ceremony finally came to a close and the graduates led the gathered throng out of the chapel, the staff stood together just outside to form a receiving line for the first lady. Since I hadn't been informed this would happen and was dragged at the last minute into the line by another staff member, I felt ill prepared as I stood with my hands sweating watching others before me first curtsy (women) or bow (men) to the extremely refined woman before shaking her hand and exchanging short pleasantries. The staff had insisted Mark participate in the receiving line too, so we stood together as we awaited the first lady.

As usual, I hoped my hair didn't look too wild and that I didn't have grass stains on my dress. Like others before me, I curtsied and shook her hand, and then Mark bowed and also shook her hand.

She asked us, blessedly in English, "What do you do at this school?"

I squeaked out, "I am an English teacher."

She smiled warmly, nodded, and looked at Mark for a response.

"I teach mathematics at Moringe Sokoine Secondary School," he said.

"Thank you for your work on behalf of Tanzanian children," she intoned before moving to the next teacher.

I let out the breath I'd been holding since she walked up to us and began to feel eminently important because I'd just met the first lady. Now I really had something to brag about.

As we milled around with the hundreds of other people who were waiting for food to be served, several of my Form I students sought me out, dragged me over to a patch of open grass, and pulled me down onto it. Mark discreetly wandered off to find Marv and a cup of coffee, perceptively knowing that I shared something special with this particular group of students and not wanting to intrude.

My students and I sat in a tight ring as they struggled to form questions in English, but mostly, I realized, they just wanted to sit near me for a while, and then to get their pictures taken with me in every possible configuration—individually, groups of two, groups of three, groups of four, then a different group of four, and on and on. I didn't mind, and they found it eminently amusing to shove one another into various groups around me and hand the camera off to one another as they took turns learning to operate it.

Between these photo shoots, several of my Form IV students came over to greet me, to introduce me to their parents, or just to say hello. A few also wanted their pictures taken with me, or with their parents. I felt surprised and encouraged by the fact that a few of them specifically sought me out, suggesting that maybe I had made more progress with them than I'd thought.

I also found a quiet, private delight in watching my Form I students respond to the older girls. Whenever one of the graduates would walk up, the group of squirrelly youngsters would literally straighten up, get very quiet, and feign cool nonchalance. As soon as the Form IV student walked away, it was silly shenanigans, pushing and shoving, laughing at each other, and making jokes—mostly in Maa or Swahili. Several of them tried to communicate with me in English, laughing at their own discomfort with the language and goading me into trying to speak Swahili. And whenever I did, they laughed even harder. Though I wasn't sure why my Swahili was so funny, their giggles were contagious, and soon we were all snickering and grinning at one another.

As I smiled and wiped the corner of my eye, Neng'ida, who'd been the first to gently twirl a lock of my hair around her finger so many months ago, sidled up to me and took my hand in hers as she leaned against me and rested her head against my shoulder. We stood like that for a long time, as if she knew how out of place and uncomfortable I'd been feeling all day and sought to let me know that I wasn't alone—that perhaps I was more a part of them than I understood. Even without common words, Neng'ida found a way to communicate.

Just as the spell was broken and the group scattered, Miriam, another of my Form IV students, walked up to me with two very Maasai-looking people—one a somewhat wrinkled woman in a well-worn shuka, and the other a younger man with a Maasai blanket draped around his shoulders. Miriam slowly guided them in my direction in her quiet, reserved way. They were, I would learn, her mother and brother.

In the classroom, there were a handful of Form IV students who stood out from the group, and Miriam was one of them. Among the first to raise her hand to answer questions, she always sat in the front row. She had a quiet but ambitious demeanor, and she always earned top grades. From time to time, I suspected that she scolded her fellow students. More than once, she'd let out a stream of sharp Swahili words aimed not at me, but at the students sitting behind her. It seemed to me that she regularly told others to get to work, to pay attention, or to generally pull it together. Miriam was a serious student, and she didn't tolerate apathy in others.

As she walked toward me, Miriam said, "Shikamoo, mwalimu. I want to introduce you to my special guests. This is my mother and my older brother."

I responded with the customary Swahili greetings and shook hands with both of them before I said, "Miriam, I think you will have to translate, but tell them that they should be very proud of you because you are one of the top students in the class."

Miriam shyly translated this, and then her mother nodded with a smile. Her brother, however, looked off into the distance as if it pained him to listen. Miriam's mother responded in Maa, and then Miriam again served as translator.

"She says she is thankful that I have good teachers."

I smiled and nodded, saying in English, "Miriam makes teaching easy."

After more smiling and nodding, Miriam directed them toward the dining hall.

As they turned to walk off, she held back a moment, turned back to me, and said, "Mwalimu, I never thought they would come. They have not supported my education, but they have come today. I can't believe they have come. Maybe now I can go home."

I didn't know what to say in response to her unprecedented candor, so I thought about what my mother might do if she were in my shoes. I took Miriam's hand, squeezed it lightly, and gently said, "Congratulations, Miriam. You deserve all the support in the world. You are a very determined young woman with a bright future."

She smiled warmly at me, turned, and bounded off to catch up with her family. In the coming months and years, she would need that determination. With her family, not everything was as supportive as it appeared that day.

CHAPTER 16:

MAMA *MACHUNGWA*

I studied the damp coffee trees in front of the house as the early morning sky slowly lightened. After graduation, it seemed as if the short rains would finally bring some much-needed moisture. Everyone at both schools talked hopefully of crops they'd already planted. Still, so far, we'd only seen a couple mornings of slow drizzle that had turned the pervasive, fine dust that coated everything into a sticky, thick, brownish-red mud. In the last week, I'd rarely left the house without rubber boots on my feet and an umbrella in my hand, even though the land had yet to receive the nourishing soak required for maize and bean crops to sprout.

This early morning—Thanksgiving morning, to be precise—I wrapped a sweater tightly around my shoulders as I shivered in front of my bedroom window. Clouds and mist clung to the Monduli Mountains, making the day feel cold and heavy. Even the roosters were strangely silent today, as if they didn't want to break the vigil I'd been holding most of the night. Soon I'd put the rubber boots on, grab the umbrella, and begin walking toward Mark's house.

Clad in his own rubber boots and rain jacket, Mark had left my house after dark the night before. It had been raining lightly. As usual, we'd eaten dinner around seven, and then he'd helped me wash the dishes before heading home. Even though it was the night before Thanksgiving, we still both had to teach as usual this week, since American holidays didn't matter in Tanzania. Nonetheless, we planned to take the bus to Arusha today to eat a turkey—a rare and much anticipated treat—at Doug and Linda's house. Last night, Mark had left a bit earlier than usual to get a good night's rest in advance of today's busy schedule.

After the requisite thirty minutes I knew it took him to walk between my house and his, I'd tried to reach him on the two-way radios we'd brought from the United States. He hadn't answered, and, even later, he hadn't radioed me before going to bed, as he normally did. After that, I'd stood looking out my bedroom window as if I might be able to see him through the darkness. I pressed the call button over and over, even though I knew that if Mark had switched off his radio, which he often did to save on batteries, then no amount of calling would raise him.

I felt as if I'd swallowed something heavy that sat deep in my stomach. The portion of my brain governed by logic told me Mark had probably arrived home tired and had just forgotten to call me, but that niggling other part, the part prone toward worst-case scenarios, became increasingly unhinged as visions of every possible horror that could have befallen him passed through my mind. In fact, these very visions were all that had kept me from forming my own little search party of one and following him into the darkness.

From the beginning, neither of us thought walking around Monduli after dark a particularly good idea, but it seemed a necessary risk. Dinner had become the one time of day when we reliably touched base with each other. Since Mark's house was ill-equipped for indoor cooking, it didn't take long before a pattern of nightly meals at my house emerged. Since Monduli sat relatively close to the equator, twilight began at six and full darkness descended by seven year-round. Thus, it became a rare night that Mark didn't walk from my house to his after dark.

Monduli after dark didn't exactly feel unsafe, but it didn't feel benign either. If nothing else, the uneven roads and pathways meant the most likely, though certainly not the greatest, dangers came from twisting, tripping, or tumbling. The greatest peril, however, I was certain, came not from going bump in the night, but from encountering living, breathing, and, in some cases, slithering threats.

Tanzania's highly venomous and aggressive black mambas remained at the top of my most feared list, followed closely by spitting cobras, honey badgers, hyenas, wild dogs, bats, and further down the list: thieves, drunks, and other riffraff of the *Homo sapiens* variety. Monduli didn't have lions, leopards, cheetahs, or any other large cats or carnivores, but the wildlife it did have still gave me pause.

One afternoon, while walking back to my house I'd noticed movement in a coffee tree about twenty yards away. As I looked closer, a snake fell from one of the low branches to the ground. I imagined I looked pretty ridiculous—a white lady in a dress sprinting through the coffee fields—but when it came to snakes, terror reigned supreme. I felt pretty confident I couldn't outrun a black mamba—known to chase motorcycles, people, and other animals at speeds up to fifteen miles per hour—but I was damn sure going to give it my best effort, and I certainly wasn't going to wait around to see what kind of snake it actually was.

As if the wildlife wasn't enough to worry about, we were wazungu. We stood out in every way, even in the dark. Neither Mark nor I could walk anywhere, day or night, without people stopping us to say hello, to ask us where we were from and why we were there, or to patiently cobble together whatever other questions and answers their fluent and our broken Swahili allowed. For the most part, this made us feel welcomed into Monduli's community, particularly as people started to recognize us and then greet us by name or by the respectful title "mwalimu" or "teacher." Whether it was true or not, it felt as if all these friendly people would surely look out for us. However, we also knew many Tanzanians saw us and immediately had visions of vast wealth flowing from us to them. No doubt, even in what seemed like the sleepy community of Monduli, as wazungu we could certainly be targets for robbery. Thus, the guards at both schools kept a particularly close watch on our houses, not because we'd asked them to, but because they too knew how the minds of would-be robbers worked.

Though I hadn't fully realized it until the previous night, I obviously lived with an unspoken but persistent fear that something sinister lurked outside after dark. I remained tense each night from the time Mark left until that two-way radio beeped, and he let me know he was safely on the other end. Last night, tension had grown to worry sprinkled with intermittent bouts of panic.

Though my concerns seemed less paralyzing in the light of day, worry still clung to me like the sagging dark clouds outside my window. At least now I felt it was safe enough for me to follow the path I knew Mark had taken in hopes of finding his sleep-filled eyes on the other end, rather than his bloodied and broken body somewhere along the way. However, as I threw on some clothes thinking there wouldn't be time for a bucket bath today if I were to walk up to Mark's house and get back in time to teach, the radio came to life with a series of quick beeps. In a matter of moments, worry turned to anger.

"Julie, are you there?" came Mark's cautious voice.

I considered not answering.

"Are you there?" he repeated.

I picked up the two-way radio and asserted, "So you're not dead."

"I'm really sorry. I totally forgot to call you," he replied sheepishly.

"I didn't sleep much and now I'm really crabby," I fumed.

"Sorry. It won't happen again."

"It better not, or I'll have to kill you myself," I threatened.

He responded with a laugh. "Okay, over and out. I heard that loud and clear."

"I'm not calling you a 'good buddy' right now. I'm still mad at you."

"Okay, over and out, good buddy," he joked.

"I'll see you later," I snapped as I sat down at the desk in my bedroom and put my head in my hands with a sigh. The day had only just begun, and I was already exhausted. For a moment, I pouted before I mustered the energy to fix myself some breakfast and head up to school. It didn't seem like a very happy Thanksgiving just yet, even though I now knew Mark was safe.

Several hours later, after I'd finished teaching for the day, I changed into a relatively clean skirt and blouse. Doing laundry in a bucket meant everything I owned seemed stretched out, slightly dingy, and sun-dried stiff, not to mention that doing laundry by hand while trying to carefully conserve water meant I'd reassessed how often a garment actually needed to be washed. Even though we'd had some rain lately, that hadn't translated into abundant water in my tap. This particular skirt and blouse looked and smelled as clean as my clothes got anymore.

I then washed my face and pulled my hair into a neat pony-tail at the nape of neck. Even though I hadn't bathed in a couple of days—which had become more or less standard for me by then because of both water shortages and the tediousness of heating water, hauling it into the bathroom, and pouring it cupful by cupful over my head—I thought I should at least try to look presentable for Thanksgiving dinner at Doug and Linda's.

I knew they'd invited several other American expatriates, some of whom I knew well, others I didn't. Most of them lived in Arusha, which seemed a world away from Monduli, with its hot water and washing machines, grocery stores and restaurants. I didn't want to look, and smell, as if I'd just walked in from the bush when I sat down at the Thanksgiving table. I frowned at myself in the bathroom mirror and put on some extra deodorant for good measure.

As I trudged toward Moringe to meet Mark, at least an inch of mud was clinging to the bottoms of my shoes. I'd left the rubber boots at home thinking they'd be too bulky for the trip to Arusha, but now I was regretting it.

Mark awaited me on the road just below Moringe. Purple jacaranda blossoms fluttered down around him and filled the air with their fragrant sweet smell. He still looked chagrined after the previous night's debacle and apologized again as we walked the rest of the way to Monduli. I remained relatively quiet. Though I wasn't still mad at him, exhaustion enveloped me. It was only a matter of weeks before we'd be returning to the United States for Christmas and our wedding, but I felt as if the trip couldn't come soon enough. I longed for a time and place that felt blissfully untroubled, and I'd created an idealized version of home that I longed for, particularly on Thanksgiving Day, when I knew my family would be gathered around the table without me.

When we arrived at Monduli's bus stand, I wondered how long we'd have to wait before the bus would depart. They operated not on a schedule, but on the philosophy that the bus could not possibly leave until it was not just full, but overflowing with people who hung out every window and door. As we boarded, a few seats remained open, one near the back and another in the middle, so we sat separately and waited for more people to arrive so we could depart.

Once every seat was full and a line of people was crammed down the middle aisle, the driver climbed in, started the bus, and began honking in long, drawn-out bleats—the signal to everyone that the bus would soon depart. After five minutes of this, another ten people boarded the already-full bus. A thin, elderly Maasai man crammed himself next to me, being of the opinion that he and I were small enough to sit together in a seat meant for one. Fortunately, I was next to the window, so at least I would get some air once we started moving.

As the driver and several other men argued about how to tie a thatched cage of live chickens to the roof, a young Maasai woman boarded the bus with a baby probably about a year old. The woman looked around, and, finding little room to even stand, she handed her child to the nearest person with a few words I couldn't hear. Soon the baby was being passed from one person to the next until he or she, I wasn't sure which, arrived in my empty lap. I wasn't sure why I'd been designated as the person to hold the baby, perhaps because the passengers thought it might be novel for the child to ride with a mzungu, or maybe just because my lap was empty and it looked like there might be a few extra inches of space around me. Nevertheless, I now had a little more responsibility than I'd bargained for.

The baby and I stared wide-eyed at each other. It wasn't clear from the look in his or her eyes whether fear or curiosity prevailed, so I quickly smiled and tried to look friendly. One day in Arusha, I'd overheard a Tanzanian mother telling her little boy, when the child was being naughty, that white people ate children for dinner and she'd hand the boy over for food if he didn't start behaving.

I hoped the child in my lap hadn't heard that tale, and I urgently hoped he or she wouldn't start crying because I didn't know what to do in that case. I glanced back at Mark, whom I could barely see through all the bodies, with a look that said, *So now what?* As I did so, the baby reached out and painfully tugged on one of the dangling earrings Bibi Ruth had given me several weeks earlier.

Once we were underway and I'd removed the earrings from my ears and placed them in my pocket, the child seemed to settle in. He or she actually started laughing and smiling at me when I began a game of peekaboo—a universally amusing game to small children. Amazingly, I'd lost sight of the child's mother and hoped I could find her at the end of the bus ride.

As we bumped our way from Monduli into Arusha, more and more people flagged down the bus and boarded it. Each time

I believed we could not possibly fit another person onto the bus, another one fit. I bounced the child on my knee and surreptitiously glanced at the Maasai man sitting next to me, who seemed completely uninterested in both of us. As he leaned against his traditional walking stick and shifted in his customary red-checkered mashuka, I noticed something strange about his ears. While I knew both Maasai men and women often bore huge holes into their stretched-out lobes, this man's ears appeared to be a mass of scar tissue. I didn't want to stare, but I was curious about what had happened to him.

As I began to run through the possibilities, the man must have intuitively felt self-conscious because he reached up and began pulling on his lobes. As he did so, they straightened into long loops. Like many Maasai, the man's ears had been purposely pierced, plugged, and thereby elongated. It had never occurred to me that if stretched long enough with a wide enough hole, ear lobes might automatically twist up like a barber's pole made of flesh.

By the time we arrived in Arusha, I had the sinking and stinking feeling that my lap was wet. When I lifted the baby to carry him or her, I still didn't know which, off the bus, I discovered the child's backside and my lap were, in fact, damp. At the time, this seemed like a secondary concern to finding the baby's mother, whom I'd lost track of in the overstuffed bus. Truthfully, I wasn't exactly sure what she looked like now that I was standing in the horde of Tanzanians surrounding the bus.

As I stood there waiting for her to find me and for Mark to disembark, I shooed away vendors who wanted to sell me peanuts, chips, bananas, watches, sunglasses, and sundry other items. I held the wet baby somewhat away from my body as I began to worry about where the child's mother might be. When she eventually wandered over, completely unconcerned that a stranger had her baby in a busy bus stand, she warmly thanked me, took the child, wrapped him or her in a kanga, and slung the child onto her back in a hammock-like arrangement.

As I watched the piggybacked baby bounce away, I shook out my skirt in hopes that the walk to Doug and Linda's would dry me out. I sighed deeply as I assessed the damage. Between the mud on my shoes, the urine on my skirt, and the wind-blown tangle of my hair, which I tried to recapture into a new ponytail, I felt certain my appearance and smell harkened more to a homeless street person than to a lovely dinner guest. As the absurdity of the day settled over me, I laughed out loud a little bit like a lunatic in the midst of a tornado. It felt as if I'd lost any semblance of control over my environment and my appearance. Then again, Tanzania had a way of regularly reminding me that control was a necessary but false illusion—case in point, my sleepless night spent pondering worst-case scenarios.

Once Mark emerged from the bus, he took one look at me and began chuckling, as I pointed at him and said tongue in cheek, "Don't laugh at me. This isn't funny."

Our moment of mirth was quickly interrupted as the vendors started afresh with their vigorous sales pitches. Eager to get out of the melee, we walked over uneven, hard-packed dirt, past piles of trash, and around large puddles that contained all manner of human detritus to the edge of what loosely qualified as Arusha's bus terminal—a square city block of open ground where diesel-fume-belching buses from all over East Africa came and went at all hours of the day and night. A determined group of vendors trailed us as we went.

The bus stand qualified as not only one of the dirtiest parts of Arusha, but also one of the places we felt most vulnerable. The crush of travelers, vendors, dala dala, taxis, and buses made it a perfect place for pickpockets and thieves. In a sea of black uniformity, we stood out like vibrant white landmarks attracting peddlers and beggars almost like flies to rubbish.

Small shops fronted the open-air bus stand, and once we reached the nearest row of mismatched, roughly constructed buildings, we paused to regroup. By this time, all but the most intrepid hawkers had given up on us, and even these turned to run back to the bus stand as another large bus pulled in.

As Mark organized his small rucksack on his back, I haphazardly studied the shops surrounding the bus stand and alighted upon an open storefront overflowing with pastel chiffon and organza, white lace and satin, and creamy taffeta and tulle. Though most Maasai weddings involved more beads than brocade, here along the dust-laden edges of Arusha's dirtiest parts sat a wedding-dress shop that specialized not in the virginal, fresh fashion favored by America's brides, but in the second-hand castoffs unearthed from the backs of America's closets.

Along the periphery of the bus terminal and in nearly every weekly market in small villages and large towns throughout Tanzania, the used-clothing market thrived, as evidenced by this small wedding shop. The hand-me-downs that didn't sell at thrift shops in America made their way on huge pallets aboard ships to all parts of Africa, including Tanzania, and this shop seemed to have gobbled up the worst of 1980s wedding fashion. Puffy, gargantuan shoulders and sleeves, as well as huge bows and sashes, made me feel like my hair needed to be permed and backcombed to enormous heights to fit with one of these lovely homages to the decade of *Pretty in Pink* and *The Breakfast Club*.

Mark and I would be making our way to the altar in about six weeks. Since I worried about finding a wedding dress once I returned to the United States a mere month before the wedding, I couldn't resist the chance to browse the options to be found at Arusha's bus terminal. As Mark snapped my picture next to one of the dresses, two street kids—a boy and a girl—wandered up behind him and watched.

I knew they were street kids because I'd already made the acquaintance of the boy, who I thought was probably seven or eight years old. He seemed to hang around the bus stand waiting for white people or wealthy-looking Tanzanians to emerge from buses. Nearly every time I'd arrived in Arusha, he'd sought me out not with the sad extended hand that many of the street kids sported, but with friendly exuberance more salesman than beggar. Each time I'd seen him, he'd been wearing the same thing, a torn white T-shirt and a pair of dirty blue shorts with dingy orange flip-flops—the strap on the right one broken and flapping loose.

The first time we'd met, I hadn't given him anything, and then I'd spent the bus ride back to Monduli going round and round with myself about why I had a fundamental aversion to giving money to beggars. Did I think he would use the money for some untoward purpose? Did I fear if I revealed my wallet he'd run off with it and everything in it? Did I wonder if maybe he was conning me and really had a nice family he returned to each night? Did I think that if I gave him money he'd enlist more and more street kids to hit me up?

In his persistent, outgoing manner, the boy had thrown question after question at me, all in Swahili, until he'd hit upon a few I could answer. Though reticent to engage with beggars, I'd found it difficult to avoid the kid's friendly direct questions, particularly since he enthusiastically danced around me while asking them. His tenacity meant he'd squeezed some information out of me. The boy knew Mark and I were teachers who lived in Monduli.

I assumed only that he lived on Arusha's streets, and, without thinking about it, I avoided learning more, inherently knowing his reality would likely shatter me into pieces I couldn't put back together, something I already felt on the verge of all too often. As someone who idealistically sought to do good in the world, knowing there were places and people beyond my reach, perhaps beyond anyone's reach, was a reality I didn't want to face even if it was regularly forced upon me in this environment.

The second time I'd met the boy, we'd volleyed back and forth, him convincing me that he only needed five hundred shillings and then dropping his price to two hundred, both amounts less than one dollar. I'd been smarter that time, putting a few coins in my pocket before I arrived at the bus terminal, and I'd given him the two hundred shillings we'd agreed on. He'd smiled broadly with the coin in his hand, jumped up and down a couple of times, and dashed off to find his next victim.

Today, he moved more slowly because he held the hand of a girl who looked to be little more than a toddler. Her nose was crusted with dried snot and her cheeks smeared with dirt. She wore what looked more like a small grain sack than a dress, and she watched me with wide brown eyes. He smiled a toothy grin at me, and I noticed he was missing one of his two front teeth.

Just before I'd gotten on the bus in Monduli, I'd stopped at a little shack along the way that sold a hodgepodge of items—laundry soap, dried beans, Coca-Cola in glass bottles, bananas, and oranges. Thinking I'd take a page from the boy I'd met at Morogoro's market many months earlier, I'd filled Mark's rucksack up with half a dozen oranges. Today, I'd come to Arusha prepared for the boy who now stood before me.

As the two children approached, I began digging around in Mark's bag while it was still on his back and emerged with two oranges. I handed one to each of them, crossed my arms, and waited for a response.

"Asante sana, walimu," he said with surprise, and then he began peeling the orange. Once he was finished, he handed it to the small girl, took her unpeeled orange, and then began peeling it.

"Karibu tena," I responded as I watched. You're welcome to ask me again.

And so it was. In the coming months, I never came or went from Arusha without oranges in my bag or in Mark's. Every time I saw this boy or any other street kids, I'd give them an orange, and this is how I came to be known among some of Arusha's street kids as "Mama *Machungwa*," or the mother of oranges.

As I left the bus terminal with Mark, I looked over my shoulder at the two kids. They'd sat down on the step just in front of the wedding shop to eat their oranges. The boy leaned toward the girl while animatedly talking and waving a juicy hand around. The juxtaposition of those kids, without a home, living in the midst of the squalor that surrounded the bus stand, against the creamy white folds of wedding-dress fabric, seemed almost more than I could bear. I had to turn away as I wiped a tear from the corner of my eye.

The very idea of shopping for a wedding dress in one of those grand dress shops with racks and racks of white fluff, glass slippers, garters, and platforms in front of full-length mirrors seemed absurd, as did the range of other decisions we'd been required to make remotely over the course of the last few months. How many flower arrangements did we want at the wedding ceremony? Should we buy or rent the centerpieces for the reception? How many place settings would we like of china? Did we want to put one or two sets of towels on our registry, and did we prefer mint green or sage?

We'd been coordinating all this remotely with my mother during infrequent telephone calls, which we had to make from Arusha accounting for a ten-hour time difference, and through a rudimentary email system whereby we typed up messages in Monduli, brought them into Arusha on a floppy disk, and then uploaded them while downloading any incoming messages at the internet service provider's office. We couldn't actually read any of the messages in Arusha, which meant there was a lag time of at least a week between when we received a message, took it back to Monduli to read it, and returned to Arusha with a response. Surfing the web was more or less out of the question.

My mother, bless her, was doing the best she could to arrange everything in our absence. We'd tried to scale the ceremony and reception down to a simple affair, but even a simple affair seemed more involved and expensive than we'd hoped. In addition, we'd learned that Mark's parents wanted to have a second reception in Minnesota since our wedding would be in Montana, and Dr. Msinjili and Mr. Kwayu were also planning a reception for us in Monduli once we returned from the wedding in January. Though we knew our families and friends loved us and wanted to celebrate our commitment to one another, it all seemed overwhelming and excessive in this context.

I knew we'd be talking to my parents and Mark's later in the day and there would be more questions to answer and decisions to make, and I knew just as surely that I'd be thinking about the two kids with their oranges in front of that wedding shop as I made those decisions and then sat down to Thanksgiving dinner.

As we walked up Ilboru Road, more wide dirt path than road, toward Doug and Linda's house, it seemed impossible to imagine a perfectly roasted, plump turkey existed anywhere in Tanzania, maybe even the world, but as usual, I imagined Doug and Linda had exercised some kind of magic in their kitchen. I tried to stay focused on this as we walked through their overcrowded, somewhat intimidating neighborhood.

The smell of hot coals floated in the air as we passed by two women who sat on small stools and roasted maize for sale to passersby. A group of haughty young men milled around in front of a bar and openly stared as we walked by. The circular saw of a furniture maker whirred, and the flash and pop of blinding light made us look away as a welder worked. Two women sat together in front of a simple one-room house, the elder braiding the younger's hair into tight cornrows.

Nearby two boys chased each other around a small ramshackle house, one shooting a plastic squirt gun at the increasingly irritated other one. As the unarmed boy threw his hands in front of his face and yelled something in Swahili, another stream of water hit him in the chest. He stomped his foot and glared at the culprit before unzipping his pants, pulling out his own personal water gun, and firing a stream of urine at the boy.

Mark and I couldn't help it. We doubled over with laughter. The melancholy bubble that had encircled us since we'd left the bus terminal broke wide open. Today's elixir seemed to be urine. I'd been baptized in it on the bus and redeemed by it on the road to despair.

As I once again considered the various horrors that could have befallen Mark the previous night, I put the earrings that Bibi Ruth had given me back in my ears, peeled one of the remaining oranges, and reminded myself, particularly in this place, there was more to be thankful for than I could even imagine.

CHAPTER 17:

AMERICASTLE

The weekend after a delicious and plentiful Thanksgiving dinner, I stood with my hands on my hips, yellow rubber gloves swamping my small fingers and stretching up beyond my elbows. I hovered over Mark, who had his head and shoulders fully inside an oven just outside of what would soon be our first home as a married couple. In a week's time, we would travel back to the United States to prepare for our upcoming nuptials, which would take place one month later on January 8. Then we would return to this house. Today we'd started moving our belongings from our respective homes to this, our new joint house, up the hill from Moringe. And we'd begun the task of cleaning the place from top to bottom.

"Don't do it, Mark. Don't do it. It isn't that bad," I joked, thinking of poor Sylvia Plath's final moments.

As I giggled to myself, Mark's muffled response came back, "You haven't seen the inside of this thing yet, so you don't know how bad it truly is."

From nearby, Gideon watched us in perplexed silence. We'd met him only the week before, but soon he'd know us in ways we would sometimes prefer he didn't. One of three Maasai guards who would be working around-the-clock just outside our front door, Gideon was the day guard, and thus the one who would see and hear all that happened during daylight hours. Even if he didn't speak a word of English, Gideon could certainly eavesdrop, whether he wanted to or not, through the relatively porous confines of our new home, and this made me patently uncomfortable, as if any shred of privacy we had enjoyed was now being peeled away. Already people noticed our white skin wherever we went. Now, even at home, our strangeness in this place would be observed and catalogued day and night—the current task as a case in point.

However, I had already gathered that Gideon was a patient, kind man—a sort of antithetical disposition for a guard, I thought, but something I found increasingly common among Maasai "warriors." Gideon, like several other Maasai men I'd met, seemed to define himself less by intimidating aggression and more by soft-spoken authority and benevolent bravery. He struck me as the type of man I'd want as my guardian, a sort of big brother of my choosing. Above and beyond safeguarding my belongings and me, Gideon would soon become my most ardent Swahili tutor.

A slight man clad in somewhat Western attire—high-water blue slacks, a 1970s zip-up tan jacket, and an American-style baseball cap—Gideon looked to be in his late thirties. Around his shoulders, he wrapped himself in a traditional red-checkered Maasai shuka, and on his feet he wore typical tire-tread sandals, or raiyo. A large machete hung from a belt at his waist, and he carried a short stick with a substantial knob on one end—a Maasai billy club—known in Swahili as a *rungu*. Though he seemed gentle and spare, both accoutrements left little doubt Gideon could crack skulls, behead snakes, and otherwise handle himself when confronted with aggression.

However, aggression of a human kind wasn't expected in our sleepy village. Here, guards were hired more to deter petty theft than as a necessity against violence. Much like doormen in New York

City, guards in Tanzania seemed to be required for people of actual or perceived wealth. This made them a prerequisite for nearly every wazungu in the country, including us.

In Monduli, we'd been told the reputation of our guards, as respected members of the Maasai community, meant our house wouldn't be bothered. However, in places like Arusha, the threat of armed robbery was all too real. Much to our dismay, we'd learned a few days earlier, over a plump Thanksgiving turkey, that Doug and Linda had very nearly experienced such an attempt at their house when, fortunately, one of their guards had chased off a team of armed robbers. Unfortunately, he'd walked away with a machete gash that required more than a few stitches.

In Tanzania's urban areas, guarding was obviously a serious and sometimes dangerous business, but in Monduli, it was just boring, which meant Gideon was already looking for things to do with his time beyond watching the days go by in front of our house.

So, with Gideon's eager help, the three of us had wedged a full-sized range out the front door and into what could loosely be described as the yard of a house that even at this early stage of our preoccupation presented many paradoxes. To Mark, it seemed a step up from where he'd been living because it actually had an oven, as well as an indoor toilet that flushed properly.

To Gideon, it must have represented something extraordinary and unattainable since he lived in the traditional Maasai way, far from town in an engang without running water or electricity. When I met Gideon, I learned he would walk about four miles each way to get to and from our house on a daily basis. When I asked him if this was too far, he emphatically told me it wasn't, as if he feared losing his new job, and so on the first day of his employment, we gave him the broken bike that rested outside our back door and told him we'd pay to have it fixed. Even though Monduli's rough roads meant Gideon would have to push the bike as much as he rode it, he thanked us as if we'd given him the moon.

To me, the house was older than my current place of residence and more cluttered with the random detritus of volunteers past—old flashlights that didn't work, dead batteries that had no place to go, half-used medications, and more than a dozen partially full bottles of bug repellent, sunscreen, and assorted other liquids. However, the simply constructed, cinderblock home had its charms. First and foremost, it was the place Mark and I would live together starting in January. No more walkie-talkie communication and late-night walks between houses.

Beyond that, the house held the promise of hot showers. One of Mark's first orders of business had been to install a "steamy," or an alarmingly counterintuitive shower head that when plugged in instantaneously heated passing water, even if it left one wondering about the wisdom of standing under a device that purposely mixed water and electricity. After nearly a year of bucket baths, I found myself saying with conviction, "It can't be that dangerous if they sell it to people," as Mark raised his eyebrows at me and screwed it into place. The caveat to the whole delicate equation, however, was that power and somewhat significant water pressure were required for the device to actually produce hot water, something I felt confident might just be possible if all the stars properly aligned.

In one half of the home, the living room ceiling vaulted upward to create a large, airy space. The adjacent quaint yet well-appointed kitchen had shiny wooden countertops with a large pantry. Three bedrooms, the smallest of which became our office, and the bathroom resided down a hallway off the living room. Since we would now have a room for guests, both Mark's parents and mine were already planning visits to this, our first home, during our first year of marriage.

Even beyond the house's ability to meet our very basic needs, it maintained a commanding position above Monduli on the initial rise of the mountains. From its louvered living room window, we could see the Moringe campus and several homes of Moringe's teachers directly below us, and beyond that, hundreds of miles of acacia scrublands and open grasslands stretched as far as the eye could see.

David Simonson, the same man responsible for building the Maasai Secondary School for Girls, had built the home some five years earlier as a place for American volunteer teachers to live. Since that time, it had housed volunteers for both Moringe and the girls' school. Due to its size, location, and wazungu occupants, locals had coined the place "Americastle." However, among its residents, the citadel above Monduli had gained a less-than-ostentatious reputation for rodents of the flying and scampering variety—a decidedly negative mark for the house in my book and one that gave me pause even if I might get a hot shower once in a while.

By air, previous occupants had been assaulted by bats, while rats launched a ground incursion. We'd been told the bat problem had been solved, even though—we would soon learn—guano still floated down from the rafters. The rats, however, seemed entrenched. I'd chosen to meet this challenge with a show of force, which explained why the oven was in the yard.

A full-sized gas range was extremely unusual in Tanzania; even the rats thought so. A few of them had deemed it a palatial choice for a nest, while others had carried off its bright yellow insulation as construction material for lairs elsewhere around our house. I imagined the range had probably arrived via a large shipping container from the United States, a donation from some charitable American donor who'd remodeled her kitchen and thought her lovely old range might find a second life in Africa. If only she could see it now.

The oven door lay unhinged against the side of the house in a stone-lined, disorderly tangle of flowers, vines, and tropical plants that edged the front door. Four burners were stacked on the metal stovetop, which lay in the grass nearby. Mark unscrewed metal pieces off the back of the range in order to locate the nexus of the rats' nest and remove the remaining insulation, as I sloshed soapy bleach water over every surface I could see and earnestly hoped no rats, dead or alive, would come running out over my toes.

Having left us to our own harebrained wazungu devices, Gideon nevertheless kept a watchful eye on us as he whacked at the weeds and grass in our yard with a long machete-like tool—the Tanzanian version of mowing the lawn. From under the brim of his cap, amused eyes peered at us. Gideon paused from time to time to contemplate our work, grinning discreetly to himself as if he were watching a Charlie Chaplin movie. When I caught his eye, I huffed, "*Panya si wazuri.*" Rats are no good—an understatement given our current predicament. Gideon nodded curtly, smiled, and turned his head to the side as he let out a buoyant chuckle.

As I worked, my face felt stretched and taut, mostly because my hair was pulled up so tightly on top of my skull that my head ached. Nevertheless, loose pieces of flyaway hair hung in my flushed face, but rather than touch them with my filthy rubber-gloved hands, I blew at them, only to have them return to tickle my nose or hang in my eyes moments later. Since the neighbors, and Gideon, were certainly watching, I'd covered my threadbare baggy khaki pants and a ratty old gray T-shirt with a long kanga that I'd wrapped high around my waist. Even with my meager attempt at culturally appropriate attire, I knew I was an absolute vision, but I didn't care. This, I thought with a sense of irony, wasn't exactly what most brides did in the weeks before their weddings. Like most brides, I felt eager to see my family and friends and over the moon about marrying the man I loved. I worried, though, about what to say about my experiences in Tanzania. I struggled to understand what this all meant to me, so it felt hopeless to try to articulate anything meaningful about this experience to someone else.

It took most of the day, but the end result seemed workable. After stripping the range to its bones, thoroughly cleaning it, stuffing it with new insulation, and then reassembling it, we bolted chicken wire over the entire undercarriage and rear of the range to, as Mark said, "keep the little buggers out." Just for good measure, we ran the burners and the oven at full force for a good two hours after we wedged the range back through the front door and into its place in the kitchen. Little did we know we'd only fought the first battle in what would be an ongoing war, but at least we'd eat well as we tussled with the enemy because the rats never retook the oven, even if they overran the castle.

CHAPTER 18:

KARIBU TENA

As I walked onto campus with Mark, I heard a surge of bubbling chatter and a few excited squeals coming from the Form II classroom. I smiled to myself. We'd been spotted. As I listened to the students giggle and jabber, presumably about seeing Mark and me—the newlyweds—together, I realized that I expected to return to an easier, more familiar Tanzania, and in many ways, I had. These girls, who'd moved from Form I to Form II in the New Year, represented one of the most joyful parts of returning. I couldn't wait to see them.

However, before I turned toward the buzzing group of girls who had now gathered just outside their classroom, I pointed Mark toward the building where he would be teaching mathematics, much as Susan had done months earlier when I'd first arrived. With little else to offer when it came to math, I gave him a pat on the shoulder and a "good luck."

Upon our return as a married couple, the headmistress had deemed Mark as trustworthy enough to teach at the girls' school—one of the few males allowed to do so. In exchange for Mark's handful of hours at "my" school, I would teach Form II English at "his" school in addition to my classes here, which included a brand-new group of Form I students, my eagerly waiting Form II students, and a special class for several of the recent Form IV graduates. About one-third of the recent graduates were on campus awaiting their national exam results because they could not safely return home without risking forced marriages during the time they waited to begin Form V, which would start in six months for those who qualified.

Those who didn't qualify were another, yet-to-be-discussed, matter that already weighed heavily on me. I'd watched them graduate and then take the national exam under the watchful eyes of heavily armed guards—something that had, at first, shocked and scared me and then angered me. The students' anxiety about how the national exam would shape their futures was already palpable enough without the presence of military-grade assault rifles. Apparently, Tanzanians took cheating on the national exam seriously.

Even while busily going about the business of getting married, I'd thought about what would happen to the girls who would inevitably fail the exam. Statistics told me that less than one-third of Tanzanian Form IV students passed the national exam with high enough marks to continue to Form V. I wondered how my former Form IV students—that proud, top-of-the-heap bunch—would feel about going back to a traditional Maasai life after four years of secondary school. Would they be able to reconcile their education, and what they'd come to hope for as a result of that education, with the realities of forced marriages, polygamy, and the unrelenting hard labor required of most Maasai women? In light of this, I didn't know what I could possibly offer them that would be of value in my special six-month waiting-for-the-results class, and based on experience, I had a hunch they might feel the same way.

However, today was my first day back, after an almost six-week break, and all seemed golden and bright as I walked toward my

Form II students. Several ran out to take my small book bag and, more importantly, to greet me with all kinds of questions.

"Oh, mwalimu, karibu tena. Welcome back. How was America?"

"I missed you so much. When did you get back?"

"How is Dr. Mark?"

"Where are you living now?"

"Was your wedding nice? I bet it was so nice."

"We're so glad you came back. Please, tell us all about the wedding. What did you wear?"

Wound up and giddy, they danced around me, jostling for the positions closest to me and beaming with the glow of unconditional affection. I spread my arms wide and herded them toward the classroom door. "Let's go inside, and I'll tell you all about it," I said with a warm smile.

When we got inside, they quickly reverted back to the expected classroom behavior—hushed, each in their appointed places, standing, and in unison chanting, "Good morning, teacher."

"Good morning!" I bellowed with purposely overdone enthusiasm.

A few of them giggled at this. Others looked away in shy embarrassment. I knew I was more unpredictable and less proper than most of their Tanzanian teachers. I guessed that I remained a mystery to most of them because I often responded in ways they didn't expect and because I didn't quite know the appropriate protocols, but this no longer bothered me the way it once had, even if it did exasperate Gladness, the class monitor, from time to time.

"I'm so glad to be back," I continued in a more subdued and sincere tone. "I think we should first discuss our holidays before we get to the lessons. What do you think?"

With a genuine cheer and several exuberant nods, we agreed it would be difficult to get much done until we spent some time properly greeting one another in true Tanzanian fashion. Rather than stand behind the table at the front of the classroom as I normally did, I walked around to the front and hoisted myself up to sit on it. At this, several students in the back of the classroom moved to the front, forcing students on the benches in the front two rows to squeeze together. Much like a wave that starts small and gains strength, soon they were all in the front squeezed together, sitting on one another's laps, and otherwise piled on top of one another.

As they jostled about trying to get comfortable, Elisipha raised her hand with intent. "Mwalimu," she exclaimed, "what is the difference between 'scoot your butt' and 'squeeze your butt'?"

I felt my face flush as I thought about how I was going to answer this one. With Elisipha, it was as likely as not that she'd asked the question in a mischievous attempt to draw laughs, but this time, her earnest face told me she had no idea about the meaning of an idiomatic expression she'd probably heard from one of the older students. Even though a couple of the girls put their heads down with embarrassed snickers and Gladness let out an indignant huff, Elisipha and most of the rest of the class stared at me unwaveringly waiting for an answer.

I walked up to Elisipha, who was sitting on the end of a bench, and bumped her with my hip as I sat down next to her on the wooden plank. "That is a 'scoot,'" I said. Then I gently squeezed her upper arm. "That, my dear," I revealed with a meaningful look, "is a 'squeeze.'"

I watched as my explanation registered with her and others in the classroom—first looks of puzzlement, then horror, followed by uncontrollable laughter. I couldn't help myself. I too laughed so hard that tears flowed freely down my face. It took a full five minutes before we all regained ourselves enough to continue our question-and-answer session.

Following our laughing spree, I asked several of the students to tell me what they had done over the break. They took turns eagerly waving their hands in the air to be called on, standing up, and saying one or two sentences about traveling home, seeing their families, hauling water, tending animals, or eating good home-cooked food. After ten minutes of this, it seemed they could stand it no longer.

"Mwalimu, stop, please, you must now let us ask the questions," chided Dinah with a broad smile.

"Okay, okay . . . go ahead," I replied.

They asked about the wedding ceremony, the music, my dress—a simple floor-length cream-colored sheath with a beaded bodice, something they seemed to understand and approve of— Mark's attire, the party, the food, and my family. Though it wasn't always easy for them to formulate the questions, I found it remarkable how much their English had improved, even though most of them had spent several weeks away from school during the holidays. Even Neng'ida, who'd been so far behind the others, stood and haltingly asked a question, "Mwalimu, pictures . . . can you show to me? I want . . . to look . . . your dress?"

I promised to bring some photos to show them in the coming days, and then, satisfied they'd extracted enough information from me, they all clapped in excitement and slowly started to reorganize themselves into proper rows, to shuffle papers and books around, and to get out pens and notebooks as they continued to chatter, now mostly in Swahili, about what they'd heard from me.

As they did this, I reflected on all I hadn't told them—things I hadn't told anyone, in part, because I hadn't yet been able to assemble the feelings and experiences into words that made sense. I didn't yet know how to talk about the fact that I'd felt disjointed and unsettled for most of my time in the United States, as if I'd walked from one world into another, where I seemed to fit in better, but where, inexplicably, nothing made sense anymore. That, in response to a pre-Christmas trip to a shopping mall, I'd found myself urgently slipping out of a busy shop to find a bench where I sat, lightheaded, gasping for breath, my heart racing, unable to cope with the crush of people, the garlands and the lights, the tinny pervasive Christmas tunes, and the smell of burnt sugar. That later, I'd felt resentful and angry at the blissful ignorance of all those shoppers—even as I'd recognized myself in them—spending all that money on unnecessary tchotchke while kids in Arusha lived on the street.

I also didn't tell them about the day I found myself standing under stark florescent lights amid aisles of neatly categorized, priced, and arranged food—a typical American supermarket. Chunky, smooth, light, extra chunky, Skippy, Jiffy, Peter Pan, 25-percent-less fat, super-sized—there were probably thirty options from which to choose. But I couldn't choose. Instead, I stood there staring, motionless, unable to contain my tears, overwhelmed by peanut butter.

All this happened even before the wedding, which was beautiful and full of all the people who loved us, but even in this, I felt as if I'd floated through the event as two separate people—one who was smiling and radiant as she gamely participated in wedding showers, greeted friends and family, and opened gifts, and another who was confused and agitated as she watched events unfold from a distance, caught up in the swift moving current of a culture—hers but no longer hers.

My only anchor in the turbulence was Mark, but even he had seemed inaccessible—first physically, when he spent more than a week in Minnesota with his family while I went to Montana to celebrate Christmas with mine and make final wedding arrangements, and later emotionally, when neither of us could find the time nor space to do more than discuss whether we should serve hors d'oeuvres before the groom's dinner, what time the cake should be delivered, and how long the quartet should play during the reception.

After the wedding, we'd spent less than forty-eight hours together in a small cabin, mostly sleeping, before we packed up, said our goodbyes, and boarded a plane for Tanzania. When we'd arrived at Americastle some thirty hours later, we'd done little more than fall into bed with exhaustion and the shared belief that together we'd walked through some kind of hole in the space-time continuum.

Fortunately, we'd had a few days to collect ourselves before we'd been expected to appear at either school, and today I was starting to feel more normal, or at least as normal as I could feel in this culture, which was not mine, but somehow was becoming mine, or at least becoming one for which I had a deep and abiding appreciation.

After teaching Form II, I wandered with Mark toward Moringe for morning chai, which was an important daily event there—a time when the entire staff gathered to socialize, discuss important school business, and drink tea. Much like my Form II students, Moringe's staff became atwitter with exclamations, questions, and congratulations when Mark and I walked in.

We beamed and shook hands and made the rounds until the group was called to order by Dr. Msinjili, who started the meeting by welcoming back "the married couple," which provoked clapping and ululation from the group. When the noise died down, he reminded everyone about the wedding reception planned for later that afternoon after classes had finished for the day. I had no idea what to expect, but I felt decidedly uncomfortable at the idea of being the focus of attention for not only the entire Moringe staff, but also for the girls' school staff, as it was a joint party to be held in Moringe's newly constructed school library.

Before the party, though, I taught my first class at Moringe, which was a discernibly different experience from teaching at the girls' school. While there were parallels—all the students wore uniforms, sat in rows, and stood when I walked in, chanting, "Good afternoon, teacher,"—the similarities ended there.

Moringe was a coed school, which meant I now taught boys as well as girls, though even on the first day, it felt more like I taught boys with a few female observers. The boys outnumbered the girls three to one, and even beyond that, the boys were generally eager, aggressive learners, while the girls remained passive and timid. When I asked questions, the girls never raised their hands, only the boys. Even when I specifically called on the girls, they spoke so quietly I could barely hear them, even after I facetiously wandered to the farthest corner of the classroom and made one of them speak loudly enough that I could clearly hear her.

Unlike the Maasai Secondary School for Girls, which got its funding predominantly from American donors, Moringe relied on local Tanzanian parents to pay school fees, which meant they had to maintain a much larger, more diverse school population in order to cover the school's operating costs. It also meant that there were fewer girls—and even fewer Maasai girls—because parents with limited resources were more likely to send their sons to school rather than their daughters, if they had to choose. The larger school population also meant that I had about twice as many students packed inside an older and much smaller classroom with fewer desks, chairs, and books than at the girls' school. In fact, some of Moringe's girls precariously perched themselves together on one chair because there weren't enough to go around.

Nonetheless, most of my students at Moringe seemed eager to learn. They carefully listened, took notes, and seemed quick to demonstrate their knowledge, which meant I found myself caught entirely by surprise when one of the boys sitting in the very back of the classroom defiantly refused to answer a question when asked and then proceeded to get up and walk out of the room without explanation. Unsure if the boy's behavior was typical and unclear about what had caused the behavior—lack of confidence, frustration with me, teenage defiance, difficulty understanding English, or perhaps that he simply felt unwell, something that often happened to Tanzanian students—I sought out Mr. Kwayu, the school's second master, after class to discuss what had happened.

When I explained the situation, Mr. Kwayu responded apologetically, "Don't worry, Mwalimu Julie. Don't you worry. I will get to the bottom of it and let you know. Some of our students are not disciplined enough. We have to teach them this too. Pole sana. I'm very sorry for this. Please, forgive us. Pole sana."

I tried to convey nonchalance about the whole incident, which was, in fact, minor compared to some of the experiences I'd had in an American public high school during my student teaching. Mostly, I wanted to understand what had happened—if I'd unknowingly made a cultural misstep that had provoked his response. Mr. Kwayu wouldn't let me accept any blame, but rather shushed me and sent me on my way with a conciliatory pat on the shoulder.

Later that day, I found myself still thinking about the boy even as I sat next to Mark at a long, linen-covered table facing several neat rows of metal chairs filled with teachers from both schools, nearly all of whom were staring at us while whispering quietly to one another. Much as I'd observed at the Form IV graduation reception, our wedding reception had a head table, where, in Mr. Kwayu's words, the "big potatoes" sat—in this case, it wasn't the first lady or the bishop, but merely Mark and me—the groom and his bride—as well as Doug and Linda on one side of us and Jean and Marv on the other.

The older couples had been deemed our adoptive parents for the event, and admittedly they both frequently took on this role. In our first year in Tanzania, I'd lost count of the number of times I'd ended up down at Jean and Marv's house looking for a good cup of coffee and guidance on one issue or another, and the same was true of Doug and Linda. Mark and I had spent numerous weekends at their house in Arusha eating their food, playing *You Don't Know Jack*, watching *Die Hard* for the umpteenth time, and generally trying to feel connected to something familiar and easy for a few hours.

The wedding reception, like every formal event I'd attended in Tanzania, had a *ratiba*, or a timetable of events, that had been carefully typed up and included introductions by Mr. Kwayu, a speech by Dr. Msinjili, another speech by Mama Mkuu, an open mic for sharing, presentation of gifts, a prayer by Chaplain Jean, and cutting the *keki*, which in Tanzania did not mean flower-bedecked frosted sweetness, but rather meant a roasted goat, which I felt decidedly less excited about eating. Fortunately, while Mark sat on one side of me, Marv sat on the other, so I'd already devised a plan to inconspicuously offload some of my goat meat to Marv, who I firmly believed would eat it without hesitation. As the honored guest, I knew Mark and I would get the biggest plates in the room, well more than I could eat.

Having become somewhat accustomed to only semi-understanding things that in my own culture were perfectly clear, such as how a bride and groom should behave at an event such as this, I felt surprisingly calm, even if my palms were sweaty.

At wedding-related events in the United States, I'd suffered from a foggy sense of dissociation, where one part of me felt grounded in a profound sense of appreciation for the many people who wanted to share in Mark's and my union, while the other part of me wanted to behave much like the shy, nocturnal bat-eared foxes around Monduli, who dashed off whenever their enormous ears picked up the rumblings of people in order to happily sleep in the solitude of their dens. This event felt no different.

As I listened to heartfelt speeches and humbly accepted thoughtful gifts, I realized that no matter where the celebrations occurred, many people had gone out of their way to express their care and their love for us, this community included. Though I still felt culturally awkward, linguistically challenged, and socially clumsy, I realized this community had come to embrace Mark and me, and we them, in a relatively short period of time, seemingly without my noticing. Even though I often still felt myself to be an outsider, I realized many people had gathered here today to make me feel otherwise, and, for the first time, I did. I felt as if I belonged.

Even Mama Mkuu sought me out during a quiet moment at the reception to tell me in her halting, reserved way that she understood we'd had a bumpy start—alluding to our "welcome" at the diocese office—but that she felt "we'd come to understand one another." As she said this, she grabbed my hand and squeezed it, looking me right in the eyes as if she truly did understand me—my insecurities, my struggles, and all. In truth, she probably did understand me more than many people in the room. Like me, she'd lived in a culture not her own, having spent several years studying in America. She obviously wanted the best for all the students at the Maasai Secondary School for Girls, even though I guessed she sometimes felt inadequately prepared for the challenges she faced. In this, we definitely understood one another.

After our generous welcome back, I felt buoyed by returning to what felt like an easier, more familiar Tanzania; however, I would soon realize not all is as it at first appears. During the next morning's chai, Mr. Kwayu pulled me aside and quietly whispered to me, "Don't you worry, mwalimu. We have dealt with this boy, and he won't give you trouble anymore."

At the time, I didn't know exactly what this meant, but I would later piece together that, not yet knowing all my students' names, I'd identified the wrong student to Mr. Kwayu. A different boy named Clarence, who'd had nothing to do with the incident in class, had subsequently endured several swift licks from a switch during the daily school-wide *baraza*, or morning call-to-order, where all the students gathered around the flag pole to sing the national anthem, share announcements, and witness discipline meted out.

Though I'd known corporal punishment to be common in Tanzania and I'd known many of the teachers at both schools carried sticks or rulers into the classroom, I'd never thought I'd be responsible for a public lashing, let alone the lashing of the wrong student. I spent days feeling mortified and remorseful, and I even tried to apologize to Clarence, though his English was so poor, I'm not sure he fully understood me.

The boy who had actually walked out of my class never made another misstep. He'd gotten the message even if he didn't bear the licks—though I didn't carry a stick, my classroom operated under the protection of the headmaster, the second master, and the discipline master. I never had another problem in class, at least none that I ever spoke to anyone about.

CHAPTER 19:

HONEYMOONING AT LAKE MANYARA

E lephant legs, thick as ancient tree trunks, rapidly closed in on the Land Rover where Doug, Linda, Mark, and I sat half frozen. It seemed these usually ambling beasts could move a whole lot faster than expected, particularly when angry. Holding my breath, I watched as the distance between a set of strong, gleaming-white tusks and our vehicle became uncomfortably short—less than thirty feet, which in elephant-sized terms represented little more than the length of one large male from trunk to tail.

Granted, the creature's aggression hadn't been entirely unprovoked, but none of us had expected full-on road rage from the wrinkled gray giant. We'd been slowly plodding along behind the lone male for more than ten minutes, his weighty girth charmingly swaying from side to side, when he'd stopped, decidedly unconcerned about blocking our way, and lazily lifted his trunk into a leafy branch that overhung the gravel road. In mock annoyance, Doug had sighed loudly, lifted his hands off the steering wheel in a gesture of exasperation, and grumbled, "African traffic jams can be so annoying." Then he'd revved the engine.

Startled by the sudden roar of our diesel beast, the elephant had spun around, eyed us warily, and started flapping his ears. "That got his attention," Doug said with a grin as he revved the engine again. The elephant shifted his weight forward, lowered his head, and snorted, ears still flapping, now more rapidly.

"Doug, I'm not sure challenging an elephant to a duel is a good idea," I squeaked from the back seat, while Linda grabbed the dashboard and looked sideways at Doug, who was now staring intently at the animal as if deciding whether to accept the challenge that was obviously passing between them. Doug paused, poised for action, and then he revved the engine for a third time.

At this, the animal pinned his ears back, let out an indignant blare, and then charged us, all while Doug spun the vehicle around with a skid and hit the gas. Off we roared, an angry elephant hot on our tail.

I gripped the back of the driver's seat in front of me and squealed with a mixture of alarm and delight as I looked from the road in front of us to the elephant behind the vehicle. I imagined the headline: *Newlyweds die in freak elephant encounter.*

"Doug, go faster. Faster!" I yipped between nervous giggles as the elephant gained on us.

Next to me, Mark blanched as he quickly rolled up his window, while Linda, still holding tight to the dashboard, looked at Doug and dryly said, "Well, that wasn't the smartest thing you've done this week."

At this, Doug rapidly shifted from third to fourth and began laughing maniacally as we quite literally left the elephant in the dust. "Check your trousers, ladies and gentleman. Anybody need a bathroom after that?" Doug chortled.

After our wedding reception in Monduli, Doug and Linda had offered to take us on a "pseudo-honeymoon," as Linda called it. "What could be more fun than honeymooning with your quasi-parents?" she'd asked. A couple of weeks later, we'd all headed to Lake Manyara National Park for the weekend. After the elephant encounter, I just hoped we would all survive the honeymoon.

Before our close encounter of the pachyderm kind, we'd spent the day cruising the lake's salt-flat perimeter looking for its famous fuchsia-colored flamingos, as well as driving the park's lush forests in search of a glimpse of its more elusive tree-climbing lions. Along the way, we'd seen hundreds and hundreds of other birds and animals, so many that I'd found myself saying things like, "Wait . . . stop," as Doug slowed the Land Rover and I put the binoculars to my eyes. Then, "Never mind, it's just another giraffe," as if one could tire of watching a wild giraffe's rhythmic long-legged strides across a dusty, golden plain. In truth, I found I could sit for hours and watch the landscape unfold before me. Lovebirds atwitter. Warthogs trotting along, tails upright as flag poles. Baboons carefully parting each other's fur in search of fat ticks. Hippos napping in the sun.

Though far from home, I found a certain kinship with Tanzania's terrain and the wildlife it revealed. It reminded me of my childhood in Montana, where the Great Plains housed bison instead of buffalo, and I searched out antelope instead of impala. Where grizzly bears and mountain lions reminded me that I was not, in fact, all powerful and invincible, as lions and leopards did here.

As we left the park to visit what we'd heard from other expatriates was the best T-shirt shack on the safari circuit, we cranked up Aretha Franklin and rolled down the windows. Doug and Linda bobbed and swayed along in the front seat, and I smiled at Mark, who sat next to me in the back, tapping his foot to the music. For the first time in months, I felt carefree and relaxed.

Perhaps this should have served as a warning, but it wasn't until Doug slowed the vehicle that I noticed a bike lying in the road askew, the back wheel bent and broken. What I saw next would forever mar this short "pseudo-honeymoon"—our breezy, wistful adventure giving way to an image that would indelibly sear itself into our memories of Lake Manyara.

Beside the bike lay the unmistakable form of a fallen child, his skinny, bare legs situated as if still reaching for the pedals, though his small body remained still. The bike had been much too big for his size—he was only a boy, probably not even ten years old, and yet already riding a man's bike. His arms had come to rest above his head outstretched on the ground. As we pulled up and stopped, a cloud of dust floated past the Land Rover and settled over his lean, little body. His head was bent at an unnatural angle, so his ashy face, eyes closed and mouth open, confronted us. A trickle of blood flowed from his nose.

From my seat inside the Land Rover, I remember something like a gasp and then a muted wail emerging from deep within me, as if unbidden from my very soul. Nobody had to tell me. I already knew this boy was dead, or on the verge of death.

"My God," whispered Doug—a plea rather than a curse—as we all sat staring. I heard Linda begin to quietly cry and watched as Doug leaned his forehead against the steering wheel and put his hands on top of his head. Abruptly, he sat back up and slammed his palms against the steering wheel.

"Damn those safari drivers. They go too damned fast through here," he said, clenching his jaw, quietly seething.

Though I'd heard grisly tales about buses colliding head-on as they roared between points near and far on Tanzania's sketchy roadways, pedestrian fatalities weren't something I'd considered, though now this seemed logical—the result of vehicles traveling at speeds far too fast over poor roads used as often by pedestrians, donkeys, and bikes as by cars.

We, and this boy, had been traversing a particularly bad stretch of dirt road that ran between Lake Manyara National Park and the Ngorongoro Conservation Area. At the time, it was the only passable land route between Arusha, where tourists arrived, and the Serengeti, where most tourists were going, often via Lake Manyara and the Ngorongoro Crater. Not all, but many safari drivers drove this route as if it were an interstate highway rather than a dusty, one-lane gravel road, ever in a hurry to get impatient tourists to the next interesting site. Now the cost seemed self-evident.

"Where in the world did he come from?" choked Mark as we all looked around for a nearby boma or building, or for any indication of other people. There was nothing but an occasional scrubby acacia tree and dust for as far as we could see.

"And where was he going?" asked Doug.

From the boy's attire, we couldn't tell much about him. He wasn't wearing traditional Maasai clothing, but that didn't necessarily mean he wasn't Maasai. Instead, he wore a brown T-shirt that had twisted up around his chest to expose his delicately still midriff, and a pair of blue shorts that revealed blood-smeared legs scraped raw in places. Had he been wearing a white button-down shirt, we would have assumed he'd been coming home from school because white shirts and blue shorts were the uniform of choice for schoolboys, but the T-shirt, as well as two large, empty plastic jugs that now lay sideways beside his broken bike, suggested he might have been looking for water even though we saw no shimmering indicator of water on the horizon, or herds of cattle moving toward a common destination.

A series of thoughts hurdled through my mind. One was to call for help. But even on this well-traveled road, our phones would not work. We lived in a Tanzania where mobile phones had just arrived. Ours only worked in Arusha, and even then, service wasn't always guaranteed. Out here, we'd be lucky to find a signal. And even if we got a signal, there was no ambulance to call. No helicopter would show up and airlift this boy to safety. Emergency medical services seemed like some kind of futuristic, science-fiction fantasy in this part of the world. In short, we had no idea who we would call even if we could.

As Mark took my suddenly cold hand, I began going through the assessment protocols I'd learned during my EMT training—evaluate responsiveness, initiate spinal immobilization, assess airway and breathing, check pulse, stop bleeding—even as I realized we were miles from the nearest passable hospital. If this child was alive, which I thought doubtful, the only place he might receive the care he would obviously need would be back in Arusha—a three- to four-hour drive over rough roads from our location. Furthermore, we had no medical supplies with us—no rubber gloves, no bandages, and nothing to effectively immobilize his neck and spine. I pondered the risks of HIV and hepatitis. I knew the statistics—about one in twenty-five Tanzanians were HIV positive.[1]

"Should we get out?" I asked, my voice quivering. Doug began rapidly drumming his fingers on the steering wheel as he swiveled his head, looking to see if anyone was coming.

In the front seat, a different kind of assessment was taking place. In whispers and gasps, Doug and Linda were undertaking the heart-wrenching work of assessing the personal risk of stopping. They knew if another vehicle came upon us, its passengers might assume we'd hit this boy even though we'd found him this way.

We had all heard that tangling with Tanzania's justice system should be zealously avoided. If the police came to the scene, would we be detained as suspects? As the driver, could Doug face jail time? This was an unpleasant thought in any country, but particularly in a developing country, where white skin and foreign citizenship put us squarely in the minority, albeit a privileged, wealthy minority. For this reason, would the embassy need to be involved? Would bribes need to be paid? Could the boy's family hold us liable?

As I listened to this assessment, I started looking around the vehicle with more urgency. I began to recall the stories of mob justice I'd heard—a thief in Dar es Salaam captured by a mob and burned alive with gasoline, a man nearly beaten to death for causing a car crash near Arusha's main market. My imagination started to conjure up dramatic possibilities if a group of Tanzanians came upon us—a sole vehicle of wazungu casting a long shadow over a Tanzanian boy's broken and bleeding body.

"No," Doug said flatly. "We can't get out."

Linda continued, "There's nothing we can do. We have to keep driving."

We'd been stopped for little more than a minute when we slowly backed up, turned around, and headed back the way we'd come, the T-shirt shack a long-lost thought. Aretha Franklin silenced.

For several minutes, no one said anything. Hot tears began to roll down my cheeks as I squeezed Mark's hand and silently wondered who would find the boy and what they would do. I wondered how many more cars would pass him by, as we had, spectators adding another layer of sandy grit to his body. I thought about the parable of the Good Samaritan, as bile rose in my throat. Beyond this moment, I no longer lived in the realm of tidy morals and self-righteous intentions. I was no hero, no savior.

Ashes to ashes, dust to dust, and so the honeymoon ended.

CHAPTER 20:

DINAH'S EDUCATION

The trip to Lake Manyara now more than a month behind us, I found I didn't think of the boy every morning, though from time to time, he still haunted the ethereal predawn hours between sleeping and waking. I suspected that years from now this boy would still come to me in my dreams, and, in fact, he did. For me, atonement would not come easily.

This day, however, his memory stayed at bay, and it started as I'd come to expect most days to begin, with the hope that there would be enough water for a shower before I trekked down to one or the other of the schools. Unfortunately, the water came out in a trickle before coming to a complete halt, so I found myself unshowered but dressed nonetheless.

After that, I stood just outside the front door quietly drinking a cup of coffee and contemplating the concrete water tank on the hill just above Americastle. How long before more water flowed down the Monduli Mountains and entered the tank? How long could we go without water? And what would we do if the drought persisted?

The short rains, typical of November and December, had started with promise but then fizzled. Now, in March, it seemed to me that I, and the very earth I stood upon, called out for the long rains to begin. On the road into Monduli town, at daily chai, and even in the classrooms, everyone talked about the crops that had failed in January and the dry conditions now, even as we cautiously encouraged one another that the long rains would begin any day. The fields were full of that hope—for seeds had again been planted in advance of March, April, and May long rains. Now, as March began, we all waited for water.

As I stood there, Gideon, the day guard at Americastle, came over to stand next to me, as he did most mornings. I handed him a thermos of chai as we went through the daily litany.

"*Habari za Mama Tumaini na mtoto?*" I asked. How are Mama Tumaini and the newborn?

Gideon and his second wife, Mama Tumaini, had just welcomed their fifth child, a girl named Grace, and he'd invited Mark and me to his engang to meet the child in the coming weeks. We hadn't yet visited a Maasai engang, and while I looked forward to the experience, I'd also been fighting a long series of intestinal bugs, so I felt some trepidation about eating unfamiliar foods, as well as some nervousness about walking four miles each way without a bathroom. Even with the aid of a bike, Gideon made this journey nearly every day, though I imagined squatting in the bushes attracted a bit less attention for him than it would for me—a woman with a snowy white behind.

In the short time I'd known Gideon, we'd developed a pidgin form of communication that consisted of short, simple Swahili phrases with a lot of between-the-lines meaning. Gideon had become an ally and a friend of both Mark and me, and we'd all come to the conclusion that just standing together in silence over morning coffee for us and chai for him was enough to solidify our friendship. Words weren't always necessary.

"*Safi kabisa,*" he smiled. Mama Tumaini and the baby are very fine.

"*Nzuri. Nemefurahi sana,*" I replied with a grin. I feel very happy to know they are well.

We stood shoulder to shoulder looking at the water tank for several minutes, quietly drinking from our mugs.

In a serious tone, I broached the subject of rain. "*Vipi kuhusu hali ya maji hapo nyumbani kwako?*" How is the water situation at your house?

"*Si nzuri,*" Gideon said with a shrug. Not good.

More silence, then, "*Pole sana,* Gideon." I'm very sorry.

Tea and coffee finished, we wandered off to continue our daily morning rounds. I to gather my books for a day of teaching, and he to feed the dog Torchi, who was a new addition to our house—a puppy acquired shortly after we moved to Americastle, when an expatriate friend of a friend needed to find homes for a litter of squirming, rambunctious fur balls.

Torchi had found an unusual life with us. Most Tanzanian dogs seemed to fend for themselves, traveling in unruly, often ruthless packs. Many were scrawny, nervous creatures, perpetually scavenging and ever watchful of humans who were as apt to brusquely shoo them away as to scratch their ears. Dogs were largely viewed as nuisances, or as utilitarian animals that should be shown limited kindness if they were to remain good guard dogs. Torchi, however, enjoyed the benefits of a more American understanding of pets.

When we sought to get Torchi spayed because we did not want all the village dogs visiting her whenever she went into heat, Dr. Msinjili summoned Monduli's local vet on our behalf. A few days later, the vet showed up at our front door with a small medical bag for what he assured me was a simple procedure. After he'd anesthetized Torchi, he told me, "Don't worry. She will be fine," as I held open her back legs on our dining room table and assisted in my first and only ovariohysterectomy. She and I both survived the surgery, though Mark and I took turns sleeping on the concrete living room floor next to her as she recovered from the anesthesia, and neither of us felt much like eating dinner on the dining-room-turned-operating table for a few days.

Torchi, unlike many Tanzanian dogs, hadn't had the mischievous, playful puppy beaten out of her, which seemed to confuse and perturb Gideon in equal parts, as did the fact that we ran around talking to her while playing chase in the yard. Nonetheless, he saw her as a confident, friendly presence around the house, with a much different demeanor from most Tanzanian dogs, and the differences seemed to interest him, as if he thought Torchi a fascinating experiment in human—albeit strange wazungu—and animal behavior. I'd even caught Gideon talking to Torchi in the same high-pitched, cutesy voice I sometimes used with her when he didn't think I was around.

As I walked down to the girls' school that morning, I waved goodbye to Gideon and Torchi before I passed by the homes of two of Moringe's teachers who lived just below us. Since Mark and I had moved in up the hill, we'd been the source of much curiosity and interest among the three small children who lived in these homes, two boys and a girl—the youngest barely walking and the oldest maybe five or six. I still wasn't exactly sure which children belonged in which homes.

At first, the youngsters would stop whatever they were doing—usually playing soccer—and stare at one or both of us as we walked by. We'd pause and greet them in our best Swahili, which typically sent them skittering off in different directions with giggles. To them, we seemed to be an odd novelty—white-skinned adults who dressed, spoke, and behaved in strange and unusual ways. We'd now been playing this little game with one another for a few months, and it had become a routine that I think we all looked forward to. They usually waited and watched for us to come down each morning so that they could run out and greet us.

As I neared the homes today, I heard one of them yell from inside, "Okay," which had become their mantra since they didn't know any other English words. At this, all three of them came running from different directions. They ran in a circle around me as I kept walking, smiling, and waving at them. In unison, they laughed and yelled, "Okay, okay, okay ..." as they waved back at me. I'd started calling them "the okay kids" because they now did this nearly every day. I don't think they realized it, but they often cheered me beyond measure.

After my experience near Lake Manyara, I'd found myself wanting to hug these children, to treasure their liveliness and enthusiasm, but they had yet to let me get close enough to even shake their hands. I was different and interesting and seemingly friendly, but also a little bit scary, I realized.

When I reached the girls' school, I almost immediately sensed trouble in the air, as if my recent experiences had sharpened my nose for tragedy. All the students were still gathered in the chapel for morning announcements, but as I entered, I noticed most of my Form II students sat with their heads in their hands, and a few looked as if they'd been crying.

Over my shoulder, the matron was patrolling the upper part of campus, a look of foul displeasure on her face. She was giving tardy girls the what for as they scurried past her. By now she'd come to generally approach me with cautious warmth, as if she wanted to embrace me but couldn't quite give up her authoritative elderly demeanor. Today, it seemed better to steer clear of her.

After chapel ended, I spent several minutes greeting each of the teachers before I followed my Form II students up the hill and into the classroom. When I entered the room, they rose from their seats as usual and chanted, "Good morning, madam," but today the greeting seemed somewhat tarnished, as if their enthusiasm had been drained out.

"Is it a good morning?" I asked as I signaled with my hands that they should sit down. Because this was an atypical response, most of them stood looking at one another and me with confused faces. It was Gladness, the class monitor, who spoke first: "Yes, mwalimu, it is a good morning."

"Are you sure? Because it doesn't seem like it's a good morning for some of you," I pressed.

By this time, a few students had picked up on my line of questioning and were talking to one another in whispered Swahili about how to respond, I presumed. Neng'ida raised her hand and then stood when I called on her. Her eyes were red as she whispered, "We are sad today, mwalimu."

"Why?" I asked.

Neng'ida responded, "Dinah must go home today."

As I noticed Dinah's empty seat, I could hear the breath catch in more than one student's throat. A couple of heads dropped down onto the tables to be cradled in folded arms.

"Why?" I asked again.

At this, Neng'ida covered her mouth and looked at me sideways. It seemed as if she were waiting for someone else to respond.

"Why is Dinah going home?" I repeated.

Neng'ida slowly sat down as a murmur of conversation filtered across the classroom. Finally, a student at the back blurted out, "She is going to have a baby."

At this, I walked around the table that I'd been standing behind at the front of the room. I leaned against it and looked with concern at one of the smallest girls in the front row, who had huge tears rolling down her cheeks. I paused for a moment to gather my thoughts. I wasn't sure how to respond to this.

"Is it her choice to go home?" I asked.

At this, a chorus of emphatically stated noes rose up.

Gladness remained in her seat—it seemed we'd passed the point of social decorum now—and said quietly, "When a student is pregnant, she must go home."

"Is this a school rule?" I asked.

"Yes," Gladness responded.

"Will she come back after she has the baby?" I asked.

"No," Gladness whispered.

"Why not?" I asked.

"It isn't possible," Gladness simply stated.

"Why?" I asked again.

"Girls who have babies are not allowed to go to school," Gladness explained.

"Who made this rule?" I asked.

"The government," said Gladness.

"Oh," I responded as I contemplated how to ask my next question. I looked at my shoes for a moment as I gathered my thoughts. Here, it seemed, was another example of something I wanted to change, something that would have lasting consequences for a student who had demonstrated promise and eager determination, and yet I was powerless in the face of an unjust system I didn't fully understand. In a place where education was already extremely difficult to obtain, particularly for girls and even more so for Maasai girls, this girl would be denied access to education for a decision that may not have been hers if she'd been promised in marriage. The room remained silent save for a couple of quiet sniffles.

"Is Dinah promised in marriage?" I asked.

"No," Gladness whispered, "but she didn't choose this."

My blood ran cold as it occurred to me what all these girls already knew—someone had raped Dinah, which probably wasn't that unusual to them, but it made me want to scream and weep and beat my chest. I wanted the responsible party held accountable. Instead, Dinah would be held accountable.

I hung my head and remained silent. Where could I go from here? Teaching was my job, but that didn't feel like it made much difference today. Subject-verb agreement would have to wait. I knew I needed to find Dinah before she left.

"I'm very sad to hear this," I said. "I think, if possible, we should write some letters to Dinah. You can write a letter to her in

English telling her whatever you want to tell her. You don't have to give it to her or to me if you don't want to, but it will be a good chance for you to practice writing in English and to express your thoughts and feelings. You can work alone or in small groups to write the letters, whatever you choose. While you begin, I'm going to go see what time Dinah is leaving."

After I got them started on their letters, most somberly working in groups of two or three, I walked over to the school office to see if I could find the headmistress, and she was there.

"I've heard Dinah must go home," I said after I greeted her in the customary way.

"Yes. This is very unfortunate," she responded.

"Is there anything we can do to help Dinah?" I asked.

The headmistress looked at the floor and said, "Not really. Schools are legally required to expel pregnant girls and are not allowed to readmit them. We will take her to her family. The matron is helping her pack now."

"This doesn't seem fair," I said, unable to keep my feelings in check. When the headmistress didn't respond, I continued, "Where is her family?"

"In Arusha. It seems she lives with her aunt because she is an orphan. Her parents died some years ago. Even most of her siblings died. I'm told a strange disease passed through her engang and took most of her family."

"What time will she leave?" I asked, as the weight of the loss this girl had already endured settled over me. "I would like to go with her."

"In about an hour," said the headmistress. "The matron and I will ride with her to Arusha. Jean will drive us. Marv will ride along too. . . . You can join us, if you like."

I knew Marv would sit in the rear of the Land Cruiser, in the area normally reserved for luggage, as he often did on journeys to and from Arusha. He'd be propped against the spare tire, quietly doodling in his journal, listening, and waiting for the moment when his substantial size or booming voice might be required. Only the week before, a would-be thief had reached into Jean and Marv's parked Land Cruiser, grabbed Mark's backpack, laden with our laptop, and taken off running. In a matter of seconds, Marv had emerged from the rear of the Land Cruiser and shouted, "Drop that bag," in a way that turned every head within a one-block radius. Apparently, the thief mistook Marv's bellow for the very voice of God because he dropped the bag and kept running.

The headmistress, and nearly everyone else, knew she could either take along a Maasai guard, or she could take along Marv. Either way, anyone with less than friendly intentions would be compelled to behave, which I thought somewhat ironic given that I viewed Marv to be about as threatening as a big teddy bear. Apparently not everyone saw him that way.

I went back to the classroom, my composure barely held together by quickly unraveling threads. By the time I stood before the unsettled group of Form II students, I wasn't sure if I could speak, and in fact I couldn't. What could I say in the face of this? What words of comfort could I offer Dinah or these students? They and I knew that what had happened to Dinah could easily happen to any one of them. So I stood before them with tears in my eyes. That day, I could not be the unflappable, self-possessed leader they expected at the front of the classroom, and so we all fell apart together before I left them to find Dinah.

When I saw her, she looked smaller than I remembered, as if the prospect of motherhood at the age of fourteen had diminished her, rather than enlarged her. But, more concerning than this, her very face and posture had changed. Dinah no longer sparkled— there was no bright smile, no eager light, and no self-assured stance. She had folded into herself in every way, and I realized as soon as I saw her that I had to remain composed, and so I took a deep breath and pulled myself together. I walked up to her, placed my hand on her arm, and then hugged her. She limply leaned into me, her eyes roving over the ground, her arms clutching a small duffle bag. "I'm sorry," I said. "I'm so very sorry."

We arrived at her aunt's home around ten o'clock in the morning. The headmistress got out first and walked up to the house. Dinah, the matron, Jean, and I followed her. Marv remained watchful in the Land Cruiser. A woman, presumably Dinah's aunt, sat on the stoop of a small rectangular mud-walled house. The headmistress and the matron spoke to her in quiet Swahili for several minutes while Dinah, Jean, and I stood mutely behind them. Dinah's aunt kept her eyes on the ground, and she nodded from time to time. When they'd finished speaking, the aunt said something to Dinah in Swahili that I didn't understand. In response, Dinah quickly walked past her aunt and into the house, and then she was gone. Just like that.

After she entered, three men stumbled out of the house, glassy-eyed and loud. They laughed and gaped at me for a moment before speaking to me in slurred Swahili. I didn't understand them, so I dumbly smiled and nodded as I inched closer to the headmistress. I heard Marv get out of the Land Cruiser behind us. A silent, meaningful look passed between Jean and me, and then we all turned and left. Though no one said it out loud, we all knew these men were either drunk or high, it wasn't clear which, and one or more of them was probably responsible for Dinah's untimely departure from school—another layer of iniquity to which we bore witness.

We rode back to the school speechless, each of us caught up in our own thoughts. I imagine Marv might have been thinking about the Alcoholics Anonymous program he'd successfully launched in Tanzania and the need for it in light of what we'd just experienced. Even Jean, usually full of repartee and stoically unflappable, remained quiet. Normally, I could depend on her to make conversation with the headmistress and the matron, something I sometimes found difficult, but nobody felt like talking, and after the day we'd had, this didn't feel awkward. It felt like the appropriate response.

In the silence, I leaned my head against the back of the seat and closed my eyes. The all-day effort to tamp down my emotions and squeeze back my tears had left me with a dull, persistent ache that radiated from my skull downward into my shoulders. I knew from experience that only sleep would ease this pain, and even then, it would only ease the corporal pain. The visceral ache would remain.

As I sat with my eyes closed, I began to picture Dinah. She'd recently started sitting right in the middle of the classroom, a bright sunflower in a field of daisies. Dinah had one of the most beautiful smiles I'd ever seen—the perfect mix of earnest joy and unmitigated happiness. Her eyes seemed to vibrate with energy, and from looking at her, I'd have never known she'd endured the loss of her family. I wondered what she did with all that grief and how that smile survived the devastation. Today seemed to have tested its limits.

Though Dinah wasn't my best student, she wasn't my worst either. Much like her choice of seats in the classroom, Dinah sat squarely in the middle of the field academically, but she was quick—quicker than most. In the year I'd known her, Dinah had made astounding progress, going from knowing virtually no English to being able to roughly communicate. But Dinah's unabated enthusiasm impressed me most. When I asked a question, she'd turn on that charismatic smile as her hand rocketed into the air. "Mwalimu, mwalimu. Me, me. Call on me," she'd say, even when she didn't know the answer. I knew the classroom would be a little duller without her—that she'd been plucked out far too soon.

CHAPTER 21:

HOPING FOR SCHOOL CHOICE

Shortly after Dinah left school, the Tanzanian Ministry of Education released the Form IV national exam results—a much anticipated event each year because it determines not only if students can continue their education to the next level, but also the rank of schools regionally and nationally, the latter influencing a school's ability to attract quality students.

For the Maasai Secondary School for Girls, recruitment was not an issue since the school served a very specific, underserved population. There were always more girls who wanted to attend the school than available spaces. However, the success of the much-watched school would be determined by the performance of its students on the national exam. Among the Maasai, there were many who rooted for the school's success and others who hoped the exams would once and for all prove that educating Maasai girls was a ridiculous endeavor. Among Tanzanians in general, there seemed to be a morbid curiosity around whether a tribe many of them viewed as backward could change. I'd heard this view from the park rangers at Tarangire National Park many months earlier.

Now I worried less about the implications of the results for the school and more about what the results would mean for my students. I knew that going home would be difficult for some of them, and that many of them wanted to continue their schooling. A handful were eager to finish school and go back home, where they would start their lives as wives and mothers.

Statistics told me that in Tanzania's education system—a system with few resources to accommodate the advancement of more than the smartest, luckiest students—less than 30 percent of young people typically pass the exam with high enough marks to continue to Form V.[1] That meant 70 percent, or about thirty of the recent graduates, would likely not pass beyond an eleventh-grade education. I'd spent the last several months wondering what their futures would hold, as I'm certain they had too.

Without doubt, there was adequate evidence within the international community that educating women and girls could be life-changing, helping women to develop to their full potential and putting them on a path to marry later; have fewer, healthier children; earn more money; and play more active roles in leading their communities. In fact, the United Nations had declared education a basic human right, so even beyond the developmental improvements it offered, education fell into the same category as freedom, justice, and equality—rights that every human regardless of race, creed, tribe, gender, social status, or nationality should enjoy.

At the time, though, I knew we still had a lot of work to do when it came to providing these young women with access to support systems and infrastructure that would help them claim their rights and work for changes within their communities. I wondered how these young, educated women would navigate a Maasai world that hadn't yet caught up to the change they represented.

Among the Tanzanian teaching staff, there was a general acceptance that many students would fail the exam. It seemed to be a tough-love approach that dictated students needed to work hard to pass the exam. No matter their success or failure, students were expected to go out into the world and struggle and fight to use what they'd learned—as each and every one of the Tanzanian teaching staff had done—something I realized as I recognized my own relatively easy path to education and employment.

Although I wished we could do more for the students, in a place where there were so many needs and so few resources, I understood that we all felt as if we needed to realistically define the scope of our impact. There was much we couldn't change; we had to hope that what we'd given these young women would be enough.

While about two-thirds of the Form IV students had supportive parents and were able to await their exam results at home, the other third—or about fifteen students—could not safely return home, so they remained on campus. From their graduation in October until March, I'd watched as these postgraduates wandered around campus aimlessly waiting for whatever fate the national exam would bring.

One Monday morning in March, with no warning, I arrived on campus to find that several of the remaining Form IV graduates had left over the weekend. Most of these, I would never see again, nor would I know what happened to many of the students who received their results at home. On the previous Friday afternoon, the long-anticipated exam results had arrived. Though I hadn't been there to witness it, I imagined a group of nervous girls huddled around a single sheet of paper that listed their entire class from highest to lowest performing.

That Monday, Miriam sought me out with tears. "Mwalimu, I don't know what to do. The exam results are out, but I can't go home. *Kweli kabisa*, I don't know what to do," she said as she stared at me imploringly.

She showed me where the exam results were posted, and we spent several minutes examining them together. As I studied the results, a small group of students huddled around me. No one smiled. One student shuffled her feet and looked at the floor. Another sniffled and covered her eyes with her hands. Miriam kept leaning into me as if she thought I might buoy her up.

In most cases, I wasn't surprised by the results. Those students I expected to be at the top of the list were there, but still the results didn't make sense to me. I, like the girls now gathered around me, didn't know how to interpret what I saw. The list clearly ranked the students, but even those at the top of the list had scored low in some subjects, but high in others. I asked the group, but nobody could tell me the overall score required to begin Form V.

After finding out that the headmistress was away from campus for the week, I got a copy of the results from the school's secretary and immediately walked up the hill to Moringe to discuss the situation with Dr. Msinjili. Even though the Maasai Secondary School for Girls was neither under his purview nor his responsibility, Dr. Msinjili would always open his office to me, clear his busy schedule, and patiently answer my questions.

As with most things in Tanzania's education system, the answers seemed complex. In O-level, or Forms I-IV, students studied all subjects within the curriculum. However, in A-level, or Forms V and VI, students had to choose a focus based predominantly on their test results. Different secondary schools offered different focuses.

For example, one school might offer a history, civics, and geography, or HCG, focus, and another school might offer a physics, chemistry, and biology, or PCB, focus. A student's focus in A-level also determined what career paths were open to her beyond secondary school. So, for the Maasai Secondary School for Girls, it wasn't as simple as deciding whether to offer Form V or not. The school also needed to determine which disciplines to focus on, and even then, only some of the girls who qualified for Form V would be able to choose this focus. Others would have to find a different school elsewhere.

For the next several hours, Dr. Msinjili and I engaged in what seemed like an endless game of alphabet soup. Could we create two focuses—one in the humanities, and one in math and science—for the Maasai Secondary School for Girls that would allow all the girls who passed the national exam—which was surprisingly high at nearly 50 percent—to continue their studies at the school? And if not, could those that didn't fit at the Maasai Secondary School for Girls be accommodated at Moringe or elsewhere?

We also discussed what opportunities were available to those girls who had not scored high enough to continue to Form V. Dr. Msinjili informed me that some of them could continue on to trade schools, nursery and primary school teacher training programs, nurses-aide school, secretarial school, and other technical programs in agriculture, cookery, and tailoring. Dr. Msinjili helped to create a list of potential schools and offered to personally contact the people he knew at these schools. As we discussed this, I wondered how we might find funding to help all the girls who wanted to continue on with their schooling.

In the coming days, I would discuss all these ideas with the headmistress and with Operation Bootstrap Africa, the US-based nonprofit organization responsible for fundraising for scholarships. Dr. Msinjili and the headmistress would meet with education officials at the diocese. In the end, the girls' school would offer two focuses—one in humanities and one in science. To the great credit of the leadership of Operation Bootstrap Africa, in short order, they sent encouraging words—they would find the funding. With this news came a sense of relief that reduced me to tears.

As these plans unfolded, I also continued to talk with the remaining Form IV graduates. I had to tell some of them that they did not qualify to continue to Form V—a dream most of them had clung to since they'd started at the school. For most of those who didn't qualify, I had other options, but some of them did not want to pursue an alternate vision to their dream—a career path not of their choosing but of their circumstance.

Miriam wept with relief when I told her she qualified for Form V. Then she said excitedly, "Mwalimu, I think I can go home for a visit now because I can tell my brother and my mother that I can't be married yet because I still have to finish school. They came to my graduation, so I think they understand now." I hoped she was right.

After this conversation with Miriam, she bounded off toward the dormitory to begin packing, and I sat alone on the steps of a classroom and watched the sun begin to slide down the horizon. I reflected on the fate of these girls for a long while before I stuffed my detailed yet messy notes of the options different students would pursue into my backpack to begin what felt like a much-too-long walk back up the hill beyond Moringe to Americastle.

As I trudged along in thought, I didn't even see them, but they had spotted me and they must have sensed something different about me that day. Perhaps even as small children, "the okay kids" could read the slump of my shoulders, or the pallor of my complexion, or the gait of my walk. Usually I heard them yelling their typical greeting—"okay, okay, okay"—from some distance, but not today. Instead, the littlest among them ran toward me and before I knew what had happened she wrapped her arms around my knees and smiled up at me. She blinked twice and whispered, "Okay?" as if she knew what it really meant.

I smiled and nodded. "I am now," I said, even though I knew she wouldn't understand me.

This was the first time any of "the okay kids" had touched me. Before this, they'd been too uncertain of my differences to get very close. But now that the barrier between us had been broken, all three of them wrapped themselves around me as I knelt down with a smile. They touched my hair, held my hands, and pulled me down into the grass, where we sat huddled together. They opened my backpack and dumped its contents onto the grass. The messy notes cast aside, they focused on a children's picture book I'd been using to teach vocabulary to my new Form I students.

"Banana," I said, as I pointed to the picture.

"Ba-nan-a," they sang back to me.

Then one of the boys pointed at the same picture and said "*ndizi*," or the Swahili version of "banana."

"*Ndizi*," I dutifully repeated.

We did this over and over for the next half hour or so, until we were all grinning and laughing at one another.

When we finally parted, they circled me as they had done so many times before while chanting, "Okay, okay, okay," a blessing and a mantra from the mouths of children.

CHAPTER 22:

GIDEON THE MIGHTY WARRIOR

"E hhhhh . . . wazungu!"
"Wazungu, wazungu . . . wazungu!"

In myriad little voices, the cry had gone up. White people were nearby, and every child within earshot knew it.

As the newest group of children took notice of Mark and me, I stopped walking to remove my sweater. When I'd dressed this morning in the cool concrete interior of Americastle's mountainside perch, I'd optimistically thought I might need a rain jacket and a sweater on today's trek. Now I tied the sweater around my waist and shook out my ankle-length dress. Though overcast, it appeared the rain jacket would remain stuffed in my backpack unused. My feet and lower legs had attracted a fine layer of dingy silt. Despite my best intentions, I knew I would show up looking dusty, rumpled, and a little sweaty when I arrived at Gideon's house.

It was April already, but the long rains had still failed to arrive. Every day, cool mornings gave way to warm afternoons. As the clouds failed to gather, the worry etched itself deeper and deeper into the faces of those without access to plentiful water. I saw more women and children wandering the roads with empty buckets and more Maasai herds searching the countryside—all in pursuit of water.

I'd heard the anxious chatter too. Although Monduli had a long history of water shortages and little infrastructure to address the problem, everybody seemed to think it was getting worse. Rather than experiencing a drought every decade, it seemed to be happening every two or three years now, with little time for recovery between disasters. And disaster seemed to be floating in the air, almost like the pervasive dust particles that invaded every nook and cranny of my existence. If the rains didn't come soon, disaster whispered that hunger would soon follow.

Mark and I were walking nearly four miles outside of Monduli to visit Gideon and his family at their engang, and the farther outside of Monduli we got, the more interest we seemed to attract. In these parts, we were as rarified as two giraffes would have been walking down the streets in Montana—worthy of exclamation, stares, and, if possible, a closer look.

Most adults were polite enough only to gape surreptitiously, but the children were a different story. As we went, we'd picked up nearly a dozen of them, who followed us as if we were the leaders of a curio parade. A group of schoolboys ran ahead, slowed to let us catch up, fell behind us, and then ran ahead again. They did this over and over, smiling at us each time we passed them and then giggling as they ran past us. They reminded me of slightly older versions of "the okay kids."

Several girls danced around us, smiling and chattering in a Swahili we didn't really understand before one of them said, "Give me pen," with a relatively innocent smile and an outstretched hand.

I smiled back as I chided, "*Hapana. Hamna. Nafikiri si vizuri kusema* 'give me pen' *kwa wageni. Je, huyu si hivyo?*" I'd learned this Swahili response relatively soon after our arrival in Tanzania: No, I don't have a pen. It isn't polite to ask people for pens. Is this not so?

I just had to substitute "pen" with money, notebook, school fees, shirt, bag, or any number of other things I'd been asked for during my stay in Tanzania. Though younger children, such as these, most frequently asked me for pens. I imagined the common request the result of great waves of well-intended tourists handing out bags of pens to children along the roads here and there—their version of giving back to the locals while on an expensive African safari. Thus, for better or worse, white people had come to perpetually represent not only unimaginable wealth, but also school supplies.

Even I had been known to give out a pen here and there, but it was generally as a reward to a student who had worked extra hard, or as a thank-you to someone who'd done something nice for me. Though I regularly gave oranges to Arusha's street kids—an inconsistency based solely on my inability to say no to that particular group of destitute and persistent children—I generally avoided giving willy-nilly handouts to strangers. Though loath to admit it, I knew the most pressing and least palatable reason for my aversion to handouts was my own fear, followed closely by a general belief that handouts did little to solve the root of whatever the larger problem might be, whether poverty, homelessness, illiteracy, hunger, or disease. But really, in truth, fear loomed large. I knew from experience that giving out a simple pen often led to either much larger and more urgent requests, or to many more petitions for pens as the word got out that I was the go-to person for free writing instruments. Even with my access to resources and relative wealth, I feared I could not furnish the whole of Monduli with school supplies, nor could I meet all the other larger and more pressing needs of this community.

How, for example, could I say no to the child to whom yesterday I'd given a pen, when today she needed medical care? Furthermore, how could I decide who got pens, or medical care, or food, or water, when everyone needed these things? So it felt safer to say no to pens, and to continue to appease myself with the idea that my gift to this community was education. I'd come here to teach. They'd have to find their own pens.

I also knew from Dr. Msinjili and Mr. Kwayu that the staff at Moringe spent a good deal of time instilling in its students a sense of self-reliance. In fact, the notion of self-reliance seemed embedded in the very fabric of Tanzania. In 1967, Julius Nyerere, the first president of a newly independent Tanzania, introduced a policy of "Education for Self-Reliance." Among other things, the policy ensured universal access to primary school education. Nyerere's education policy was part of a broader philosophy he called *ujamaa*, or familyhood, that emphasized community-based solutions. For Nyerere, independence and ujamaa meant Tanzanians needed education in order to do things for themselves, and they needed to focus on what they could achieve on their own as individuals, as communities, and as a country.[1]

During his twenty-five years in office, Nyerere made self-reliance Tanzania's rallying cry, and long after his retirement, Nyerere's legacy lived on. Most Tanzanians still referred to him as mwalimu, or teacher, a term of great respect in their culture. In fact, I'd witnessed the public outpouring of grief when Nyerere, known as the father and teacher of Tanzania, died just before Mark and I returned to the United States to get married.

Dr. Msinjili, Mr. Kwayu, and many of the teachers at both schools had spent their formative years watching Tanganyika gain independence to become Tanzania under Nyerere's leadership. For this reason, Mr. Kwayu and others visibly bristled at the idea of small children asking white people for pens, or most anything else.

On the one hand, they could see the benefit of Americans providing scholarships to Tanzanian students with the idea that the students were gaining the skills to become self-reliant and support their broader communities. They could also see the value of donations that benefited the whole community, such as for the construction of classrooms.

On the other hand, Mr. Kwayu, in particular, simply could not abide the idea of a student begging for a handout, or, more specifically, begging for something that she could already provide for herself. A very inexpensive pen fell into this category. I had learned my Swahili response to the perpetual requests for handouts from Mr. Kwayu, and here on the road to Gideon's house I'd been called on to employ it once more.

After my somewhat chiding response to her question, the girl looked at me sheepishly and then began skipping around Mark and me as we walked. I obviously hadn't dampened her exuberance. The general philosophy among many Tanzanians, despite the policy of self-reliance, was that it never hurts to ask. Thus, whatever the answer, it was rarely taken personally, and so it was with this girl.

Soon, she and her friends settled into our pace, until first one and then another worked up the courage to grab my hands. Mark, as a man, was still too scary to touch, so instead the girls and I walked hand in hand grinning at one another. They jumped and wiggled along beside me, swinging my arms back and forth, until the one in need of a pen decided to examine my fingernails and trace the lines in my palms with her fingers.

Eventually, the girls set about creating a big human chain, enlisting the boys to hold hands with Mark and connecting our chain to theirs. We snaked our way down the road for a mile or so until we reached the turnoff to Gideon's engang. We went one way, and they turned back the way we'd come, probably to tell tales of the strange and unusual habits of wazungu.

When we neared Gideon's engang, he was waiting for us, knowing we would likely find the turnoff to his house from the main route out of Monduli, but that from there, we'd be setting off across a series of rough, unmarked footpaths. He leaned against a tree near where the children bade us farewell, his red shuka wrapped around his shoulders and his walking stick resting in the crook of his arm. He was chewing a long piece of dry grass as he waited in the shade. I wondered how long he'd been there, as we hadn't set a firm time for our arrival, only sometime in the afternoon.

As Gideon approached us, he spit out small bits of grass and smiled broadly. With a slight bow, he said, "*Hey, walimu. Karibuni sana! Nimefurahi sana kuwakaribisha nyumbani kwangu.*" Hi, teachers. Welcome! I am very happy that you've come to my house.

We were happy too. We smiled back at him as Mark expressed our gratitude for the invitation and presented him with the gifts we'd brought in a large plastic grocery sack—one kilo of rice, one kilo of sugar, and a big box of black tea. In this context, a gift felt like the appropriate response to an invitation to Gideon's home—evidence of the reciprocal relationship we shared rather than a simple handout given to a stranger on the road.

Mark had carried the five-pound load from a small store in Monduli, and I'm sure his labor had given everyone along the way more fodder for conversation. I could hear one of the children laughing in my head as she relayed, "You'll never guess what I saw today . . . two white people, and the man carried all the groceries instead of the woman!"

Gideon looked at the items in the plastic bag, grinned shyly, and said how happy Mama Tumaini, his wife, would be. Unsure of what to bring to a Maasai engang, I'd consulted one of the teachers at school that morning to get a recommendation. In my backpack, I also had a baby blanket, but I would wait until later to give that gift directly to Mama Tumaini. I wondered if we should have also given the food items to her, since Gideon had clearly indicated those items were in her domain.

Gideon politely carried the gifts the rest of the way, even after Mark insisted several times that he should carry them. The idea of two men arguing over what, in the world of the Maasai, was clearly a woman's job quietly amused me. I suspected Gideon's watchful presence at our house had taught him a thing or two about the ways of white men and women, which were far different from the ways of Maasai men and women.

In fact, I'd recently heard that the word for "white woman" in Maa literally translates as "little man." In the eyes of some Maasai, and perhaps even Gideon, this terminology reflected the fact that white women frequently behaved more like men—taking on careers, serving as leaders, speaking their minds, and refusing to take sole ownership of many of the chores traditionally in the domain of women, such as carrying water, hunting for firewood, and caring for children. Thus, even though white women were quite obviously not men, they were still referred to as "little men," and that seemed okay to me given the alternative.

We covered the remaining distance to Gideon's engang at a quick pace, much quicker than the pace we'd been walking with the children on the main road. I sensed from his brisk, long strides that Gideon might be as nervous about having us at his home as we were about visiting our first Maasai engang. We walked mostly in silence, more out of necessity than awkwardness. Swahili conversation was difficult for Mark and me under the best of circumstances, and the terrain required us to walk more or less in single file and to pay attention to where we stepped.

As we walked, I wondered how we would effectively communicate with one another once at the engang. What would we eat and drink, and would it involve *pombe*, a strong beer-like drink the Maasai made by fermenting honey, or would we be offered cow's blood, which the Maasai were known to drink mixed with milk? Would we unknowingly offend Gideon by saying or doing something we shouldn't? What if I had to go to the bathroom? How was that going to work? Even though I was a "little man," I still had to squat when I peed.

As we neared what Gideon had pointed out from a distance as his engang, a group of people began walking out to meet us. They'd obviously been watching for us and awaiting our arrival, which might also have explained Gideon's purposeful pace. Nearby, several children from a neighboring engang also took notice of our arrival, letting out the typical "wazungu" rally cry. Gideon laughed at them, slightly embarrassed, as he told us in Swahili that the children in this area were very happy to see us. In this case, "us" meant white people. We laughed too.

As the group from Gideon's engang neared, I noticed it included a young man dressed in more Western than Maasai attire, and a slight Maasai woman who looked to be about my age. Traditional Maasai beadwork swung from her ears and encircled her wrists. A simple chain of triangular white beads hung around her neck, and even with the warmer temperatures, she wore a button-down sweater over her traditional Maasai mashuka, probably her nicest clothing, worn, I suspected, for the occasion of our arrival.

Like most Maasai women I'd met, her clean-shaven head only emphasized the striking natural beauty of her face. She'd used a kanga to strap an infant to her back. The little body, almost the same size and shape as the tightly wrapped kilo of sugar we'd brought, lay so still and quiet, it could almost have gone unnoticed. Two other children trailed a few paces behind her. When she stopped in front of us, they clung to her legs and stared at us from behind her. She beamed at us with a wide, nervous grin. It seemed even her eyes smiled, as Gideon introduced her as Mama Tumaini. They exchanged words in Maa, and Gideon handed her our bag of gifts. Though she thanked us in Swahili, I realized immediately that, like me, she was uncomfortable using the language. At home, Gideon and Mama Tumaini spoke Maa.

The children at her feet, as well as those who by now had reached us from the neighbor's engang, differed from the ones we'd seen on the road, as well as from "the okay kids" in our own neighborhood. Each one of the seven or eight children who now surrounded us stood wide-eyed and stock-still. Their eyes expressed seemingly morbid curiosity, as if before them stood something so strange and odd that they felt drawn to look at it and yet were disquieted by its presence.

None of them wore school uniforms, though some of them were certainly of school age. While Gideon's children looked as if they might have been scrubbed clean and dressed up in advance of our arrival, the neighbor's children wore tattered and dirty swaths of fabric tied toga-style over one shoulder and little else. Much like a cliché photo from a humanitarian fundraising campaign, the younger ones had crusty eyes and runny noses that seemed perpetually visited by large, black flies. I smiled kindly at them, though I inherently knew that if I moved toward any one of them, they would all scatter in different directions with cries of fear.

As we left the neighborhood children and their stares behind, Gideon introduced us to the young man with Mama Tumaini. His name was Godwin, and he looked to be in his teens. In English, Godwin explained that he was Gideon's neighbor and that he'd come to help with communication, though as I began to ask him some basic questions, such as where he went to school, it became apparent that his English might be only slightly better than our Swahili. Nonetheless, already, it was abundantly clear to us that Gideon and his family had gone to great lengths to prepare for our arrival.

Gideon's engang consisted of several round and rectangular mud-walled buildings configured in a semicircle facing a steep embankment. In the center of the buildings, a treacherous-looking thorn fence encircled an area where I imagined a few cows and goats spent the night. Now the corral stood empty, the livestock likely off to graze with one of Gideon's older children. On the hillside, I noticed three or four Maasai men sitting on small stools and stumps in the grass, apparently chatting with one another. They waved at us from a distance as we walked up to one of the buildings.

I already knew that Gideon had two wives, though he didn't like to talk about this. He'd converted to Catholicism sometime before we'd met him, and though he still provided for his first wife—in fact, he'd built a separate engang for her and the six children they had together—he rarely spoke of her and spent most of his time with his second wife, Mama Tumaini. Between his two wives, Gideon had eleven children—the most recent only a couple of months old. This meant that Mama Tumaini, who was in fact exactly my age, now had five children. Her first one, Tumaini, to whom she owed her name, had been born as I started high school. And, at twenty-six years old, she certainly wasn't done having children yet.

Despite the size of Gideon's family, the engang seemed surprisingly quiet. I'd expected a hub of activity—children's voices, a crying baby, women bustling about, and perhaps a braying donkey or a crowing rooster. But Mama Tumaini, the baby, and the two children we'd met had disappeared into one of the buildings while we headed for another, making the engang feel sleepy, sluggish, and above all silent in the afternoon haze.

Inside the cool, dark interior of the mud-walled structure, it smelled as if a nearby wood fire had recently been snuffed out. It took a moment for our eyes to adjust after having been outside. The small building seemed larger from the inside than I'd expected. A partition divided it into two rooms. In the largest room, a wooden couch with cushions stood against the back wall. In front of it, a coffee table sat on the hard-packed dirt floor. Gideon and Godwin guided us to the couch, made sure we were comfortably settled, and then left us, promising to return shortly.

"This is bigger than I thought it would be," Mark commented.

"And I didn't expect furniture," I said, referring to the couch that looked almost new. "I wonder how they got it out here."

"Good question," Mark responded. "How are you doing?"

"Tired," I replied. "How about you?"

"Same," he said. "That was a long walk."

"Yes. I can't believe Gideon does that every day, even with a bike," I said out loud as I thought about the four-mile walk back home.

At that, we settled into silence as we continued to study the room. The handmade walls contained a network of supporting posts and crossbeams constructed of tree branches about two inches in diameter. These branches served as the framework for thickly packed, dried earth. This building, probably because of its rectangular shape, had a bati, or corrugated metal, roof rather than a grass roof, as the adjacent round buildings had. Above the couch behind us, a neatly painted sky-blue shutter had been flung open. It matched the building's wooden front door, which now stood ajar. Between the window and the door, a slight breeze passed.

The interior walls had been decorated with various pictures from newspapers and with landscape scenes from what appeared to be an old calendar, the pages seemingly glued to the walls like wallpaper—the Grand Canyon here, the Great Wall of China there. Two skinny yellow dogs hovered just outside the door before scampering off when Gideon shooed them away as he entered, Godwin and Mama Tumaini following closely behind him.

Mama Tumaini, still with the quiet baby on her back, carried a tray with four bottles of soda—two Coca-Colas, a Fanta Orange, and a Sprite. Gideon first offered Mark his choice of soda, then me. He placed a Coca-Cola and a Sprite on the table in front of us and stepped back to let Mama Tumaini open the glass bottles with an opener. For himself, he opened a bottle of Fanta and then he gave Godwin, who had stepped outside only to quickly return with two wooden stools, the remaining Coca-Cola. They both perched themselves on the stools at either end of the coffee table, as Mama Tumaini stood near the door staring at me with a broad smile. We sipped our sodas in what felt like awkward silence. As Mark began a faltering conversation with Godwin, Mama Tumaini slipped out again.

"How many cows does Gideon have?" Mark unsuccessfully asked once, twice, and then on the third time in broken Swahili, "*Ng'ombe . . . wa ngapi?*"

At this point, the question didn't need translation, so Gideon answered it. He had two cows, and six goats, he added.

"How long has he lived here?" I asked. This Godwin understood and translated. His whole life, came the answer, so I guessed "here" meant in this general vicinity since I was fairly sure Gideon would have built his own engang once he got married, though I imagined many of his relatives lived nearby.

As if on cue, the men we'd seen on the hillside appeared in the doorway. They first exchanged traditional Maasai greetings with Gideon and Godwin and then tried the same with us, with little success. As they filed in one by one and politely shook our hands, the room started to feel a lot smaller than it had when Mark and I were sitting in it alone. All of a sudden, we found ourselves surrounded by not a couple of Maasai men, but by nearly half a dozen tall, lean warriors. All but Godwin wore traditional red mashuka, and each of them had either a sheathed, foot-long machete belted to his waist or a short stick with a substantial knob on one end known as a rungu. Though I knew better than to feel frightened, in that moment I certainly recognized how little control I had over the situation. As they made conversation with one another, Godwin told us the men were Gideon's friends and relatives who'd come to greet us.

It wasn't long before Mama Tumaini showed up in the doorway with a covered bowl and two spoons. After greeting her, the men filed back outside, to return to their perch on the hillside. Godwin told us they would eat there because there wasn't enough room inside. Mama Tumaini placed the bowl in front of us, uncovered it, and handed us each a spoon.

"Karibuni sana," she said. You are most welcome.

She, Gideon, and Godwin all looked at us expectantly, as we looked back thinking we should surely wait until everyone had a spoon. The bowl was mounded high with a mixture of rice and chicken, and we assumed that we would all share the food before us. Gideon encouraged us to eat when Mark asked, "But aren't you going to eat too?"

At this they laughed, and Godwin assured us they would also eat, but that we should start. As we awkwardly dug in, feeling watched, they seemed to breathe a collective sigh of relief. Mama Tumaini left and returned with two similarly full bowls of chicken and rice, which she gave to Gideon and Godwin. It dawned on me that Mark and I would need to eat every morsel of the substantial amount of food we'd been served. Though it was delicious, it was more food than we were used to eating.

I was very aware that Mama Tumaini stood just inside the door without any food while we ate. She had pulled the baby off her back and now rocked it in her arms. I could hear it making the gurgling, bubbly noises of a baby. When we'd finished, Mama Tumaini walked over and handed me the baby. Gideon laughed. "*Huyu ni Grace*," he said. This is Grace.

While Mama Tumaini cleared away our dishes, I held Grace, whose little pink tongue came in and out of her mouth and whose eyes stayed fixed on me. Even as a baby, she seemed to register that I looked different from anyone she'd ever seen before. Holding Grace and knowing her father as I did, I believed Grace would be allowed to go to school, if that's what she wanted and the family could find the funds to send her. I silently vowed to help, if I could. Today, this seemed to make all the things I couldn't change, such as Dinah's circumstance, seem less important. I held Grace for a little longer before tightly wrapping her small body in the blanket I'd brought and handing her back to her mother.

As I did this, Mama Tumaini's response, translated from Maa to English through Godwin, shocked me into stammering, stuttering speechlessness. Rather than a simple thank-you for the blanket, she asked, "Do you want her?"

As Godwin translated, Gideon smiled and laughed at my stunned response, as if offering up one's child was the most natural thing in the world. I would later learn that among the Maasai this tradition is not uncommon. Children are frequently raised by relatives rather than by their parents, particularly if those relatives don't have their own children, something viewed as a tremendous misfortune among not only the Maasai, but also most Tanzanians.

After regaining my composure, I carefully explained that as generous and kind as the offer was, I could not possibly take Grace. "She belongs with you, her parents," I said with a smile.

"Okay, but then I think you will be her second parents," Gideon responded, as translated by Godwin.

We nodded and continued to smile, as we quickly steered the conversation away from rearing someone else's child.

As the afternoon unfolded, there was no pombe, nor cow's blood. In fact, we'd been served soda and chicken, something the Maasai rarely eat and drink, paired with rice, which was a rare luxury for most Maasai families. Gideon's family would normally have eaten ugali, a paste-like ground maize substance, with beans. For a celebration, they might have slaughtered and eaten a goat. However, Gideon had bought soda and a chicken in town. No one had to tell me this was an extra expense. It was, and I wondered what Gideon and his family would have to skimp on because of our visit.

I felt humbled and deeply moved by the many gestures Gideon and Mama Tumaini had made to ensure we would feel welcomed and comfortable in their home, and we had felt that way. Gideon had invited Godwin so we could better communicate with one another. We'd been served food and drink that they knew would be more familiar to us even though it was costly for them, and they'd invited their friends and relatives to meet us.

And, as if that wasn't enough, before we left, Mama Tumaini anointed us with beads. She took the bracelets off her wrists and put them on mine. She brought out a pair of earrings she'd made for me and put them in my ears. Not wanting Mark to be left out, Gideon took off the single string of beads he wore every day and put it over Mark's head. To them, we were obviously foreign and different, but they wanted us to know they'd claimed us.

Then they both stood back and admired us before Gideon began to quietly speak, as Godwin translated. Gideon told us that he'd built the structure we'd had lunch in as a result of the income we'd provided, and that he'd invited his friends and relatives today as a sign of respect and appreciation to us. He said we were more than employers; we were now counted among his relatives. Gideon closed his speech by putting his hand over his heart and saying, "*Asante sana. Kweli. Asante sana.*"

This didn't need translation. We knew he'd thanked us from the bottom of his heart. He'd conveyed that to us in many, many ways that day—ways we felt we would never be able to repay. He'd shown us kindness and a willingness to give beyond what we could imagine.

As we walked home, just the two of us, we felt so overwhelmed we could barely speak. The relatively small income we provided to Gideon seemed like so little to us, and yet he'd made us feel as if we'd transformed his life, and perhaps we had. Without thinking about it, we'd given him self-reliance, and he'd granted us Grace.

CHAPTER 23:

NEVER A STRANGER, ALWAYS A GUEST

I could speak fluently when it came to rats, so I found describing their presence in our house to Gideon, or anyone else who would listen, an easy task. While I might struggle with the names of fruits and vegetables at the market, I knew all the Swahili words associated with rodents. Describing their sizes, shapes, speeds, colors, favorite hangouts, and potential modes of demise was no challenge.

However, I was entirely unprepared for snakes, which is why I stood in stunned silence one morning in early June when, after proudly announcing to Gideon that it had been many weeks since we'd seen a rat inside our house, he intoned, as if it was no big deal, "You probably have a snake."

"A what?" I asked, even though I'd clearly heard him. I had no words for snakes.

I'd been hoping to minimize the rat problem during the several weeks when Mark's and my parents would be visiting us in Tanzania because, though our accommodations in Monduli were rustic and simple, I wanted our parents to see the charm in our situation, rather than the difficulties. If I had to choose between rats or snakes, though, I was certain the rats would win. Snakes weren't on my list of rat-control options.

For most of the June school break, we had *wageni*, or guests. Mark's parents visited Monduli first, overlapped with my parents for a weeklong trip to Ngorongoro Crater and the Serengeti, and then my mom and dad came to stay with us in Monduli.

Mark and I carefully orchestrated their time so they would see the very best Monduli and Tanzania had to offer, including sweeping views of Mount Kilimanjaro and a hot-air balloon ride over the Serengeti. They were warmly welcomed in Monduli, enjoying meals at Dr. Msinjili's and Mr. Kwayu's respective homes. At the girls' school, they met Mama Mkuu and Bibi Ruth, as well as Neng'ida and a handful of other students, who'd stayed on campus during the school break rather than face a forced marriage or other risks at home.

The visits went smoothly. Both sets of parents handled the limited access to water without complaint. No rats appeared, and I thought we were home free. However, the day before my parents ended their stay, we came home to find that Gideon had proudly demonstrated his Maasai prowess by hanging a headless six-foot spitting cobra in a tree in our yard.

My parents took it in stride, even if I didn't. To them, it was just another part of their African adventure. To me, it was just part of home sweet home. My parents left, and the rats returned, but at least we didn't have a snake anymore.

Just before my mom and dad left, however, we once again stood at an airport together. This time, I'd been in Tanzania for more than a year, and they for more than two weeks. Though they now had an authentic picture of Tanzania, instead of some imagined place created by the media's portrayal of Africa, it didn't make saying goodbye any easier. Even though the real Tanzania seemed less threatening to them than the imagined one, the distance between Monduli and Montana still remained vast.

Usually the stoic one, my father typically let my mom do the crying when it came to goodbyes, but not this time. Though I could count on one hand the number of times I'd seen my father cry, Tanzania had seemingly weaseled its way into his heart in the same way it had mine, for as he hugged me goodbye, his voice cracked and his eyes reddened.

"I understand why you came here now," he choked. "I'm proud of you."

He couldn't say more than that, and he didn't have to. I knew what he meant. Though he had originally all but forbidden me to come here, in the end, he had recognized the need to let me go. Though I would always be his daughter, I was no longer a child. At our wedding, I'd overheard him telling a friend, "I raised her to be strong and independent, but this isn't exactly what I had in mind," when describing my choice to teach in Tanzania.

Now, after sitting among my students, enjoying dinner with our Tanzanian friends and colleagues, walking the streets of Monduli, meeting Gideon, and driving the plains of Maasailand, my father understood something of what I'd sought here and what I'd found. My parents had experienced the deep sense of community in this place and the tacit welcome that resonated through nearly everyone they met. Here, we'd all experienced radical hospitality—in the midst of economic poverty, generosity overflowed.

I'd explained to them that in Swahili, there was no word for "stranger." The word translated as "guest." As someone who'd spent many years studying the English language, I understood that language followed culture. In Tanzania, we got a glimpse of a world where fear receded and every encounter came with a smile and an invitation to friendship. We'd come to help, and we'd been helped. We'd come to teach, and we'd been taught. We'd come as strangers, and we'd been welcomed as guests.

Neither of my parents lived under any illusion that what Mark and I had found in Tanzania was simple or easy. They knew we viewed the world with different eyes now, and they had glimpsed that world too. For that, I was grateful. We would need someone back home who had seen at least a part of our lives here.

Increasingly, Mark and I talked about our return to America, about six months away, with conflicted feelings as our experiences in Tanzania continued to weigh heavily upon us—a dead boy on the side of the road; street kids for whom oranges and pocket change were simply not enough; girls like Neng'ida, Dinah, and Miriam who faced weighty challenges at home; national exam results that dictated possibilities, or lack thereof; and water shortages with no end in sight.

We'd shared some of these stories with our parents, but most of them we'd kept to ourselves. We knew these events would never leave us. In truth, we had no idea how we might carry these stories back to America—how we could live there knowing what we knew here. We realized we would leave with too much undone, even as we yearned for the familiarity of life in our own country and culture.

For all these reasons, in the weeks following my parents' departure, I found myself frequently feeling melancholy, even when there were signs of hope. For example, Moringe had started building a large water tank to hold some 100,000 gallons of water with funds raised through school fees and by donations generously gathered by Mark's parents. Dr. Msinjili, Mr. Kwayu, and other leaders at Moringe had recognized that regular droughts and water shortages were becoming a way of life in Monduli, as the region's population continued to grow and the annual rainfall seemed to get more and more irregular. I watched as the tank grew, cinder block by cinder block, just below our house. It would serve the entire school community and would certainly mitigate future drought situations. However, sometimes I found it difficult to see beyond the immediate needs of the many women looking for water around Monduli in the here and now.

Likewise, Form V had started at the girls' school with a group of about twenty young women, and several other students had started in technical programs, but I often thought about those whose hopes of higher education had fallen short. I continued to feel powerless and out of my depth in many situations, including Dinah's.

I'd been visiting her in Arusha every few weeks since she left school, and though Dinah's situation still worried me, I looked forward to seeing her, in part, because she once again beamed with her characteristic bright smile. As she grew fuller, rounder, and more and more eager for her baby's arrival, Dinah seemed to settle in and become comfortable with her impending motherhood. She rarely asked about her classmates or school anymore, and in fact, she now seemed more at ease than I'd ever seen her at school.

Dinah had moved into a traditional-looking round Maasai boma near her aunt's house in Arusha. She told me she lived there with one of her female cousins, though I never saw anyone else around. While I felt glad to know that Dinah was no longer in the same house as the drunken men I'd seen the day we'd taken her home, I hoped she wasn't being left on her own. I imagined Dinah all by herself in that small hut giving birth to a baby on the hard-packed, earthen floor.

Other than visiting from time to time with small, functional gifts, such as food, I didn't know how else to help Dinah. I encouraged her to visit the clinic in Arusha for a checkup, but as far as I knew she hadn't done it. I even offered to pay for the visit, which had been met with a silent stare—whether this was due to our ongoing difficulty in effectively communicating with each other in either English or Swahili, or whether it was due to some other unknown reason, I wasn't sure. No matter, I hoped Dinah would get the help she needed when the time came to deliver the baby, which I guessed could be soon.

On a day in late August, when I suspected Dinah's baby might have arrived, I left Mark happily drinking coffee and reading a book in the shady outdoor seating area of one of our favorite restaurants in Arusha. Dinah resided on the north side of the city in what seemed like a completely different world. Visiting her required a dala dala ride to get to the rough dirt road where I began the mile-long hike uphill to where she lived.

Though I worried about encountering the intoxicated, lewd men that I'd seen at Dinah's aunt's house, during daylight hours many people populated this road. Because I stood out as the only mzungu walking the road, this also meant many eyes followed me. I was neither isolated nor unnoticed, and this gave me a sense of security. Nevertheless, I stayed on guard and walked quickly to get to Dinah's small boma.

When I arrived, I could hear someone bustling about inside.

"Hodi, hodi, hodi," I called to announce my arrival.

A young woman, even younger than Dinah, came out of the hut.

"*Habari yako?*" I asked. How are you?

"*Nzuri sana, mwalimu. Karibu sana. Mtoto amefika,*" she responded with a smile. Very well, teacher. You are welcome here. The baby has arrived.

Though I hadn't met this young woman, I assumed she was Dinah's cousin. Dinah had obviously told her about me since she referred to me as "teacher." As the only white woman to visit Dinah, I was easily recognizable.

"*Hongera sana, sana, sana! Je, Dinah na mtoto wake wanaendelea vizuri?*" I exclaimed. Congratulations! Are Dinah and the baby doing well?

"*Ndiyo. Wanaendelea vizuri sana. Utawaona,*" she said as she gestured for me to come inside. Yes. Very well. See for yourself.

It took a moment for my eyes to adjust to the darkness inside the boma, and as they did, Dinah spoke to me. She lay on a small cot with a very small baby sleeping across her chest.

"Hi, mwalimu. Karibu sana. Meet Upendo."

I smiled warmly and walked over to them. Dinah sat up and handed me Upendo, which means "love" in Swahili. Dinah leaned against me as I held the sleeping infant. They both looked healthy.

"*Hongera sana,*" I whispered. "She is beautiful. When did she arrive?"

"Two days ago," responded Dinah.

"Was the delivery okay? Is everything okay now?" I asked.

"Yes, mwalimu. We are both doing great," she said with a smile.

As Dinah stood up and rewrapped her kanga tightly about her waist, I looked more closely at Upendo. Her tiny fingers wiggled even as she slept. She'd been born with a full head of black hair.

I had hoped Dinah might go back to school after the baby's arrival and had even talked with Dr. Msinjili about quietly admitting her to Moringe. Many schools, including Moringe, didn't ask too many questions when it came to young mothers. In this way, many girls found their way back to school after they'd had their babies, even though this was against the law.

As I now held Upendo and reflected on Dinah's situation, I knew my aspirations for Dinah differed from her own. Education, for all its benefits, could also be a wedge between students and their parents. For this and so many other reasons—including violence in its many insidious forms—education remained unattainable for too many girls.

As an orphan, Dinah didn't face family opposition to her education, but she didn't have support either. The untenable situation at her aunt's house meant she had no one to care for her baby while she attended classes, and no financial resources to support her education.

I watched Dinah look at the child in my arms, her face radiating tenderness and joy. Out of difficult circumstances, she had made her own family, and this gave me some measure of peace. In motherhood, I believed Dinah had found this peace too.

CHAPTER 24:

WITHOUT WATER

I'd been to visit Dinah the week before, and though it was Saturday and I could sleep in, getting out of bed felt particularly difficult today. A leaden heaviness sat squarely in my gut.

Like the parched landscape around me, I felt as if I'd dried up and bits of me were slowly flaking away—as if my mood were a reflection of my environment. August was coming to a close, and the dry winter months still dragged on—June to September in the Southern Hemisphere.

The Monduli Mountains remained burnt brown. The long rains had never fully arrived, so the mountains had failed to turn lush and green this year. The short rains, if they came, wouldn't start until October or November, so we still had to endure at least another month or two of drought. Northern Tanzania had now experienced nearly a full year without consistent precipitation.

In the past few months, fledgling bean and maize crops had quickly withered, dust swallowing their tiny shoots and leaves. In fact, dust had enveloped everything, and because water taps ran dry, there was nothing to do to combat it. As I watched tiny floating particles dance in the air of our sunlit bedroom, I imagined my lungs filling up with fine silt until I could no longer breathe. I closed my eyes and sighed deeply.

Already, we were witnessing the secondary effect of water shortages—people not only didn't have enough water; now they didn't have enough food either. The price of beans and vegetables had gone up in the market, and many families had already begun to ration food since their crops had failed.

In fact, I'd overheard Dr. Msinjili and Mr. Kwayu debating how to reallocate already-limited school funds to ensure that the students had enough food and water until the end of the term, still several months away. The school grew its own maize and bean crops, but since those crops had failed, the school now needed to buy increasingly expensive food, as well as haul water in for students to use on a system of strict allotment. Just the previous week, the school staff had chosen to temporarily halt construction on the new water tank in order to buy food for the students—a choice made to meet immediate needs in lieu of a long-term solution; something that seemed all too frequent here.

Though lost in my thoughts, I now heard Mark rustling around in the kitchen and thought I'd better get up, whether I wanted to or not. Mark often rose early on the weekends to prepare something special for breakfast. From the smell, I guessed it was either cinnamon rolls or homemade bagels today. Even with little water and simple ingredients, these were achievable in our kitchen. Mark knew I'd been battling the blues in recent weeks, and his care often came in the form of food. For this, I loved him even more.

When we had enough water, Gideon's wife, Mama Tumaini, came to our house on Saturdays with a donkey harnessed with two large plastic containers. I heard her outside now—the dull thud of water filling up the empty containers an unmistakable sign of her presence. As I sat up and looked out the window, I noticed that she herself was harnessed with Grace, whose fuzzy head poked out of the top of the kanga with which she was strapped to her mother's back. Mama Tumaini must have risen before dawn to be here this early, and I could guess why. She hoped to get water and be on her way back home before too many other women noticed where she'd gotten it. This relieved me as much as it made me feel guilty.

Though Mark and I had been rationing our use of the water in Americastle's concrete tank and we'd already paid to have water hauled in twice, we knew Gideon's situation and most everyone else's was much worse than ours. Gideon had already lost one of his cows about two weeks ago. He'd told me it had just refused to continue the search for green grass and water. Falling on its knees, then its haunches, its breathing labored and its eyes rolling, it had never gotten up again. Gideon didn't have to tell me that this scared him. I knew it did. Animals were Maasai commodities, and without them, Gideon would have nothing.

Though I worried about how Mark and I would continue to cope with our own shortage of water, I knew we'd find a way to get more water if we had to. Come what may, we'd told Gideon and the two other Maasai guards who worked for us—the night guard and the swing-shift guard—they could use the water in our tank.

That said, we all knew that women at our water tap had the potential for exponential growth, so every day Gideon, Mark, or I politely refused at least one or two women who walked into our yard with an empty bucket, eyeing our water tank, and hoping to avoid the search for a working tap farther into town and the long line of women that would certainly be waiting their turn for a bucketful.

In fact, Gideon had padlocked the spigot to our tank, and he wore the key on a string around his neck, hidden under his shuka. As Mark, Gideon, and I had peered into the nearly empty tank a few weeks ago, Gideon had warned us in Swahili, "Today, you give water to one woman, tomorrow ten, and the next day one hundred. There isn't enough water for everyone, and they will all come."

The next day, the padlock had appeared. Gideon's primary job as our guard had now become protecting our water source, something that felt reprehensible and yet necessary. Difficult decisions with profound moral underpinnings kept coming our way, and I yearned for them to stop.

Once I'd gotten out of bed and eaten a leisurely brunch with Mark, I started to feel better. I decided to wander down to visit Jean and Marv, mostly because they'd graciously offered to let me use their shower, if they had water. For the last week or so, they'd been getting water for one to two hours each afternoon, during which time they hastily showered and filled up various containers and buckets in their house for later use.

I hadn't had a shower in more than a week because the water level in our tank was so low that it didn't provide enough pressure to keep water flowing to the showerhead. I'd reverted back to bucket baths, as had Mark, but I longed for a hot shower, so I stuffed a relatively clean towel and fresh clothes in a bag and made my way toward Jean and Marv's house. I thought I'd show up at their door with a bar of soap on a rope around my neck—an obvious metaphor for my state of mind—and beg for a shower.

Mark had other plans for the day. He'd been cajoled into helping Moringe manage a volunteer group that had arrived a few days earlier from America. They'd written to Dr. Msinjili several months ago indicating they wanted to come to the school to do a work project. Both schools in Monduli seemed to regularly host groups like this one. They showed up eager to roll up their sleeves and do something meaningful with their time, but sometimes their expectations of the experience didn't quite match up with the realities of the local context—something I could admittedly relate to.

Arriving in the middle of a drought they probably knew nothing about, this particular group came with the intention of painting classrooms, which seemed to be the go-to project at Moringe, even if the school had other more pressing needs. In a matter of two short days, the group had already used up all the water in the tank set aside for their entire weeklong stay, and they'd spent their first day on campus waiting around for the school to buy different paintbrushes for them because they didn't like the ones that had already been purchased. Their various wants, needs, and desires had consumed the time of at least two of Moringe's staff members, who were paid to be teachers, not volunteer gofers. Ultimately, I knew that the classrooms didn't really need to be painted since two other groups had already painted them in the last twelve months, and even if they did need painting, it would have been much more cost effective and a significantly lighter burden on the school to hire local people who needed employment to do the work.

Normally, I might have taken some time to talk with the group, but today they felt like just another in a long line of groups that I'd watched pass through one or the other of the schools. In fact, a few weeks earlier, a visiting retired teacher had toured the girls' school one morning and, after stopping in my classroom, had earnestly asked, "Do you know that computer-assisted learning is improving test scores in Minnesota?"

I'd smiled and nodded while I thought about our irregular electricity, lack of internet connection, and hand-me-down, circa-1990 computers without functional software that were still in storage. I also knew that most of the students had never seen a computer; thus they'd have to learn how to use a keyboard and mouse long before any "computer-assisted learning" would take place. Admittedly, the schools could have benefited from functional computers in the long run, but in the short run, we didn't even have enough books and were struggling to find the resources to feed students in the midst of a drought.

I found myself frequently wondering how well-intentioned people in the West, like me and other short-term volunteers, could best help the Maasai, or Tanzanians in general. The answers didn't always seem clear. Certainly, I'd come to recognize that some of the most pressing problems were vast, complex, and systemic. When I became overwhelmed by these types of problems, I tried to focus on the singularity of one student. I'd witnessed the growth and development of many students like Neng'ida and Miriam, and I recognized that their achievements came from the work of many people, most of them Tanzanians in partnership with generous donors.

I'd also come to firmly believe that true giving had to be reciprocal. I'd certainly received far more from my experiences in Tanzania than I would probably ever give back, and that humbled me. In sometimes stark and painful moments of clarity. I'd experienced my own deficiencies and had begun to see the poverty in my own culture. I'd learned about the challenges of walking together in common community, caring for one another, and weighing the moral responsibility of my privilege.

Certainly, I believed in the power of one person or a small group of people to profoundly change the world, particularly when I stayed focused on individual students, a single school, or a small community. I'd witnessed it here in the work of Dr. Msinjili, Mama Mkuu, Jean and Marv, and so many more, but I knew it wasn't easy, in-and-out kind of work. It required sustained, ongoing, mutually beneficial relationships, and donations given in the spirit of empowering local people.

Today, Mark would try to ease the burden Dr. Msinjili bore by serving as a friendly buffer between the volunteer group and the school's staff. Mark operated under the philosophy that his job was to help subtly and gently educate the group about the context in which they found themselves. As we left the house together, I patted him on the back, grateful for his diplomatic and generous spirit, and continued my journey toward Jean and Marv's house.

While Mark painted, I benefited from a hot shower, and I felt slightly guilty about that, but not too guilty. Jean even offered me a ride back up the hill to Americastle so that I wouldn't get sweaty and dusty on the walk home. While the hot shower had momentarily transported me into a happier, more carefree state, my transformation was indeed fleeting because just as Jean and I rounded the first corner beyond her house, we noticed two women struggling down the hill toward the road.

As they saw us, one woman waved her arms wildly while the other wailed with alarm, a child's limp body in her arms. I felt the woman's wail reverberate in my chest almost as if it had come from my own lungs, and the effect was immediate—the blood drained from my face, my breath quickened, and an almost instinctual urge came over me.

Jean must have felt the same way because she immediately braked as I flung open the passenger's door and ran toward the women. They both began urgently spouting Swahili, which I couldn't understand, but it didn't matter. The problem seemed self-evident.

The unconscious child, a girl, I thought, looked to be four or five years old. Her ashen, round face was taut, her cheeks hollow, and saliva ran out the side of her mouth. Her eyes were half-closed and rolled toward the top of her head. As the women continued to make their way toward the Land Cruiser, I cradled the girl's head in my hands, trying to lighten the burden of the woman who was carrying the child, her mother, I assumed. Even in the shuffling chaos of movement and limbs, I noticed tears had traced lines in the dust on the woman's cheeks. Though she kept moving, she never took her eyes off the girl in her arms.

Once we arrived at the Land Cruiser, a handful of yards from where I'd first met the women, we all struggled to get the girl into the vehicle, which sat too high off the ground for any of us to easily hop in with her. Jean leaned over from inside the vehicle and pulled on the woman carrying the child, while I did my best to boost the girl and her mother into the front seat from the outside. Once they were in, the second woman crammed in next to them, while I quickly hopped into the back.

Jean hit the gas, the wheels spun, and we took off as fast as the road would allow toward Monduli Clinic, only three to four miles away. As we hurtled along, I leaned over the front seat, squeezed between the two women's shoulders, and once again took the child's head in my hands. This time I put my ear as close to her nose and mouth as possible, listening for breath sounds. If she was breathing, it was only shallowly. I felt for a pulse, but the road was either too rough for me to find one, or the girl didn't have one. I couldn't be sure.

As I turned to look at the girl's mother, the woman and I were literally eyeball-to-eyeball, and her eyes spoke louder than any words, Swahili or otherwise, could have. *Please, dear God, save her.*

Though I knew she couldn't understand me, I said as calmly as I could in English, "I need to clear her airway. Can I do that? Will you let me do that?"

When the woman didn't answer but moved farther aside to let me squeeze past her, I put my thumbs behind the girl's lower jaw and squeezed upward in order to force her mouth open and her tongue down, while tipping her head back. Even from my awkward position hanging over the seat, I was able to hold her head like this until just before we reached the clinic, when to my amazement and hers, the girl opened her eyes and looked directly at me. Even in her weakened state, first shock and then fear registered on her face. I imagined waking up to find a strange mzungu woman hanging over her face gave her quite the start—perhaps the kind of adrenaline start she needed right then.

When the girl began to wiggle out of my hold and reach for her mother, I let go of her head and leaned back against my own seat. Her mother lifted the girl and cradled her in an upright position as she began to cough and choke forcefully, all the while looking over her mother's shoulder at me. I gazed back with a worried smile, as I tried to slow the tremor that seemed to be overtaking my body.

I had never been to Monduli Clinic and had hoped I'd never have occasion to go. When we pulled up, I quickly hopped out of the

Land Cruiser and ran toward the simple rectangular concrete block building. I was looking for someone, anyone, to help us. I looked in one room and then another, but the place seemed deserted.

"Hello," I yelled. "Is anyone here?"

From around the back of the building, two women in pink smocks emerged at a decidedly unhurried pace.

"I have a sick girl in the car," I blurted.

They both looked at me as if confused.

"*Kuna mtoto mgonjwa,*" I emphasized while impatiently pointing at the Land Cruiser, where by now the women, as well as Jean, were already walking rapidly toward us. The girl now clung to her mother while resting her head against her mother's shoulder.

The nurses ambled as if unconcerned a few steps in their direction before stopping and waiting for the group to come to them. There was no emergency-room urgency, no gurney or stretcher, no code red to match my perception of the situation—only a sleepy clinic where I felt increasingly impatient and uncertain of adequate medical care.

As Jean and I hung back, the four women conversed with one another about the child's condition—all in Swahili that seemed entirely too calm for the current situation. I wondered if sick children, even dying children, were so common in this place that they didn't warrant urgent, rapid-fire communication and action. Now that the child was conscious and at the clinic, her mother seemed calm, almost passive, in the presence of the nurses.

Jean and I stared at one another in confusion as if asking one another, *Now what?*

As the group of Tanzanians walked onward, Jean said, "We've done what we can."

"Okay, but let me see if there is a doctor around," I said.

I jogged to catch up to the group and gently grabbed one of the nurse's arms.

"*Kuna daktari hapa sasa?*" I asked. Is there a doctor here now?

"*Hapana. Kesho kutwa,*" she responded. Not until the day after tomorrow.

I frowned, but I didn't know what else to ask. Even if I'd had the language skills to communicate my questions, I wasn't sure this woman could help. They were bigger questions than she could answer.

In my silence, the nurse focused her attention back on the woman and her child. I stood there a moment, just outside their circle, watching them. The girl lifted her head off her mother's shoulder for a moment and looked back at me and then she waved. I waved back and watched them walk away.

The next day, I walked back down to where we'd first seen the two women and the girl. I knew there was a small rectangular house just up the hill from the road, and I suspected that was where they'd come from, but I wasn't sure.

I'd filled my backpack with bananas and a small blanket for the girl, hoping to find her mother or the other woman who'd been with them. I wanted to know what had happened to the girl, and to provide more help, if I could. I didn't really know the Tanzanian protocol for what to do when a child was sick, so I did what I would have done in America. I brought gifts and well wishes, and I quietly prayed that I didn't find the house overrun with relatives grieving the loss of a child. I'd also put some money in an envelope, but I had mixed feelings about giving it to the family. I wanted to help, but I didn't want to make them feel like some kind of charity case. I thought I'd wait and see what the situation was before I revealed any of the things I'd stowed in my backpack.

When I arrived at the house, all looked quiet and still, save for a curtain that fluttered across the opening where the front door should have been had there been one. I stood just outside and called, "Hodi, hodi, hodi," the equivalent of a knock in Tanzania. After several volleys, a woman I didn't recognize appeared from behind the curtain.

She had a sad, weary look about her, and my presence at her door only seemed to deepen the lines in her haggard face. I hadn't really thought through what I would say, but I did my best to explain in Swahili that I'd come to find out about a sick girl I'd seen nearby yesterday.

Though we struggled mightily to understand one another, I gathered that the girl did live at this house, that she was still at the clinic, and that she would be okay over time. I still didn't have a clear understanding of what had happened to the girl, only that the woman kept pointing to her own lungs and saying, "*Mbaya*," or "bad." She would then cough and say, "*Mafua*," or "flu." What I'd seen yesterday seemed to go beyond a bad flu, but I didn't have much hope of getting to the bottom of what was actually going on.

Since I didn't know this woman, I decided to leave the blanket and the bananas with her. The money I would either deliver directly to the clinic or give to the girl's mother, if I saw her again.

For the next week, I carefully studied the house each day as I walked by on my way to and from the girls' school. It remained quiet except for the flutter of that curtain, until one day, I heard the laughter of children, and just like that, the house sprang to life again. In the coming weeks, I noticed that the girl and two younger children often played in front of or behind the house. Sometimes, when they saw me, I would hear the usual chorus of "mzungu," and I would wave at them, but they kept their distance and so did I.

I also saw the girl's mother working around the house from time to time, but if she recognized me, she didn't let on that she did. It was as if the emergency on the road had never happened, and that was okay with me. Just like the incident with the boy near Lake Manyara, I locked this memory away in the part of me that I only let a handful of people see—namely Mark. Though this child had survived, I didn't feel redeemed. I'm not sure I wanted to feel redeemed, so I kept counting—counting children who had been lost and children who had been saved, counting the days without rain, and counting the remaining days until my return home.

CHAPTER 25:

A SAFE HOUSE FOR MIRIAM

"Why Miriam?" I whispered to myself. "Why her?" I stood by the window in our living room and cast a watery gaze down the hill to Moringe and then beyond to the vast plain that stretched into the hazy midmorning horizon.

I felt like I was teetering on the edge of coming completely apart. Miriam's situation seemed to magnify the already unsettled feelings that kept creeping up on me as our departure for the United States drew closer and closer. In a mere six weeks, we would leave Monduli.

I suspected Gideon could hear me crying because he kept shuffling around near the front door. He knew I was alone because he'd seen Mark leave this morning to teach an early class. I knew I needed to pull myself together before I saw Gideon and went down the hill to talk to Dr. Msinjili, but it seemed like the tears wouldn't stop flowing this morning. I sighed and walked toward the bathroom, where I knew the shower wouldn't work but at least I could brush my teeth.

Dr. Msinjili had become my go-to person on really tough issues. To me, he held an almost mystical wisdom, embodying the idea of a spiritual elder in a way I'd never experienced before. In truth, I couldn't envision what our lives in Monduli would be like without his presence. In many ways, he seemed like the glue that held so much together at Moringe and beyond.

Today, I would tell Dr. Msinjili about Miriam to find out if we could do anything for her. Yesterday, I'd learned from the headmistress that Miriam was pregnant, just a few months after she'd started Form V. Today, she would be sent home. One of the top students in her class, I thought Miriam's departure marked another promising future cut short.

However, several years later, Dr. Msinjili would remind me that first appearances can sometimes be deceiving. Miracles take time, and over the years, I would come to learn that Dr. Msinjili played the long game. He worked miracles, and for Miriam, he did just that.

■ ■ ■ ■ ■ ■ ■ ■

Somewhere down the hill, Monduli's dogs engaged in the nightly routine of barked calls and responses as Dr. Msinjili stood by his wife in their simple, utilitarian kitchen. Even though it was already after ten at night, they had just begun to clear the dinner dishes when the phone rang.

Dr. Msinjili deliberately wiped his hands on a towel before pulling his reading glasses from his breast pocket and putting them on the end of his nose. While the phone kept urgently chiming, he studied the buttons on this piece of mobile technology that both amazed and baffled him. He carefully pushed the answer button and lifted the phone to his ear.

"Hello . . . hello?" he said in a tentative voice. All he heard was quiet static on the other end.

Dr. Msinjili pulled the phone away from his ear and looked at the screen, which indicated that the call was connected. His brow furrowed.

"Hello?" he tried again.

It was a rare night that he went to bed before midnight, despite getting up before the sun rose. Since the arrival of mobile phone technology in Monduli, evening phone calls weren't that unusual—a new convenience and yet an added demand. As the head of a boarding school, Dr. Msinjili seemed to be on call, no matter the time of day or night. He expected this, though, and he didn't complain.

Despite the fact that his two children were nearly grown, Dr. Msinjili still had many responsibilities at home. He had recently moved his family from a small, spare apartment on the grounds of the teachers' college, where his wife worked, to a house just up the hill from Moringe where the family could raise more beans and keep chickens.

The neatly painted yellow concrete-block building served as home not only to his immediate family, but also to several members of his extended family, including his mother-in-law, who required ongoing care, and his nephew, a mere toddler. They filled this new house to full capacity and then some, particularly during school breaks, when they frequently took in one or more young Maasai women who were students at Moringe and yet couldn't risk going home for fear of being circumcised, married off, beaten, or raped.

"Hello?" he spoke, more loudly now.

A tremulous voice whispered through the static, "Dr. Msinjili . . . my engang is surrounded by morani. . . . My brother has arranged for my marriage tomorrow. Please . . . Dr. Msinjili . . . do what you can to save me."

As the line went dead, Dr. Msinjili closed his eyes, hung his head, and sighed raggedly. Miriam was in trouble.

Situations like Miriam's had always been part of his experience as a teacher and headmaster, but it wasn't until recently that he'd begun to more actively work on behalf of these young women. Rather unexpectedly, he'd gotten a reputation for helping predominantly Maasai girl students who had nowhere else to turn, which seemed illogical, even to him, given that he was neither a woman nor a Maasai, but to many of these girls he had become like a grandfather. He still wondered how this had happened as he thought back to when he'd initially met Miriam, who had been among the first girls he'd helped. At the time, she hadn't even been one of his students.

More than three years earlier, Miriam had graduated from Form IV at the Maasai Secondary School for Girls, where she'd been one of my students. It was from me that Dr. Msinjili first heard Miriam's story, relayed to him with a sense of urgency and anguish in the weeks before I left Monduli.

Dr. Msinjili knew that I'd come to care deeply about many girls like Miriam. Though I imagined he sometimes found my criticisms of Tanzania too pointed—its strange, often unfair, systems and its pervasive gender discrimination—I hoped he knew they came from the right place.

When Dr. Msinjili heard Miriam's story, I think he believed he had to help her, if for no other reason than to help me. Before I returned to the United States, Dr. Msinjili had promised me that he would watch out for Miriam, and I knew he took that promise seriously. That particular night, as he walked into the living room and sat down, I imagine Dr. Msinjili probably wondered how he was going to keep that promise.

He first tried to call Miriam back, but after three unsuccessful attempts, he gave up. Then he hesitantly dialed the number for Edward Lowassa, Monduli's representative to parliament, a longtime friend, and an elder within the Maasai community. Dr. Msinjili knew that one only called Lowassa if it was an emergency, but tonight seemed like the kind of night to call in the powerful and the political, both of which described Lowassa. Dr. Msinjili knew from personal experience that one didn't trifle with the man.

When Lowassa answered, Dr. Msinjili quickly apologized for the lateness of his call and tried to explain the situation. He reminded Lowassa that Miriam was the tenacious, smart girl who'd traveled to his office in Dodoma to beg for help to attend secondary school many years earlier. Dr. Msinjili then summarized the details of Miriam's history. He explained that Miriam had thought it was safe to return home after she'd finished Form IV, but that she'd been wrong. Her brother still owed her husband-to-be several cows, and now that she'd finished Form IV, it seemed to him that she could finally be married off and his debt settled. While she awaited her chance to continue her schooling with Form V, Miriam's husband-to-be had raped her. She'd once again run away, fearing an impending marriage to a man she barely knew. She'd returned to the Maasai Secondary School for Girls, and later discovered she was pregnant. Following the government's policy, the school had expelled Miriam.

Though he'd felt somewhat awkward about helping Miriam when the Maasai Secondary School for Girls had made it clear they couldn't, Dr. Msinjili had been moved by my conviction and passion about the need for girls like Miriam to have options to continue their schooling. He had agreed to quietly admit Miriam to Moringe once she'd had her baby, and this he had done long after I'd left Tanzania.

On this night, though, Dr. Msinjili glossed over many of these details, unsure how Lowassa, as a representative to the government, would view the fact that he had technically broken the law. When Dr. Msinjili paused and Lowassa remained silent, he took a deep breath and continued.

Fortunately, Miriam had been able to go to a sympathetic relative's engang to have her baby. Even this had been a big risk. At the time, Dr. Msinjili had doubted Miriam's safety, but Miriam had quietly hidden at her relative's engang until she'd had her baby—a girl. As was common in Tanzania, this relative had agreed to care for Miriam's daughter when she went back to school.

Miriam had completed her final years of secondary school at Moringe, and though she'd struggled, her scores still remained promising. During school breaks, she'd stayed at Dr. Msinjili's house. Even though she had yearned to see her daughter, both Miriam and Dr. Msinjili knew the risk of leaving Monduli was too great if she wanted to finish school.

Just a month earlier, Miriam had finished Form VI, but her future had still been unclear. Dr. Msinjili suspected that she had scored high enough marks on her Form VI national exam to continue on to college, but the official results were yet to be released.

Once again, her mother and brother had attended her graduation, from Form VI this time. After this, Miriam had begged Dr. Msinjili to let her go home, arguing that she was now too old, at just over twenty, to be married off. She also wanted to see her daughter, who was by now a toddler. Dr. Msinjili had warned her against it, but in the end, he'd let her make her own decision. In this instance, he hadn't wanted to be right.

"What can we do to help her now?" Lowassa interjected. "Her family will not understand why she cannot be married now that she's finished secondary school."

"Please, listen though. She is not finished with school. This girl is not yet economically self-sufficient. I believe we must help her obtain enough education so that she can find employment, and then she will be out of the reach of these men who want to control her. In fact, then her family will be dependent on her," explained Dr. Msinjili.

After some discussion, Lowassa agreed to call both the regional commissioner for Arusha and the district councillor for Miriam's village. Both men were also Maasai. Lowassa promised one or both of them would call Dr. Msinjili back.

By now, it was nearing midnight, but Dr. Msinjili made one more call to Jean and Marv, who offered to do whatever they could to help. They too knew Miriam from her days at the

Maasai Secondary School for Girls. Then the headmaster-turned-unlikely-hero lay in bed, the phone by his pillow, and waited.

At nearly two in the morning, the phone sprang to life again. Arusha's regional commissioner called to tell Dr. Msinjili that he was sending his car to Monduli with two armed police officers. They would be at Dr. Msinjili's front door before six to pick him up and take him to Miriam's village.

On the heels of this call, the district councillor called to say he would arrive at Miriam's engang at six o'clock to start negotiating with the family—to help them understand that Miriam still wanted to go to college.

For a few brief, restless hours, Dr. Msinjili tried to sleep.

At six thirty the next morning, just as Dr. Msinjili was preparing to leave with the police officers, the district councillor once again called Dr. Msinjili to warn him that more than fifty morani with spears and other weapons had surrounded the engang.

"Please, dear headmaster, you cannot bring the police here. You cannot even bring the regional commissioner's car here. It will be recognized and attacked. I am negotiating, but they are very hostile. This will take time," the man cautioned.

At this point, Dr. Msinjili called Jean and Marv to explain the situation and ask if they would be willing to drive him and the police officers to the engang. They needed a plain, unmarked vehicle. Even the school's truck had the school's logo emblazoned on the door. Jean and Marv immediately agreed. By seven, they were on their way.

For two hours, they drove toward Miriam's engang, short volleys of small talk punctuated by long stretches of tense silence. As usual, Jean drove and Marv rode in the very back of the vehicle, where the luggage would normally have gone, quietly writing in his notebook and waiting for the moment when his stature might be called upon. Though armed, the police officers were slight, as was Dr. Msinjili. Marv stood nearly a foot taller than anyone else in the car, but even he seemed nervous about what this day might hold.

At nine o'clock, Jean pulled over where the main road inter-sected the rough dirt road out to Miriam's engang. She turned off the ignition, and they began to wait.

Throughout the day, Dr. Msinjili and the district councillor exchanged a handful of messages, all indicating that negotiations were still taking place, that the family was still hostile, and that Dr. Msinjili and the group with him should remain out of sight.

The tense silence in the vehicle stretched on and on.

At three o'clock, Dr. Msinjili jumped as his phone rang. "It's the district councillor," he said warily before answering the phone.

A tense voice came over the line: "I am through with negoti-ations. They have agreed to let me leave the engang with the girl. I have told the family that you are here to take her back to school. She is being allowed to leave on the condition that she will eventually come back to the village."

With that, the district councillor instructed Dr. Msinjili to drive within a half mile of the engang, to leave the police and the wazungu in the car, and to walk toward the engang alone.

As the late afternoon sun radiated off the arid, acacia-dotted landscape surrounding Miriam's engang, Dr. Msinjili, in his typical attire—a button-down shirt, dark slacks, and sensible shoes—steadily and deliberately walked toward the engang, his head bowed as if in thoughtful meditation. It was as if he didn't see the district councillor and Miriam walking away from the engang followed by what seemed almost like a mirage. For out of the landscape behind them, a great wave of red mashuka fluttered in the breeze as too many men to count followed the Maasai girl who refused to stay put.

Dr. Msinjili did see them though, and he saw Miriam too. Dressed in traditional Maasai attire, rather than the school uniform he usually saw her wearing, she stood taller than he remembered, her jaw set firmly, and her face tilted toward the sun. A simple string of white beads swung from her neck. Though she'd been at the very center of these negotiations, it was likely that she hadn't spoken a single word today—these negotiations were the realm of men—so instead she seemed to speak with her body. She would not bend. She would not turn back. She wore her Maasai heritage with the hubris common to her tribe—her appearance left little doubt that she would walk her own path in spite of the fact that she was Maasai, and because she was Maasai.

They met halfway between Jean and Marv's Land Cruiser and the engang. Dr. Msinjili greeted the district councillor in the customary way, and then he walked onward right up to the substantial group of Maasai warriors—a short, mild-mannered man with a spine of steel amid an expanse of tall, sinewy warriors. He found Miriam's brother, greeted him with a slight bow, and thanked him for agreeing to let Miriam go to school.

The young man begrudgingly nodded, and then Dr. Msinjili smiled and, though he was the elder, offered his outstretched hands to the man in a show of respect. Their eyes met, they shook hands, and then Dr. Msinjili walked away with Miriam.

Miriam would eventually return to this village, but not before studying at Tanzania's Institute for Rural Development Planning and starting her own nonprofit organization to assist the Maasai with planning for their own future. This work would take her to the United Nations Permanent Forum on Indigenous Issues to discuss economic and social development, her culture, the environment, education, and health and human rights. Though she returned home, she never married the man her brother chose for her. She chose for herself.

Miriam was among the first Maasai girls Dr. Msinjili helped, but she would be far from the last. After Miriam's dramatic return to Monduli, she lived on and off in Dr. Msinjili's home for the next several years, as did many other Maasai girls, until Dr. Msinjili and I, with the help of many generous donors, raised enough money to fund the Safe Initiative, which provides housing, training, and mentoring to girls like Miriam.

Dr. Msinjili is now called "*babu*," or "grandfather," by the girls in his care, and he remains committed to helping Maasai girls gain education and economic self-sufficiency, so much so that in 2010, only one year after he retired as headmaster of Moringe Sokoine Secondary School, he was called out of retirement by Bishop Laiser and Edward Lowassa, by then former prime minister of Tanzania, to serve as headmaster at the Maasai Secondary School for Girls.

◾◾◾◾◾◾◾◾

That day, though, as I sat in Dr. Msinjili's office feeling as if I could not say goodbye to Miriam, having just walked the same path with Dinah, I don't think either of us realized the ways our lives would remain intertwined. Miriam and other girls like her would bind us together. This work, finding a safe place for the most vulnerable, at-risk girls, would be our joint calling—that thing that would not leave us. Together, we would change lives, though Dr. Msinjili is due the credit. I would just raise money and show up from time to time to witness the work.

Though I didn't realize it until many years later, during my time in Tanzania I became one of Dr. Msinjili's girls too—one of the young women whose lives he would irrevocably shape with his kindness and wisdom. I have learned more than I can say from this remarkable man, this babu.

CHAPTER 26:

NEVER SAY GOODBYE

At the beginning of December, just two weeks before our departure, Mark and I dragged the trunks we'd brought to Tanzania
into our living room where they stood in a neat row and gaped at
us—a daily reminder of our departure. We'd started filling them
with the objects that represented our lives here—the ilturesh I'd
bought from Bibi Ruth; the dress Moringe's staff had given me as
a wedding gift; a stack of handmade baskets I'd picked up at mar-
kets here and there; and a short, bead-encrusted ebony stick with
a substantial knob on one end, a rungu that Gideon had given to
Mark last week—just in case we ran into any trouble without him
in America. I imagined the latter with amusement.

I didn't know it yet, but years from now I would open one of
these trunks where I still stored kitenge fabric, and Tanzania would
waft out at me. I would sit back on my heels, tears filling my eyes,
and I would breathe in deeply as dust and smoke mingled with
jacaranda blossoms, dry grass, leather, and memories.

Already, Mark and I knew we wouldn't fill up all the trunks
we'd brought over. Some of them would remain here. A few of them

had already traveled back to the United States with visitors who'd offered to courier them. Still, we would leave Tanzania with fewer belongings than we had arrived with. We'd brought many things we didn't need—foolish items that had little use here, such as the portable stove that required fuel we couldn't purchase in Tanzania. At the time, we didn't know any better. Most of these things, we'd already sent home.

Then there were the other items we'd brought that were so valuable that we would purposely leave them behind. To Jean and Marv, we would give our pizza pan with a recipe that had been well tested in Tanzania, though Marv claimed it wouldn't taste the same if it didn't come out of our chicken-wire-clad oven.

To Doug and Linda, we would leave a stack of DVDs that Mark and I had watched while huddled together around his laptop. Since our collection was limited, we'd watched the same movies so many times that we'd created a whole inside language based on movie quotes. Some Saturday mornings, we would try to cook breakfast while using only cinematic expressions from our deep knowledge of about ten films.

Mr. Kwayu's eldest son would get Mark's laptop. My earnest, good-natured husband had spent many hours coaching the keen young man on how to use it, while also introducing him to Italian-style espresso, which was Mark's answer to Tanzania's pervasive instant Africafé coffee. The stovetop espresso maker, though, Mark wouldn't give up. It would return to America with us.

The Maasai Secondary School for Girls would get most of my clothes and shoes, which I imagined my students would wear around campus on the weekends long after I'd gone, and Moringe's library, for which Mark's parents had raised funds to build, would get almost all of our books.

Before we'd left for Tanzania, Mark had carefully packed more than one hundred pounds of math textbooks into the United States Postal Service's M-bags, or large cream-colored canvas duffel bags designed for cheaply sending printed materials overseas. These books would now go to Simon Panga, the head of Moringe's math department, with whom Mark had developed a close relationship based on their mutual desire to teach students a love of mathematics. I'd often seen them walking across campus together, deep in conversation, and I always knew they were probably talking about how to change the pervasive negative opinion toward mathematics among Tanzanian students. Since Mark regarded his books as if they were dear old friends, I knew leaving his treasure trove behind was a testimony to how much he cared about Simon and the math program at Moringe. This bond reminded me, once again, of the many tested-by-fire friends we would leave in Tanzania.

Today, in fact, the goodbyes would begin, for it was my last day of teaching at the Maasai Secondary School for Girls. I planned to give my students a small token of my presence among them. Weeks earlier, I'd hired Gideon's wife, Mama Tumaini, to make more than fifty identical beaded bracelets. Today, I would take the hand of each of the girls before me and slide a beaded Maasai bracelet around her wrist to match the one I already wore around my own.

Over the upcoming weekend, most of my students would return home for the December school break, and I would board a plane that would take me thousands of miles from Monduli. I didn't know if I would ever return, nor if I would see any of them again, but I wanted them to know, if only symbolically, that I'd been marked by my experiences among them. Though we came from vastly different places, we'd lived, and grown, and learned together for a brief but important moment in time. I knew I was the better for this, and I hoped they were too.

As I stood behind the simple wooden table at the front of the classroom for the last time, I realized that though I'd been counting the days until my departure, now that it was upon me I didn't know how to say goodbye. I folded my hands in front of me and looked down. My stomach felt unsettled, and saliva filled my mouth.

Whether from emotion or another bout of food-borne illness, or a combination of the two, I realized I felt sick.

I hadn't rehearsed what I would say today. Nevertheless, I cleared my throat and looked up at them. They already knew today was my final day on campus, and they knew this was the end of our last hour together. Tears streamed down Neng'ida's face as she looked at me. Paulina's head rested in her hands, and Riziki slowly rocked back and forth in her chair.

I felt like doing the same thing, but I knew my composure was like a leaky dam held together by temporary, ill-conceived patches. I'd done my best to shut down my emotions in the last few weeks, knowing that if a single tear squeezed its way through the barricade, the whole dam would break loose. Right now, I couldn't even imagine what might pour forth, only that it would be powerful and unstoppable, so I swallowed hard and scanned each row of desks before me and the girls, now nearly young women, who filled them.

I just had to get through this, I told myself. I just had to keep breathing.

I'd stood before these girls many times trying to imagine myself in their shoes, just as I had that very first day when I'd stood outside the classroom examining their tidy rows of neatly polished black loafers, Oxfords, and Mary Janes. *What would I do in their shoes?* I'd wondered that day and many days since then.

What would it be like to come from a Maasai engang to this school? How would I feel if a foreign teacher spoke to me in a language I'd never heard before? What if I faced a forced marriage? What would happen if my future depended upon the results of a single exam? Who would I turn to if my family disowned me because I wanted to go to school?

Had I been born here, to Maasai parents, my life would have been vastly different. This I knew without question. The choices I enjoyed—the life I lived—was nothing more than the good fortune afforded to those born in Western countries. There were many things I loved about Tanzania, but I lived in the sober knowledge that for me, Tanzania had always been a choice. If I wanted to escape the drought, I could leave. If I got critically ill, I would be airlifted out. If I needed more money, I could always find a well-paid job.

I knew the reasons for this were nothing more than the station and place of my birth. Now that I was returning to my Western life in America, I felt guilty, as if by leaving these girls and this community, I was taking the easy route out, and perhaps I was, but I'd always known this was a two-year post. My presence here was never meant to be permanent.

Nonetheless, I now wondered what I could possibly say that would offer these young women hope and encouragement in the face of all the challenges that I knew many of them would endure. In the end, I don't remember what I said, and the exact words aren't important. I want to believe it was something eloquent and profound—something about how proud I was of all they'd learned and accomplished, or something about my hope that each of them would pursue her dreams. That is probably what I said, but I don't remember. I might not have said anything at all.

What I do remember is slowly walking down each row, taking each girl's hand, and looking her in the eye with the best smile I could muster. I wanted them to remember me smiling, not crying, and this took a herculean effort. I could feel the tension painfully swelling behind my eyes into a massive, unavoidable headache. Truth be told, I was feeling more and more awful by the moment, and I felt increasingly certain that it was more than just the emotion of the day. I began to think that I was truly sick, but nevertheless I pressed on.

As I handed each girl a bracelet, one or two asked me to place it on her wrist. Others quietly thanked me. A few stood and hugged me. As I went row by row, more and more sniffles filled the silence.

I knew that some of them probably thought of me as they might think of an older sister, or perhaps a devoted, benevolent aunt.

Others appreciated me as a teacher. A handful of them thought of me as a guardian angel, not because I was necessarily worthy of this title, but because I represented the many Americans who'd made this school possible. Still others didn't really understand me at all. For these students, I was still too foreign and too unconventional by Tanzanian standards to be taken seriously. These girls were probably glad to see me go. I imagined a few of them questioned my motives, wondering why I'd come so far to teach in a culture so vastly different from my own. Sometimes I'd wondered the same thing, but I'd stayed anyway.

I left the classroom that day surrounded by a small group of them. They held my hands and touched my face. They draped their arms over my shoulders, and none of this felt uncomfortable anymore. I understood these gestures as simple expressions of our sisterhood, even if in my own culture they might have felt intrusive and awkward. These young women merely wanted to *sindikiza*, or escort, me off campus. In Tanzania, I'd learned long ago that it was a polite and common practice to walk a friend, a relative, or a guest part of the way home—to sindikiza.

As we slowly meandered toward the gate, I couldn't help but think about the great privilege it had been to sindikiza these girls for a brief time on their journeys to womanhood. I'd learned so much from them about courage and strength and determination. They had taught me that wealth and poverty, blessings and hardship don't have the clear lines I'd originally thought they did. These girls, as well as Dr. Msinjili, Mr. Kwayu, Simon, Gideon, Mama Mkuu, and many other Tanzanians, had taught me the true meaning of *ujamaa*, or a "familyhood," that extends well beyond lineage and pedigree. We'd walked with each other, hand in hand, and I realized without doubt that though I would leave this place, it would never leave me.

By the time I reached Moringe, I felt weak and queasy. My stomach kept cramping up in waves, and the pain behind my eyes seemed to be keeping time with my heartbeat—a pervasive, drumbeat-like throb. Though I didn't yet know it, the full weight of the grief and loss and despair that would overwhelm me in the coming months was just beginning to settle over me, and it was as if my body rejected this sorrow as it might reject a virulent bacteria, with everything at its disposal—fever, aches, pains, diarrhea, and vomiting. I knew the fever, aches, and pains were already upon me, and I worried that the other two were soon to follow.

However, my students at Moringe had spent the last several weeks planning a goodbye party for me that I simply couldn't miss. When I'd passed by the classroom on my way down to the girls' school earlier that day, they'd been hanging streamers and setting up a sound system. They'd pushed all the desks to the sides of the room and put the chairs in neat rows facing a podium they'd dragged in from somewhere. They'd been atwitter with excitement but had quickly shooed me away, indicating that my presence was spoiling the surprise.

I'd sent the school truck into town to buy several crates of soda the day before—my contribution to the party. I'd stopped by to make sure that it had arrived, and it had. Though probably less meaningful than a beaded bracelet, a bottle of soda was still a rare treat for many of these students, and this would be my parting gift—Coca-Cola, Fanta, Sprite, or, my favorite, Stoney Tangawizi, a hot ginger soda. Right now, however, I felt sure I couldn't stomach any one of them.

I heard the party well before I reached it. The rhythm of typical celebratory Swahili anthems recorded and played at alarming volumes through an old, worn-out, popping and wheezing sound system greeted me. Today, I thought to myself, a power outage might not be so bad. I always found these types of events somewhat puzzling. Why, I wondered, was a sound system required for any proper celebration in Tanzania? I knew I'd be required to give a speech, also blared through this sound system, even though I stood at the front of this classroom every other day and spoke in an unamplified yet clearly audible voice.

Tanzanian events like this one followed a certain pattern. I'd learned this from graduation ceremonies, other going-away parties, and my own Tanzanian wedding reception. There would be a master of ceremonies, likely William, a well-liked class leader, who would have a ratiba, or schedule of speeches, music, and other presentations. These schedules always slightly amused me because, though required for every event, they were rarely followed. Most of the time, celebrations like these started late, which meant the carefully planned timeslots were wrong even before the event began. Speakers or musicians were tardy, others were long-winded, and in the end, the schedule, which had been so carefully developed so as to ensure each and every important person had his or her moment at the microphone, ended up on the floor, trampled upon by the way things really work in Tanzania.

I imagined the ratiba as some kind of remnant of colonialism, just another practice that seemed very important to nearly everyone, but that made no sense to anyone because life simply didn't follow a schedule in Tanzania. I imagined fifty years ago some stiff Brit insisting on schedules and timetables, and now everybody in the country thought that's just what you did, whether it made sense or not. Unfortunately, it seemed the country's education system followed the same pattern.

Thankfully, as I walked into the classroom with a feverish yet earnest smile, the group of students, all boys, running the sound system turned it down. The music faded to a dull roar, and everyone began shuffling around until we were all seated and awaiting the master of ceremonies. I'd been escorted to a special cushioned chair behind a table right next to the podium. Nearly immediately, a warm Coca-Cola appeared in front of me with a straw in it. As I took a dainty sip, I had to breathe in deeply through my nose to avoid choking on it. Though I didn't want to be rude, there was no way I could eat or drink anything more.

William, as the master of ceremonies, kicked off the event by welcoming all the students and me. He then introduced a group of six girls, also my students, who shuffled into the room two by two, swaying back and forth, and singing. Their little parade did a loop around the room and ended in front of the head table, where I was seated. At the conclusion, they all curtsied to me and took their seats. I nodded and clapped enthusiastically as I wiped sweat from my brow.

This is not good, I thought to myself. *Not good at all.*

I started counting backward from one hundred to keep from thinking about how much I felt like I was going to throw up.

After the singing, there were two speeches. Martha gave the first one. In class, Martha always sat in the front row, her intent eyes focused on whatever I said or did. She didn't miss much. Though I suspected Martha always knew the answers to my questions, her self-conscious nature meant she only raised her hand about half the time.

This was an important difference between the Maasai Secondary School for Girls and Moringe Sokoine Secondary School—here girls were self-conscious and reserved, I suspected because they had to both compete with the boys and also impress them. It seemed the world over that very smart, vocal women more often than not threatened men, rather than impressed them, and so it was at Moringe.

Martha was certainly among my top students, but one wouldn't know it from watching her. In fact, it surprised me that she would stand in front of her fellow students and give a speech, but now she stood before them confidently reading from a sheet of paper. She thanked me for all I'd done for the school and for the students. She said she would never forget me and that she would miss me.

By this time, much of what she said failed to register as more than simple words strung together. I just kept counting backward.

The next speaker, to my great surprise, was Clarence, the boy I'd mistakenly identified to Mr. Kwayu during my first week of teaching at Moringe. The same boy who'd wrongly endured corporal punishment because of my mistake. Perhaps it was the sickness doing its work on me, but I almost expected him to now publicly berate me for this mistake. *This could be his chance to get me back,* I thought, but deep down I knew he would never do this. I'd come to know Clarence as a gentle, eager boy who, though we'd gotten off to a bumpy start, really wanted nothing more than to impress me with his ability to learn and speak English. During class, he'd often call me over to his desk to ask me a question, or to show me his work. I always took special care to be as kind to him as I could and to give him extra attention. I figured I owed him this, at least.

The tenor of his speech followed that of Martha's. He thanked me for teaching him English. He also said he'd miss me. The rest, I can't remember, because as I reached the twenties on my downward march to zero, my mouth began to water so much that I knew, without question, that I would be sick. I held my breath, waited for him to sit back down, and wondered if maybe now the celebration would be over so I could sneak off to my house and empty the contents of my stomach in peace, but I'd forgotten: my name was still on the ratiba.

As William asked me to say a few words, I urgently stood, but rather than walking toward the podium, I raced for the door. My face felt hot, and I feared my quick departure would gravely offend my dear students who had spent so much time planning the event, but truly I had no choice.

I reached the weeds just around the corner from the block of classrooms before I doubled over and heaved. As the second wave left my stomach, I realized, at first with horror and then with amazement, that I was not alone. Martha and two other girls from my class had followed me outside. None of them said anything, but Martha put her hand on my back as I bent over with my hands on my knees, tears streaming down my face. I felt so embarrassed. I'd ruined the party and sullied their kind gesture.

As I stood upright, another student appeared with a bucket of sand and tossed it over my vomit. One of the girls handed me a bottle of water, and another a tissue. All this they did in somber silence. They seemed to know just what to do, and I was reminded that sickness was more commonplace and visible here than anywhere I'd experienced it before. Because of this, people were used to caring for one another. They knew how to handle situations like this one. They weren't embarrassed by what had happened. They understood it.

Students were frequently absent with malaria, or dysentery, or even pneumonia. It was commonplace to ask people about their health as part of daily conversation, and nobody was ever surprised to hear that you had a bad stomach, or that your head hurt. It happened to everyone, and it happened frequently.

As my mind scrambled to find a way to recover from this—to apologize for my condition and for ruining the party—I thought about how a group of American high school students might have responded to what had just happened. I suspected they would not now be standing around me, taking me by the arms, shushing my clumsy apologies, and shepherding me up the hill to where they knew I lived. That was the parting gift I received from Moringe's students.

The next forty-eight hours passed by in a blur. There was more sickness and more goodbyes, and by the time Doug and Linda arrived, liked bookends on our experience, to pack up our belongings and take us to the airport, I felt like a shell of my former self, as if I'd been hollowed out completely.

The night before, Mark and I had stopped by Mr. Kwayu's house to say farewell. He'd taken the opportunity for one last sindikiza, walking with us the relatively short distance between his house and ours. We'd mostly walked in silence, until he'd quietly said, "You know, we never say 'goodbye' here. We only say 'see you later,' so I'm not going to say goodbye to you."

He was right. In Swahili, it is common to say *tutaonana*, see you later, and that had become my mantra in these last hours in Monduli: I won't say goodbye. I'll only say see you later.

As Doug and Linda's Land Rover bumped down the hill away from Americastle for the last time, I turned and looked out the back window. Gideon stood on the stoop watching us go, his shoulders hunched in a way I'd never seen before. "Tutaonana, Gideon," I whispered to myself as tears streamed down my face. "Tutaonana."

I reached for Mark's hand as I turned and faced forward, toward whatever was coming. I knew we were leaving with mixed feelings, both ready to return home, if for nothing but the creature comforts we would have, and yet unwilling to leave behind all we'd learned and experienced with a group of people we held dear. Neither of us had any idea what we would do once we arrived in the United States. We didn't have a place to live or jobs, and already we felt adrift as if we belonged neither here nor there.

Little did we know, this was only the beginning of our displacement. Though we were welcome guests in Tanzania, we would come to feel like strangers in our own country.

CHAPTER 27:

NO LONGER A GIRL

Ten years is a long time, but it passed by seemingly without my noticing. When I think back on the first months and years after we returned from Tanzania, I struggle to remember much of anything. It was as if a thick veil had descended over those early years back in the United States.

Mostly, I remember feeling isolated and alone, as if nothing we'd experienced in Tanzania translated to our American lives. The stories we told about our students, or about our experiences, would usually be met with pity, alarm, silence, or, worse yet, disinterest. Friends and colleagues would change the subject when we spoke. Family would express worry that we'd fallen into depression, and in truth, we had. We'd lost something profound, and we didn't know how to get it back. Gradually, to survive, we started compartmentalizing our lives in Tanzania. That was then. This is now. And Mark and I desperately clung to one another because it seemed that we were the only ones who understood.

During these years, we would hear sparse reports from Tanzania. Jean and Marv would visit once a year, and for a few days, we would feel we'd reentered a special time and place in our past. Mr. Kwayu, Simon Panga, and Dr. Msinjili would all visit the United States, and we would have the chance to try to show them the same hospitality they'd shown us in their country. Eventually, a handful of former students from the Maasai Secondary School for Girls would make it to America. They would remind me why I'd gone to Tanzania in the first place and jolt me awake to the reality that, though I was far away, that community was still a part of me, and I a part of it. This would change everything for me.

■ ■ ■ ■ ■ ■ ■

I sat alone in a dimly lit gymnasium filled with good Midwesterners. Gray-haired men wore their newest Wranglers, pant legs pressed down the center by the sturdy women who accompanied them in Norwegian sweaters or woolen coats. Fresh-faced young girls wore frocks that covered their knees, and everybody seemed to know everybody else, except me.

Though I now counted myself as a Midwesterner—Mark and I had been living in Minneapolis for nearly a decade—I still felt like an outsider as I scanned the faces around me. It seemed my time in Tanzania had created a perpetual flightiness in my personality—an inability to settle in and call any place home. I watched as people smiled warmly at one another, large families gathered together and chatted, and college-aged kids dashed up to the top of the bleachers in talkative groups.

I'd come alone, in part, on purpose. I wanted to be the proverbial fly on the wall in this crowd—to watch and observe, to blend in and remember, to be among the handful of people in the room who knew the story of today's single Tanzanian graduate.

Mark had offered to skip work and join me for a long weekend away, but I felt like I needed to drive the three and a half hours from Minneapolis to Moorhead on my own. I needed to sit anonymously in this crowd and remember a girl I'd met when she was just barely past childhood—a girl who'd sat in my first Form I classroom, smiling shyly at me, her hair clipped short, in a new school uniform, unable to understand a single word I spoke and yet enamored and intrigued by the differences between us. I remembered how, so many years ago, she'd reached up and wrapped a curly lock of my hair around her finger as she'd nervously giggled. I also remembered how we'd held hands that last day, as she and several other students had walked me, for the final time, to the school's gate.

Today, Neng'ida would graduate from college, and though I'd had only a very small part in her education, I found myself almost bursting with emotion. My palms felt sweaty, and a persistent lump sat squarely in my throat. I found it difficult to sit still as I waited for the ceremony to begin, so I fiddled with the Maasai bracelet I still wore on my wrist.

I'd spent the last ten years grappling with questions about how education would really benefit my students, and how their education would affect the Maasai. In Tanzania, I'd wanted to do the right thing, but sometimes a vexing voice in my head would ask how this education was any different from the forced assimilation of North America's indigenous peoples some hundred years ago. I knew a handful of Maasai men had helped to establish the school because they sought self-determination for all their people, but I also knew the realities of a postcolonial education system. I could readily cite the international studies on girls' education that outlined its many benefits. However, deep in my gut, I felt unqualified to answer these questions, as if it were almost inappropriate for me to answer them, and as if history were yet to bear out the results.

I regularly wondered if education had relegated my students to lives of unhappiness and unrealizable dreams, or if they'd found ways to integrate what they'd learned into their own cultural realities. I wanted to know if they'd found jobs, or love, or some measure of equality—I wanted to know if they'd achieved their goals. I'd been waiting and watching for these ten years, waiting for them to grow up, go out into the world, and report back. Neng'ida marked the beginning of this, and I knew she would hold answers to what had happened to many others.

Neng'ida knew I would be here today, but we hadn't seen each other since my last day at the Maasai Secondary School for Girls, nearly ten years earlier. When I'd emailed her to ask if I could attend her graduation, which I'd heard about through the grapevine, I'd felt uncertain about how she would respond. In typical Tanzanian fashion, she had been gracious and welcoming, yet I didn't know what to expect when I saw her. I imagined she would look different than I remembered, but I figured it wouldn't be difficult to pick her out in this predominantly white crowd. I kept scanning the room looking for any person of color. I knew that a couple of other Maasai Secondary School for Girls graduates might be in attendance, but I didn't see anyone who looked familiar.

I'd heard about Neng'ida's graduation through an old friend— one of the pastors who had married Mark and me and who now served as the campus pastor at Concordia College, a small Lutheran college that was the alma mater of David Simonson, one of the founders of the Maasai Secondary School for Girls. For several years, Concordia had been granting a few highly sought-after scholarships to the top-performing students from the girls' school, and Neng'ida had been among the lucky recipients.

As the opening notes of "Pomp and Circumstance" began, I spotted my friend leading the faculty and graduates into the gymnasium. He wore a white pastor's robe and a bright red stole—*The color of the Maasai*, I thought to myself.

As I eagerly scanned the faces of the graduates, looking for Neng'ida, I thought about the differences between this graduation and the ones I'd witnessed at the Maasai Secondary School for Girls. I smiled to myself as I wondered how all these Midwesterners would respond to the striking spectacle of fifty Maasai girls, dressed in full garb—beads dripping from nearly every part of their bodies—heads held high, processing to drums and celebratory Swahili calls and responses. I wondered if under her traditional black cap and gown, Neng'ida might be wearing this very thing, and I wondered if she too might be reflecting on a different graduation in a different place.

About halfway through the processional, I spotted her, and to me, she looked just as majestic as she would have had she been wearing all her Maasai beads. Though she wore a black mortarboard, I could see that her hair was long, held together in numerous tight braids that swung loosely to the middle of her back. Appropriately, even in the low light of the gymnasium, I could see that she'd dyed the ends of her braids a subtle shade of red.

Though I'd known Neng'ida to be a determined student, as I watched her among her fellow graduates, it seemed nearly unfathomable to me how far she had come. I remembered her as a struggling student who fell somewhere in the lower half of her class, but after I'd left, she'd obviously quickly risen to the top. Now she seemed even taller than I remembered. Though she was still thin, her face had a soft roundness about it, and she carried herself no longer as the shy, uncertain girl I had known, but as a proud, regal Maasai woman.

This is when I realized that, without noticing it, I'd begun to cry. My vision blurred as tears streamed down my face. *She is one among them*, I thought to myself. *One for whom anything is now possible*.

I eagerly waited through dozens of names for hers to be read. As she walked across the stage to collect her diploma, I stood and clapped as loudly as I could. I whistled and jumped up and down as I heard the familiar ululations from one or two Tanzanians who must have been hiding in the crowd somewhere. Those around me stared, but I didn't care. I thought she deserved a standing ovation. When she retook her seat among the graduates, I sat down too, and that's when the tears really started flowing.

The emotion caught me off guard. True, I often found it hard not to shed a tear or two at big events such as weddings and graduations, but this level of emotion seemed graceless and ostentatious in this reserved, buttoned-up crowd. I found comfort in my anonymity even as the woman next to me discreetly handed me a tissue from her purse, patted me on the arm, and asked if I was okay.

"I'm just so happy," I blubbered, and I was. I felt as if the universe had just whispered in my ear, "All's well that ends well, my dear." And so it was.

After the ceremony, I ducked into the bathroom to powder my puffy eyes and reapply some mascara before I set off to find Neng'ida. She'd invited me to a reception being held in her honor by none other than the president of the college and my old pastor friend, but I hoped to find her before I went to the reception. In truth, I was nervous about seeing her, and I thought the anonymity of the large crowd might be a better place to first meet her, rather than in the quiet confines of an intimate reception being held by the college's president.

Chaos reigned in the entryway of the gymnasium. Families gathered around their graduates in tight circles or moved to and fro looking for them. Some people were pushing through the throng trying to get to the exit, and here and there groups of graduates made plans for post-event parties. I took a place along the wall near the exit and kept an eye out for Neng'ida, as people moved past me in waves.

Just as I was beginning to give up hope, thinking maybe I should just go over to the reception by myself, I heard a squeal that snapped my head, and everyone else's in the lobby, in the direction of its origin. It was Neng'ida. She was looking right at me with her hands over her mouth, as if she was trying to hold in the squeal that had obviously just escaped. As I smiled at her, she started jumping up and down, her arms wide open, and she yelled, "Mwalimu, mwalimu . . . it's you. Oh my gosh! It's you."

As everyone in the lobby watched, she ran toward me and gathered me in a huge hug that lifted my feet off the ground. I laughed and cried at the same time. Neng'ida squealed again with delight. As she put me back down, another former student, Riziki, who was also now a student at Concordia, emerged from the crowd with a series of ululations and wrapped both of us in her arms. We stood like this for what felt like a long time, without words, in a little huddle of joy.

Soon every Tanzanian in the crowd surrounded us, a small bunch of about half a dozen former Maasai Secondary School for Girls students and a few of their friends. I knew only Neng'ida and Riziki, but I spent time meeting and greeting everyone before we all walked over to the reception together. For the first time in years, I felt as if I belonged.

The next day, I met Neng'ida for chai, just the two of us. After we'd been in touch via email about her graduation, I'd asked her if I could interview her because I was considering writing a book about my experiences living and teaching in Tanzania. She had willingly agreed, and this is when I first heard her full story. The previous night, I'd placed her story in the general narrative I understood represented most of the girls who attended the school. That day, I understood the specifics.

She told me that her father had arranged for her marriage, just as she was about to finish primary school. As she relayed her story, it was as if I were sitting with her in a stark primary school classroom so very far from the ivory towers of Concordia, worrying about how she might continue her education to secondary school. My stomach churned as she told me about how she'd agonized over running away from home, and how after she did, her mother and her husband-to-be had come to the school to find her.

I sighed deeply when she told me how her mother had suffered for the decision to allow her to stay in school. With her eyes downcast, Neng'ida said more than once, "My father was furious," and I had a hunch that his fury might have manifested itself as more than harsh words.

She told me that over the years, her mother had stood by her decision, and in fact had been so proud of Neng'ida that she'd sought education for more of her children. She'd had seven girls and three boys—only two older than Neng'ida. Her mother's desire to educate her children had driven an irrevocable wedge between Neng'ida's mother and father, until eventually her father had forced her mother to leave the engang. With financial support from Neng'ida, her mother had built an independent engang in a nearby village. With a mix of pride and humility, Neng'ida quietly told me that she and her mother continued to support many of her siblings and relatives in their education.

"She is my mentor. She is so wise, and I talk to her whenever I get stuck," Neng'ida told me with a nostalgic smile.

As she finished her story, Neng'ida's voice grew hushed. She revealed that only a handful of months earlier, she'd spoken to her father by telephone. He'd been very sick, and in this sickness he'd asked to speak to Neng'ida. Though he didn't go so far as to commend her education, he did ask for her financial support, something that indicated to Neng'ida that he understood her success and felt confident that she would be there to support the family even after he was gone. Two days later, he'd died. Though she didn't cry when she told me this, the deep lines in her face and the redness around her eyes conveyed that Neng'ida's feelings about her father remained complex—a mix of love and loss, respect and regret.

This, all before the age of twenty-five, I thought to myself—the very age when I'd arrived in Tanzania, a young, naive girl ready to save the world. In the presence of Neng'ida, it seemed clear that I was well out of my league.

We spent another hour talking about the future and Neng'ida's hopes and fears for herself, for her family, for the Maasai Secondary School for Girls, and for the Maasai people. For herself, she hoped for a career in health care and perhaps a master's degree. She worried about finding a good job and what life after all these years of school might hold for her. She worried about her mother and her siblings and when she might see them again. Clearly, she felt responsible for their well-being, even from so great a distance.

When I asked her about the Maasai Secondary School for Girls, she responded, "That school is everything to me."

Then she paused for a long moment, looking at me and collecting her thoughts.

She continued, "From where I started to where I am is unbelievable. Some people say that educating Maasai girls means the destruction of our culture, but look where the world is headed. Already, we are not the same as we used to be. We will not remain primitive forever, and I don't know what that means for our culture. We will never completely westernize, but it is impossible to go back too. We are caught in the middle.

"If you leave us behind, worrying that our culture will be destroyed, you deny us the chance to choose. The Maasai are still here, and we want and need the resources to take care of our own families. We want and need to make our own decisions, and school is the pathway to this. When I tell people that I am one of the Maasai girls' school graduates, they expect more from me. Already, we are known all over the country. Without that school, so many girls would have no chance. That school is everything to me . . . it is everything to us."

I took her hand, squeezed it, and replied, "I am amazed by you, and that school has meant everything to me too." In this moment, I knew I had to go back.

EPILOGUE:

MOVING MOUNTAINS
WITH TEASPOONS

I sat alone in the dark, waiting.

I'd emerged from the guesthouse as the first birds began to twitter in the coffee fields, even before subtle oranges and pinks began to swell across the sky. I wrapped a red woolen Maasai shuka more tightly about my shoulders. Though I wore a pair of flannel pajamas, the predawn air felt cool against my cheeks, and I needed the shuka for warmth, even though I could already smell the dusty dryness of a warm afternoon to come. I'd always appreciated that here in Monduli, mornings and evenings remained pleasantly cool and afternoons blissfully warm, almost year-round.

I sat on the front stoop with a cup of coffee waiting for the sounds I knew would soon emerge. First, the morning wakeup bell would chime for several minutes. The chatter of girls rolling out of bunk beds and getting ready for school would soon follow. Running water would hit the bottom of empty buckets. Here and there, a swift riff of Maa would rise above the din. Soon, the smell of wood-fired cooking stoves would waft this way. Not long after, I'd hear desks and chairs scraping across concrete floors as the classrooms were tidied before morning chapel. And then there would be sing-ing—a cappella in multipart harmony. Its beauty would arrest me, as it always did. I would hold my breath with my eyes closed and listen, riding the wave of memory.

Since Neng'ida's college graduation five years earlier, I'd returned to the Maasai Secondary School for Girls every year for a few weeks. Each time, I'd met with more and more former students. Several of them worked for NGOs out in Maasailand on issues of health care, girls' education, land rights, and microfinance. Miriam had represented the Maasai at the United Nations more than once. One was a pastor, another a lawyer. Already, there were two doctors and several nurses. More than a dozen were teaching. In fact, four now worked at the Maasai Secondary School for Girls. Many were already wives and mothers. I held their children, if they weren't too frightened of my white skin, as we talked about their lives.

As I held these children, I often thought of another child, who so many years earlier I'd held at Gideon's engang. Grace was now a student at the Maasai Secondary School for Girls, and Mark and I would continue to support her education for as far as she wanted to go. Gideon continued to work as the guard at Dr. Msinjili's house, now just down the hill from Americastle. Both Gideon and Grace had the same knowing, warm smile, and Mark and I looked for-ward to seeing them and Mama Tumaini every year. Often, Gideon insisted on having a feast for us at his engang. We were family, after all, he would say.

Dr. Msinjili seemed busier than ever as headmaster at the Maasai Secondary School for Girls, but not too busy to continue his work with the Safe Initiative. We would sit in his living room over dinner in the evenings, and he would tell us the stories of these remarkable young safe women.

As the singing ended, I smiled as I took another sip of my coffee and remembered the many cups of coffee I'd had at Jean and

Marv's house so many years ago. Now they lived in Seattle, but they'd spent more than a decade living at this school, and it seemed strange to be here without them.

"Here's to you, Jean and Marv," I whispered as I raised my mug.

I knew Marv would probably laugh at this, and at the notion that I found some of his words to be almost prophetic. He'd been the one who'd sat with me at one of my lowest points, just near the end of my tenure in Tanzania. I'd been on the verge of tears, nearly unable to speak, and discouraged by what felt like insurmountable odds. He'd served me a warm cup of coffee, and as he'd handed me a teaspoon, he'd said, "You know, Julie, we have to remember . . . we're moving a mountain one teaspoon at a time."

He didn't need to say more than that. The metaphor was apt. Nearly fifteen years later, I could see how the mountain had been moved, even though I recognized a lot of work remained to be done. Now the graduates of the Maasai Secondary School for Girls were helping to move that mountain.

As Mark came out of the house to join me on the stoop, we leaned against one another, shoulder to shoulder, and sat in silence. *Bega kwa bega*, I thought to myself. Then as now, we would face whatever came shoulder to shoulder. The two of us together, but not alone, shoulder to shoulder with a community we'd come to love.

"Do not be daunted by the enormity of the world's grief. Do justly, now. Love mercy, now. Walk humbly, now. You are not obligated to complete the work, but neither are you free to abandon it."

—Talmud[1]

AFTERWORD

I remain committed to Monduli and its schools, and I invite you to join me in supporting the ongoing work they are doing there. Founded in 1965, **Operation Bootstrap Africa** is the US-based nonprofit organization that has provided substantial funding to build and operate the Maasai Secondary School for Girls (also known as the **MaaSAE Girls' Lutheran Secondary School**).

As of 2015, the school had served approximately 1,125 girls, the majority of whom would not have had access to secondary school education without the girls' school. The school's completion rate is 75 percent, considerably higher than the 40 percent estimated for girls in sub-Saharan Africa.[1] More than 350 graduates (about 30 percent) have received postsecondary training at universities, colleges, and vocational schools. Seventy graduates hold university degrees. Approximately fifty graduates are working or training in health care fields; several are already doctors. More than 130 graduates have received teacher training or have education degrees. Nine students hold law degrees. Several graduates have founded NGOs.[2]

Even beyond this, there are now over a thousand educated Maasai women who have gained access to a very basic human right. They will likely have fewer, healthier children, who they'll ensure attend school. They will be more economically self-sufficient than their peers. Most will protect their sisters and daughters from genital cutting, and many will work for change within their communities.

Operation Bootstrap Africa has supported all this, but they have also partnered with many other Tanzanian communities to improve access to education, including providing infrastructure support and scholarships to students at **Moringe Sokoine Secondary School**. Over the past fifty years, Operation Bootstrap Africa has built more than 3,200 primary school classrooms, as well as numerous secondary school classrooms, libraries, dormitories, computer labs, and other school buildings.

The **Safe Initiative** has grown out of Dr. Msinjili's efforts to provide housing, scholarships, and mentoring to girls like Dinah and Miriam, who face forced marriages, rape, female genital cutting, or unplanned pregnancies. While most of the girls who attend the Maasai Secondary School for Girls are considered at risk, the girls in the Safe Initiative are at particularly high risk. They typically do not have supportive families and have already faced traumatic experiences at home, or they face imminent danger of harm should they return home. The program's goal is to support these very high-risk girls as they complete secondary school, technical training, or postsecondary options until they've received the qualifications and skills necessary to support themselves.

All proceeds from the sale of this book will support causes that uplift Maasai women and girls. If you would like to further support this effort, please visit my website at www.julietcutler.com to learn more. You can also view pictures of my time in Tanzania on the website.

Finally, please keep in mind that Monduli and its schools are real communities, with real people. Let them do their work. If you visit Tanzania, go to the national parks, take your pictures there, and invest in the economy as a tourist. If you want to invest in the schools, please consider a scholarship or a gift to the Safe Initiative.

Should you be interested in volunteering in Tanzania or elsewhere in the world, consider reading *When Helping Hurts*, a book by the founders of **The Chalmers Center,** a faith-based organization that trains groups to do community-led work. The book outlines a strategy for poverty alleviation based on the idea that sustainable improvements come not from the outside in, but from the inside out.[3]

Most importantly, remember that no matter who you are or where you live, you have the power to make a difference, whether it's in your own village, neighborhood, or across the globe. Bega kwa bega (shoulder to shoulder) we can work together to make the world a better place.

ACKNOWLEDGMENTS

Writing this book and reliving my experiences in Tanzania was as much of a journey as was the original experience of living there twenty years ago. On this journey, some of the characters were the same, and others joined the adventure for the first time.

This book would not have been possible without the insights, support, and encouragement provided by many of my former Maasai students and several other graduates of the Maasai Secondary School for Girls and Moringe Sokoine Secondary School. A special thank-you to Nashipai, Milla, Lilian, Nengai, Belinda, Neema, Melaisho, Nanyorri, Endasat, Kirangwa, Sarah, Margretu, Paulina, Rebecca, Scholastica, Beatrice, Martha, Elisipha, Esther, Elisifa, Selina, Faraja, Nai, and Upendo. Neng'ida and Miriam are composite characters whose stories come directly from these women. Dinah's name was changed to protect her privacy. Thank you also to Morrie Kershner, who first told me about the Maasai Secondary School for Girls.

To Dr. Msinjili, I owe you more gratitude than words can express. One day, I hope I will grow up to be as wise and generous as you. This story would have been much different without you. I am a better person because of all you've taught me. *Asante sana, mwalimu wangu na babu yangu.*

Thank you to Ndesa Kwayu, Daudi Msseemmaa, Damaris Parsitau, Nengai Benton, Doug Dybsetter, Marvin Kananen, Jean

Wahlstrom, Ken Cushner, Camille Griep, Deb Griffin, Lisa Brochu, Tim Merriman, Kathi Oetken, Phyllis Bleiweis, and Dr. Msinjili for reading early and later drafts of the manuscript. Your thoughtful comments and encouragement were invaluable.

This book was largely written while I lived in Amsterdam—a city whose creative, breezy spirit certainly shaped my work. Thank you to Bryan Monte and *Amsterdam Quarterly* for publishing the first excerpts of the book. Also, many thanks to the ladies of the American Women's Club of Amsterdam for hearing the first reading from the book.

Herta Feely, this book is better and my writing is stronger because of you. I couldn't have completed the manuscript without you. Thank you for being a trusted advisor, mentor, and friend, not to mention my editor. You have been a champion for this project, and that made me believe it was possible. I am also grateful to Brooke Warner, Crystal Patriarche, and the team at She Writes Press for creating a space for stories like mine. I value the community of women writers you've fostered and am proud to count myself among them.

Many other people provided words of encouragement, read portions of this book, agreed to interviews, or simply made the solitude of writing a little less lonesome. Thank you to the many friends, family, and colleagues who supported this endeavor.

To my parents, Dennis and Ann Rehrig, thank you for embracing this journey, even though you were scared, and for being willing to see the world through my eyes. Your support means everything to me.

To Arnie (in memoriam) and Jan Cutler, thank you for your enthusiasm and your willingness to always jump in with both feet. Thank you, Mama Mark, for being my traveling partner in 2014.

Finally, Mark Cutler, you are my rock. I am profoundly grateful for your presence in my life. Neither my experiences in Tanzania nor this book would have been possible without you. *Wewe ni baraka kwangu.*

SWAHILI / MAA TO ENGLISH GLOSSARY

Denotes Maa words; all other words are Swahili

asante: thank you
baba: father
babu: grandfather
baraka: blessing
baraza: a public meeting or school assembly
bati: corrugated steel usually used for roofing material
bega kwa bega: shoulder to shoulder
bibi: grandmother
boma: a traditional Maasai house/dwelling made of mud, sticks, grass, cow dung, and cow urine
bwana: man, sir
chai: tea; also colloquially used to refer to a bribe
chupi: underwear
daktari: doctor
dala dala: minibus
embolet*: temporary name given to a baby when it is born

enanga*: a black cloth worn over the shoulders by Maasai girls before and during circumcision

endito*: girl(s)

eng'udi*: long wooden staff carried by a Maasai man

engamuratani*: a Maasai woman who performs circumcisions on girls

engang*: a group of dwellings (see *boma*) sometimes surrounded by a fence of thorn bushes; a single Maasai man with all his wives and children live together as a family unit inside an engang

engisaisai*: changing Maasai culture through the adaptation of traditions

habari: news (when used in a question, as in "*Habari ya safari?*" it means "What news of your journey?")

hapana: no

haraka: hurry

hodi: announces one's arrival; often said multiple times instead of knocking on a door

ikuo*: appropriate response to the Maasai greeting *takwenya*

ilturesh*: beaded necklace worn by Maasai women

jiko: a small outdoor stove that burns butane, propane, or charcoal depending on the model

jioni: evening

kabisa: entirely, utterly

kanga: a lightweight colorful patterned fabric with a Swahili proverb stamped into the pattern; usually worn by Tanzanian women as a wrap over clothing to protect from dust and dirt; sometimes wrapped around the waist, worn as a shawl, or wrapped around the head

karibu / karibuni: welcome (*-u* to one person, *-uni* to more than one person); also you're welcome

kazi: work

keki: roasted goat served at a celebration such as a wedding

kesho: tomorrow

kiazi kikubwa: big potato

kichaa: crazy

kidogo: little, small

kitenge: colorful wax-print patterned fabric often used as a wrap or a shawl by Tanzanian women; also used to make clothing, curtains, table cloths, and assorted other items

kuondoka nyumbani: to leave home

kweli: really, truthfully

lala salama: sleep well

machungwa: oranges, as in the fruit

mafua: flu, chest congestion

maji: water

mama: mother

marahaba: the appropriate response to *shikamoo*

mashuka: more than one piece of red and/or blue fabric, often checkered, that is worn in a cape-like or toga fashion by Maasai men and women

mbaya: bad

mgeni: guest

mgonjwa: a sick person

michongoma: a thorny plant used to build hedges

mji: city

mkuu: head or leader

morani*: Maasai man

mtoto: child

mwalimu: teacher

mwizi: thief

mzee: elder, old person

mzungu: white person

nafikiri: I think

ndiyo: yes

ndizi: banana

ng'ombe: cattle

nimefurahi: I have joy

njema: good

nyumbani: inside a house or home

nzuri: good

oloileti*: a type of tree that is placed in front of a Maasai home during the female circumcision ceremony as a sign that girls from that *boma* are being prepared

panya: rat

pesa: currency, money

pikipiki: motorcycle

pole: sorry; also used to refer to a kind, easygoing person or to mean slowly (*polepole* means very slowly)

pombe: beer made from fermented honey

raiyo*: shoes made from the rubber of old tires; worn by Maasai men and women

ratiba: schedule, agenda

rungu: a short stick with a substantial knob on one end typically carried by Maasai men; a Maasai billy club

safari: journey

safi: clean; also used as slang to mean cool

samahani: excuse me

sana: very

shida: problem

shikamoo / shikamooni: greeting of respect spoken to an elder or a person of authority (*-moo* to one elder; *-mooni* to more than one elder)

shuka: one piece of red and/or blue fabric, often checkered, that is worn in a cape-like or toga fashion by Maasai men and women

sindikiza: to accompany a guest partway home

takwenya*: Maasai greeting spoken to a woman

tena: again

tutaonana: see you later

ugali: ground maize usually boiled in water to make a stiff porridge; generally eaten with meat and/or vegetables

ujamaa: familyhood, brotherhood, sisterhood; also the name given by Julius Nyerere, the first president of Tanzania, to a system of village cooperatives established in the 1960s to create equal opportunities and to foster self-reliance

uji: ground maize or rice usually boiled in water to make a thin porridge; generally eaten for breakfast

umependeza: you look beautiful

upendo: love

usiku: night

vizuri: good

wageni: guests

walimu: teachers

watoto: children

wazungu: white people

wazuri: good

zawadi: gift

NOTES

Front Matter

1. Protected Planet, *The World Database on Protected Areas* (Cambridge, UK: UNEP-WCMC and IUCN, accessed January 2016), www.protectedplanet.net.

2. Julie Narimatsu, *Environmental Justice Case Study: Maasai Land Rights in Kenya and Tanzania* (Ann Arbor: University of Michigan, accessed January 2016), www.umich.edu/~snre492/Jones/maasai.htm.

3. Julius Nyerere, *Nyerere on Socialism* (Dar es Salaam: Oxford University Press, 1969), 24.

4. Malala Yousafzai, "One Child, One Teacher, One Book, and One Pen Can Change the World" (speech, United Nations Youth Assembly, New York, July 12, 2013).

Chapter 2: Leaving Home (*Kuondoka Nyumbani*)

1. Paulo Freire, *Pedagogy of the Oppressed* (New York: The Continuum Publishing Company, 1999).

Chapter 8: Life inside the Bell Jar

1. Jim Klobuchar, *The Cross under the Acacia Tree: The Story of David and Eunice Simonson's Epic Mission in Africa* (Minneapolis: Kirk House Publishers, 1998), 48–50.

2. Stan Juneau, *Indian Education for All: History and Foundation of American Indian Education Policy* (Helena, MT: Montana Office of Public Instruction, 2001).

3. Paul Spencer, "Becoming Maasai, Being in Time," in *Being Maasai*, ed. Thomas Spear and Richard Waller (London: James Currey Ltd; Dar es Salaam: Mkuki na Nyota Publishers; Nairobi: East African Educational Publishers; Athens: Ohio University Press, 1993).

Chapter 12: Diamonds in the Darkness

1. The World Bank, *Percentage of People in the World at Different Poverty Levels, 2005* (Washington, DC: World Bank Development Indicators, 2008).

2. Matthew 19:16–30.

Chapter 13: Through Maasai Eyes

1. The United Republic of Tanzania, *Tanzania Demographic Health Survey, 2010* (Dar es Salaam: National Bureau of Statistics; Calverton, MD: ICF Macro, 2011), 295.

2. 28 Too Many, *Country Profile: FGM in Tanzania* (London: 28 Too Many, 2013), www.28toomany.org/country/tanzania/.

3. World Health Organization, *Eliminating Female Genital Mutilation: An Interagency Statement* (Geneva: World Health Organization, 2008).

Chapter 15: The First Graduation

1. Jim Klobuchar, *The Cross under the Acacia Tree: The Story of David and Eunice Simonson's Epic Mission in Africa* (Minneapolis: Kirk House Publishers, 1998), 7–12, 60.

2. N. Swainson, S. Bendera, R. Gordon, and E. Kadzamira, *Promoting Girls' Education in Africa: The Design and Implementation of Policy Interventions*, Educational Paper no. 25 (London: Department for International Development, 1998).

Chapter 19: Honeymooning at Lake Manyara

1. UNAIDS, *Country Factsheet United Republic of Tanzania* (Geneva: UNAIDS, accessed January 2019), www.unaids.org/en/regionscountries/countries/unitedrepublicoftanzania; The United Republic of Tanzania, *Census Population* 1967-2002 (Dodoma: National Bureau of Statistics, accessed January 2019), www.nbs.go.tz/nbs/takwimu/references/1967popcensus.pdf.

Chapter 21: Hoping for School Choice

1. HALI Access Network, *Education Fact Sheet: Tanzania* (accessed January 2019), http://haliaccess.org/wp-content/uploads/2018/05/Tanzania-Education-Fact-Sheet.pdf; The United Republic of Tanzania, Secondary Education Master Plan, 2001-2005 (Dodoma: Ministry of Education and Culture, 2000), 14.

Chapter 22: Gideon the Mighty Warrior

1. Julius Nyerere, *Education for Self-Reliance* (Dar es Salaam: Information Services Division, Ministry of Information and Tourism, 1967).

Epilogue: Moving Mountains with Teaspoons

1. Rabbi Rami Shapiro, *Wisdom of the Jewish Sages: A Modern Reading of Pirke Avot* (New York: Harmony/Bell Tower, 1995), 41; Pirke Avot 2:20; Micah 6:8.

Afterword

1. The World Bank, *Lower Secondary Completion Rate, Female* (Washington, DC: UNESCO Institute for Statistics, accessed January 2019), https://data.worldbank.org/indicator/SE.SEC. CMPT.LO.FE.ZS?locations=ZG.

2. Operation Bootstrap Africa, unpublished data, February 2015.

3. Steve Corbett and Brian Fikkert, *When Helping Hurts: How to Alleviate Poverty Without Hurting the Poor . . . and Yourself* (Chicago: Moody Publishers, 2014).

ABOUT THE AUTHOR

Juliet Cutler is a writer, an educator, and an activist. Her teaching career began in Tanzania in 1999, and since that time, she has been an advocate for empowering at-risk girls through education.

Among the Maasai is Juliet's first book, though her literary and professional publications number more than two dozen. She has taught writing in many settings including as adjunct faculty for the College of St. Scholastica in Minnesota. She holds an MA in English from Colorado State University and a BS in education and English from the University of North Dakota.

Juliet currently lives with her husband, Mark, in a community outside Atlanta. When she's not writing, Juliet consults as an education and exhibition specialist for museums, parks, and cultural centers throughout the world. She regularly returns to Tanzania and remains a supporter of causes that uplift Maasai women and girls.

To learn more, please visit www.julietcutler.com.

Author photo © Dani Werner

SELECTED TITLES FROM SHE WRITES PRESS

She Writes Press is an independent publishing company founded to serve women writers everywhere. Visit us at www.shewritespress.com.

Renewable: One Woman's Search for Simplicity, Faithfulness, and Hope by Eileen Flanagan. $16.95, 978-1-63152-968-9. At age forty-nine, Eileen Flanagan had an aching feeling that she wasn't living up to her youthful ideals or potential, so she started trying to change the world—and in doing so, she found the courage to change her life.

The Outskirts of Hope: A Memoir by Jo Ivester. $16.95, 978-1-63152-964-1. A moving, inspirational memoir about how living and working in an all-black town during the height of the civil rights movement profoundly affected the author's entire family—and how they in turn impacted the community.

Catching Homelessness: A Nurse's Story of Falling Through the Safety Net by Josephine Ensign. $16.95, 978-1-63152-117-1. The compelling true story of a nurse's work with—and young adult passage through—homelessness.

Dearest Ones at Home: Clara Taylor's Letters from Russia, 1917–1919 edited by Katrina Maloney and Patricia Maloney. Clara Taylor's detailed, delightful letters documenting her two years in Russia teaching factory girls self-sufficiency skills—right in the middle of World War I.

(R)evolution: The Girls Write Now 2016 Anthology by Girls Write Now. $19.95, 978-1-63152-083-9. The next installment in Girls Write Now's award-winning anthology series: a stunning collection of poetry and prose written by young women and their mentors in exploration of the theme of "Revolution."

100 Under $100: One Hundred Tools for Empowering Global Women by Betsy Teutsch. $29.95, 978-1-63152-934-4. An inspiring, comprehensive look at the many tools being employed today to empower women in the developing world and help them raise themselves out of poverty.